FRONTIER JUSTICE

Frontier Justice

BY WAYNE GARD, 1899-

UNIVERSITY OF OKLAHOMA PRESS
NORMAN : 1949

By Wayne Gard

Book Reviewing (New York, 1927)
Sam Bass (Boston, 1936)
Frontier Justice (Norman, 1949)

Publishing Division of the University
Composed and printed at Norman, Oklahoma, U.S.A.
by the University of Oklahoma Press
First edition, September, 1949
Second printing, October, 1949

Foreword

CIVILIZATION took a rapid stride across the American West. In the short span of two generations settlers witnessed a rise from savagery to social stability that in some parts of the world took several thousand years. To some of the participants the taming of the West seemed slow. Certainly it was marked by violence—almost every community had its blazing guns and dangling ropes. Yet, as history goes, the transition from the bloody tomahawk of the painted savage to the polished gavel of the black-robed judge came with bounding speed.

Subduing the Indians did not end the violence. The motive of vengeance which marked most of the Indian fighting carried over into frontier feuds among the whites. In many places clashing economic interests of rival groups led to battles for grass and water. Strife arose between sheepmen and cattlemen and between stockmen who wanted fenced ranches and those determined to keep the open range.

On the prairies and in the mining camps, orthodox law enforcement often lagged behind the need to punish troublesome offenders. Where officials were helpless and jails were far away, citizens had to work together as vigilantes. They made their own laws on the spot, caught horse thieves and other outlaws, and hanged them to the nearest cottonwood. Sometimes they imposed overly severe penalties or executed the wrong men; but usually they were fair, and their activities discouraged crime. The work of the vigilance committees was a form of social action against bad men and a step toward the setting up of statutory courts.

Between the committee of vigilance and the formal court

often came the primitive justice of the peace whose decisions had scant relationship to statutory law. Much of the transition from frontier turbulence to quiet stability was the continuation of a process that had gone on east of the Mississippi in earlier generations. Conditions in most of the West, however, sharpened conflicts, brought new types of rivalry, and favored resort to violence.

Until recently the feuds, range wars, and vigilante activities that marked the taming of the West had little attention from historians. Many graphic details lay buried in court records, in almost forgotten letters and diaries, and in faded newspaper files. In the last few decades local and regional historians have begun to dig out these accounts, which help to fill conspicuous gaps in the history of the West.

This book is an informal study of the rise of order and law west of the Mississippi, where order often came before law. With abundant use of illustrative incidents and a minimum of abstract discussion, it traces the progress made from the chaotic, almost anarchic relations between many pioneers and the Indians to a state of peaceful settlement. Space limits the scope of this work not only to the West but to those forms of conflict that grew out of frontier conditions. The activities of the Ku Klux Klan, original and revived, and other discriminations against Negroes, Mexicans, Chinese, and Japanese, which sometimes resulted in violence, have no place here.

Gathering material for this work has taken the author over many western trails, including that of the invading cattlemen in Wyoming. He has gone also to the weatherbeaten shack of Roy Bean in the western plains of Texas, to the reports of dauntless Ranger captains in Austin, and to the records of Judge Isaac C. Parker's court in Fort Smith. While primary sources of information have been used as far as practicable, a book covering so wide a territory, so long a period, and so diverse a field could hardly be written without the author's relying heavily on the spade work of other searchers and writers in individual fields. Much effort has been spent in checking material, and credit to sources is given in the footnotes.

In the arrangement of chapters, it has been hard to follow

either logical or chronological order consistently, as most of the subjects overlap others and some cover several decades. Logic has seemed more important than time, since frontier conditions prevailed in various parts of the West in different periods. The gold rush, for instance, caused California to be settled earlier than some of the mountain states to its east. Thus the chapter on California's committees of vigilance is placed after the one on the cattlemen's war in Wyoming. The California events, although they occurred earlier, seemed to illustrate a later stage in the development of social order.

Generous assistance in the preparation of this work has come from many quarters. The Texas State Historical Association made available a Rockefeller Foundation research grant. Librarians and archivists in several states gave more than routine help. Collectors of western history—E. DeGolyer, Ramon F. Adams, Dan Ferguson, and the late Dr. William E. Howard of Dallas, Frank Caldwell and Captain R. W. Aldrich of Austin, and Fred A. Rosenstock of Denver—opened doors to their libraries. Authors and publishers, as credited in the notes, gave permission for quotations from copyrighted works.

Several historians took time to read and criticize chapters in their fields. Grant Foreman, Oklahoma historian and author of books on the Indians, read the initial chapter. C. L. Sonnichsen, historian of Texas feuds, read the second and third chapters. J. Evetts Haley, ranchman and biographer, read those on the sheepmen-cattlemen conflicts and the fence-cutters. Professor Walter Prescott Webb of the University of Texas, whose standard works on the Great Plains and the Texas Rangers have been widely used, read the chapters on the fence-cutters and the Texas Rangers. Miss Lola M. Homsher, archivist of the University of Wyoming library, read the account of the Johnson County invasion. Professor Carl Coke Rister of the University of Oklahoma, who has made many important contributions to western history, read the three chapters on vigilante activities.

All these and other historians gave valuable suggestions on sources and treatment of material, though they are not responsible for any statement of fact or opinion. The list includes J. Frank Dobie of Austin, Earl Vandale of Amarillo, Professor H.

Bailey Carroll of the University of Texas, Professor Edward Everett Dale and Professor W. S. Campbell (Stanley Vestal), of the University of Oklahoma, Professor William R. Hogan of Tulane University, LeRoy R. Hafen, William MacLeod Raine, and Henry Swan of Denver, John Charles Thompson, editor of the *Wyoming State Tribune,* and Alfred J. Mokler and Robert B. David of Casper.

Among those who helped round up the pictures were John Bruce, city editor of the San Francisco *Chronicle,* and Wayne C. Sellers of the Fort Worth *Star-Telegram.* The author is grateful also to his wife, Hazel D. Gard, for reading the manuscript and making many helpful suggestions.

WAYNE GARD

Dallas, Texas
June 14, 1949

Contents

Illustrations

MAP

VENGEANCE

1. Scalp for a Scalp

White men take Indians' scalps with as little compunction as the Indians take theirs.
—H. H. HALSELL, *Cowboys and Cattleland*

BESIDE a placid lake in southern Texas a small band of weary travelers had made camp. Spring was in the air on that afternoon of April 4, 1836, but it was not in the hearts of the campers. They were disappointed settlers on their way back from the Beales colony on Las Moras Creek, farther west. They had found the land assigned them too barren and had given up in despair.

The party had eleven men, two of them with families. Two days earlier they had crossed the Nueces River, where they had seen many buffalo and wild horses. On the road they had heard the shots and shouts of men they supposed to be Santa Anna's soldiers. The Mexicans, foraging for game, seemed elated by the victory at the Alamo and confident that they soon would stamp out the rebellion of Texas colonists.

In the improvised camp six oxen were grazing quietly. Some of the men were cooking venison for dinner; others were fishing, reading, or repairing their guns. John Horn, who, with his family, had come from England less than three years before, was entertaining his two sons by making holes in some alligator teeth so they could string them and wear them about their necks. John, aged five, and Joseph, three and a half, looked on, fascinated. Mrs. Horn had just bathed the three-months-old baby daughter of Mrs. Harris, who was gathering wild fruit near by. She was about to get a dress for the baby from one of the wagons when she noticed a company of strange, nearly naked, armed men approaching on mules.

Frightened, Mrs. Horn rushed to her husband. He assured her there was no danger; yet, as he spoke, an arrow pierced the breast of one of the men. The victim drew it out; but blood gushed from the wound, and he fell on his face and died. The campers ran for cover, but it was too late. They were trapped by a band of Comanches. As one of the Indians hit Horn on the back of his head with a double-barreled gun, his wife and sons watched him keel over and draw his last breath.

There were more than forty warriors in the raiding party. When they had finished with the men, they tore the Horn children from their mother, threatening them with death if they should go near her. After looting the wagons, they set off on their mules, the women and children riding behind some of the savages.

The Indians soon reached their thicket camp, two miles away, where they were greeted with shouts of joy by several hundred others. The prisoners were almost suffocated by the stench of stale horse meat. John and Joseph were stripped of their clothes; then they and the two women had their hands and ankles tied and were left for the night, without food or water, to endure the mosquitoes and other insects. The boys—frightened, hungry, and thirsty—cried most of the night; and by morning the Harris baby was wailing for food. As the mother, because of an ailment, was unable to nurse her baby, Mrs. Horn, who spoke Spanish, asked the Comanches for food for the child.

"Yes, she shall have something to eat," smilingly replied a tall, muscular brave.

With that, he took the baby, swung her as high in the air as he could, and let her fall to the ground at his feet. By the time he had done this three times, the baby was in no more need of food.

The women supposed all the men had been killed on the day before; but that day Harris and another, who had been only wounded, were brought up and shot before their eyes. The whole band of Indians then resumed their wandering across the prairies and through scratchy chaparral. They took along their prisoners. These often were forced to go two days or more without food, while the captors had plenty. The younger Horn boy, Joseph, had his shoulder badly bruised by a fall; but his mother was not allowed to treat it, even after maggots were crawling about in the sore. One of the Indian women took delight in tormenting Mrs. Harris, often taking her by the throat and choking her until she turned black in the face as if she were dead.

One day when little Joseph fell off a mule into a stream and was trying to climb up the steep bank, a savage stabbed him severely with a lance just below the eye and pushed him back into the foaming water. When Mrs. Horn upbraided him for his cruelty, he forced the child to go on foot the rest of the day. That night he gave the mother a lashing with his whip and cut off her hair.

The next day some of the Comanches took the Horn children and were gone about an hour. As they returned, the distracted mother saw them holding her sons by their hands. When they let go, as they did several times, the boys fell as if dead. They were unconscious for some time, their bodies dreadfully distended and Joseph's face swollen from his wound of the day before. The Indians had been amusing themselves by throwing the boys into a stream and taking them out only after they were nearly drowned. Later that day, when Joseph fell off his mule, the savages choked him until blood ran from his mouth and nose.

For months the Comanches wandered about, raiding and killing. Their prisoners were blistered from the sun and badly scratched by brush and thorns, especially the two boys, who were not allowed to wear any clothes. Each night the whites were bound, to prevent their escape, and thus could not defend themselves against bloodthirsty mosquitoes. The women wondered if their torture ever would cease. Finally the warriors placed the captives in semipermanent lodges but kept them separated so that they seldom saw each other. Mrs. Horn was put to work cleaning and dressing buffalo hides, and Mrs. Harris was given menial tasks. The boys were adopted into the tribe.

Late in June, 1837, the Comanches sold Mrs. Harris to some Mexican traders but refused to sell Mrs. Horn. In the following September, however, they took her across the high plains to San Miguel, New Mexico, and traded her for a horse, four bridles, two mirrors, two knives, and some tobacco, powder, and balls. She found that Mrs. Harris had gone back to Missouri with a caravan of Santa Fé traders.

Mrs. Horn stayed in San Miguel and Taos while some of the Americans and Mexicans tried to find and recover her sons. On their return they reported that Joseph could be taken only by force and that John had died. Still without clothing, he had been ordered to hold a horse through the night. The weather turned cold; and in the morning he was found in a sitting posture, chilled to death. Broken in body and spirit, Mrs. Horn left Santa Fé for the States on August 22, 1838. She arrived at Independence, Missouri, on the last day of September,[1] a scarred victim of Comanche vengeance against paleface intrusion.

Such experiences were by no means unique. For half a century, Indian forays like the one which brought tragedy to the Horn and Harris families were common on the Great Plains, from Canada to the Río Grande, and in the mountain country to the west. They repeated on a larger scale the raids and massacres perpetrated on the earlier frontier east of the Mississippi. With the whites invading their hunting grounds and killing off the buffalo and the deer, with treaties broken almost before the ink was dry, the Indians struck back in the only way they knew.[2]

Whenever the moon was full, isolated settlers kept their livestock close, bolted their doors, and saw that their rifles were loaded. But often these precautions were useless. Men were killed on the trails and in the fields. Women were tortured, mutilated, and scalped. Children were carried off to be either adopted or held for ransom. Hundreds of lonely stone chimneys on the prairies were mute evidence of the burning of settlers' cabins. Yet the wagon trains rumbled on, bringing ever more white families into the West.

If to many emigrants the bronze raiders seemed like savage beasts, it did not follow that the Indians were lawless within their own tribes. They observed strictly their unwritten laws,

[1] E. House, *A Narrative of the Captivity of Mrs. Horn and Her Two Children, With That of Mrs. Harris, by the Comanche Indians.*

[2] Rupert Norval Richardson, *The Comanche Barrier to South Plains Settlement.*

some of which fitted western life so well that early white trappers and hunters adopted them. To Indians the frontier owed the ban on the discharge of firearms within a camp, the rule that the first man to touch a stray horse became its owner, the death penalty for horse thieves, and the division of meat in which the man who killed a buffalo took the hide and the tongue, other parts going to his helpers.[3] Yet when Indians went on the warpath, they seemed to cast aside every restraint.

Most of the Indian raids were made by small parties; but sometimes they were linked in an organized campaign, as in the Sioux uprising in Minnesota in 1862. There the Santee Sioux had been nursing grievances against the whites for a long time. Crooked agents had been withholding government food intended for the Sioux, and traders had been selling them rancid bacon and wormy flour at exorbitant prices. Degenerate whites had been seducing Indian women and filling the camps with half-blood children.

Trouble loomed when three hundred Indians died from eating spoiled food issued by a government agent at Sandy Lake. For months afterward the survivors were refused either food or credit. "There will be no payment," the agent told them. "The appropriation has been entirely used up to pay traders' claims."[4] Finally, when Little Crow and other chiefs went to the agency near Fort Ridgely for promised food for their starving people, they received only rebuffs and taunts from the trader, Andrew J. Myrick.

"If they're hungry," he said, "let them eat grass."

A week later the Sioux were back with guns, knives, and war whoops. The fighting began when a family at Acton refused food to four braves. The Sioux callers then murdered several whites, and Little Crow decided to protect the killers. Traders and farmers alike were mowed down, children were butchered, babies were hacked to shreds and nailed to doorposts. More than six hundred whites were killed. Several hundred others,

[3] W. S. Campbell (Stanley Vestal), letter to the author, October 24, 1946.

[4] Meridel Le Sueur, *North Star Country*, 104.

most of them women, were carried off, some never to be heard of again.

Myrick was slain in front of his store. When his body was found, his mouth was stuffed with grass.[5]

In the wake of such massacres, whatever their cause, many of the western settlers concluded that the only good Indian was a dead Indian. The frontiersmen, when they could, repaid the red men in kind. They not only banded to chase and punish marauders but, aroused by the slaughter of their loved ones or their neighbors, tried to even the score by butchering any redskins they could find—squaws and papooses as well as braves. If the villages they decimated were not those of the raiding parties, it mattered little. The settlers would "larn 'em a lesson."

On the fringe of settlement, some of the pioneers had no qualms against shooting any redskin who happened to come within gun range. As a result of this policy of blasting away first and asking questions afterward, many a friendly Indian lost his life. Others, concluding that the whites were determined to exterminate their race, joined forces for retaliation. Both sides sought to avenge their wrongs rather than to achieve a fair and lasting adjustment of their difficult situation.

Thus frontier relations between the early settlers and the Indians became, in many places, the law of a scalp for a scalp. In an earlier period, Spaniards had offered rewards for Apache scalps, while the English and the French had paid the Indians for each other's scalps. Although the Iroquois had engaged in scalping and in torturing prisoners before the whites came, the colonists' incentives and precedents had been largely responsible for spreading these practices among the Indians of the West.

The scalping of Indians by whites had been common east of the Mississippi, where, in some sections, it was encouraged and rewarded by public bounties. New Netherlands began offering

[5] Charles M. Bryant and Abel B. Murch, *A History of the Great Massacre by the Sioux Indians in Minnesota;* C. C. Andrews, editor, *Minnesota in the Indian and Civil Wars;* William Watts Folwell, *A History of Minnesota,* II.

bounties for scalps in 1641.[6] This practice was adopted in 1704 by Connecticut and soon afterward by Massachusetts, where Cotton Mather regarded all Indians as tawny serpents and where the Reverend Solomon Stoddard of Northampton urged that the settlers hunt them with dogs as they did bears.[7] Virginia and Pennsylvania later offered bounties for Indian scalps. The last incentive of this kind was the fifty-dollar reward proclaimed by the Territory of Indiana in 1814 as an "encouragement to the enterprise and bravery of our fellow citizens."[8]

As a rule, frontiersmen west of the Mississippi needed no monetary spurs for killing Indians, although these sometimes were offered locally. In 1867 a Denver citizen promised ten dollars each for the scalps of hostile warriors; and residents of Central City, at a mass meeting, raised five thousand dollars for buying Indian scalps at twenty-five dollars each.[9] In 1876, miners at Deadwood, Dakota Territory, resentful of sniping in the hills, offered two hundred dollars for each Indian scalp; and Indian heads carried into that town brought high prices at auction.

When the Westerners removed scalps, as they often did, their purposes usually were similar to those of the red men. They wanted to humiliate Indians who might come back for the bodies, and in addition they wanted to carry home souvenirs that would give proof of their prowess. A Minnesota merchant boasted that he had taken many scalps with his own hands, removing the ears along with the skin and hair.[10] H. H. Halsell, a Texas cattleman, noted in his autobiography: "I have seen white people in Wise County at picnics exhibiting Indian scalps as trophies of conquests, and some of the scalps were of Indian women."[11]

There were many such trophies. In 1858 a party of Texans, after finding the scalped body of a white man, trailed the Indians who had killed him and found them encamped on San Domingo Creek in Bee County. Making a surprise attack, they killed all

[6] William Christie MacLeod, *The American Indian Fronter*, 223.
[7] Frederick Jackson Turner, *The Frontier in American History*, 45–46.
[8] MacLeod, *op. cit.* 488.
[9] New York *Times*, June 11, 1867, article from a Denver correspondent.
[10] Le Sueur, *op. cit.*, 91.
[11] H. H. Halsell, *Cowboys and Cattleland*, 180.

eleven of the warriors and scalped every one.[12] In another Texas clash prior to the Civil War, six men from Milam County overtook as many Indians, who were eating beside their camp fire. A hard rain had wet the priming of the white men's guns and had made the strings of the Indians' bows so slack they were useless. In a hand-to-hand encounter, the Texans clubbed to death all the Indians and took their scalps to carry home.[13]

Even the Texas Rangers sometimes scalped Indians. Curly Hatcher, who joined the Rangers in 1874, related that he was the first in his battalion to kill an Indian and that his commander, Captain Jeff Maltby, gave him fifty dollars for the scalp and took it to Austin.[14] In 1875, after a small band of Lipans had stolen some horses from Mason County, Lieutenant Dan W. Roberts led a detachment of Rangers on the marauders' trail. In a brush with these Indians on August 24, the Rangers killed one of the raiders. Ed A. Sieker promptly scalped him; and James B. Gillett, a recruit of nineteen, used the scalp to cover his pistol holster.[15]

One of the most publicized scalpings by a white man climaxed a duel between William F. Cody (Buffalo Bill) and Chief Yellow Hand of the Cheyennes, when Cody was serving as an army scout in the summer of 1876. The frontiersman dashed out ahead of the soldiers and engaged the young chief in a close-up fight. After shooting Yellow Hand, Cody scalped the youth and flaunted his trophy—with the war bonnet still attached—before the stunned warriors.[16]

[12] San Antonio *Express*, July 1, 1906.

[13] *Frontier Times*, January, 1924.

[14] *Ibid.*, July, 1924.

[15] Lieutenant Dan W. Roberts, report to Major John B. Jones, August 26, 1875, Adjutant General's papers, Austin; Carlysle Graham Raht, *The Romance of the Davis Mountains and the Big Bend Country*, 250–51; James B. Gillett, *Six Years With the Texas Rangers* (revised edition), 33–44. At the Texas Centennial Exposition in Dallas in 1936, the most popular exhibit in the Texas Ranger building was a display of scalps.

[16] William Frederick Cody, *The Life of the Hon. William F. Cody, Known as Buffalo Bill;* Joseph Mills Hanson, *The Conquest of the Missouri*, 341–42; Richard J. Walsh, *The Making of Buffalo Bill*, 190–93. The version used here is based upon eyewitness accounts. Details of this incident have been much disputed. Cody, addicted to boasting and exaggeration,

Scalp for a Scalp

White soldiers still were lifting Indians' hair as late as 1880. In November of that year, Lieutenant F. F. Kislingbury, stationed at the mouth of the Musselshell, presented to a Missouri River steamboat captain, Grant P. Marsh, the scalp of a warrior killed in a skirmish a few days earlier.[17]

Tomahawk justice, with or without actual scalping, prevailed almost everywhere in the West in the period of early settlement. In Oregon, where memory of the Whitman massacre of 1847 was still green, the appetite of the whites for Indian blood was whetted by Indian agents, the legislature, the Know-Nothing party, and the Methodist clergy. Jobless miners and others were hired as territorial soldiers and sent out to exterminate the redskins. On some occasions they clubbed women to death and dashed babies against trees.

The attitude of Oregon pioneers toward the Indians was recorded by Father John Beeson, one of the early settlers. Of his fellows, most of whom were from Missouri, he wrote: "Among them it was customary to speak of the Indian man as a buck, the woman as a squaw, until at length, in the general acceptance of the terms, they ceased to recognize the rights of humanity in those to whom they were so applied. By a natural and easy transition, from being spoken of as brutes, they came to be thought of as game to be shot or as vermin to be destroyed."

Any white man found dead was assumed to have been murdered by Indians, and often his death was made an excuse for raiding the nearest Indian village and killing all the men, women, and children found there. In one instance an elderly white miner who had refused to participate in such raids was called on by a score of men and forced to join them, Father Beeson related. "After resting on the mountains, they shot him, cut off his head, leaving it on the limb of a tree, and divided his property among themselves."[18]

In California the Indians were dispossessed, with scant com-

claimed that he dispatched Yellow Hand with a knife in a hand-to-hand combat. His more severe critics asserted that it was not he who killed the young chief.

[17] Hanson, *op. cit.*, 403.

[18] MacLeod, *op. cit.*, 485–86.

pensation; and many were wiped out in brutal butcherings. Andrew Kelsey and Charles Stone made virtual slaves of a band of Pomos on the ranch they established in Lake County in 1847. They overworked and underfed these Indians and often whipped them for minor offenses or for the amusement of visitors. When the chief tried to escape, he was made to stand for several days, with his hands and feet tied, and was fed only bread and water. When a boy stole a handful of wheat for his sick mother, Stone shot and killed him. The Pomos, unable to endure this treatment any longer, took the lives of Kelsey and Stone, looted the ranch, and fled to an island in Clear Lake. But their liberty lasted only a few weeks. In the spring of 1850, friends of the dead ranchmen obtained from San Francisco two whaleboats, each armed with a brass cannon. With these and a group of soldiers and settlers, they trapped the Pomos and mowed them down with canister and bullets.[19]

This and many like incidents led the historian Hubert Howe Bancroft to observe: "The poor natives of California had neither the strength nor the intelligence to unite in any formidable numbers; hence when now and then one of them plucked up courage to defend his wife and little ones, or to retaliate on one of the many outrages that were constantly being perpetrated upon them by white persons, sufficient excuse was offered for the miners and settlers to band and shoot down any Indians they met, young or old, innocent or guilty, friendly or hostile, until their appetite for blood was appeased."

As late as 1871, many Californians still viewed the red men as fair game. In that year, whites trailed a group of Indians with dogs, cornered them in a cave, and killed about thirty, some of them children. One of the men said he could not bear to kill the youngsters with his .56-caliber rifle because it tore them up so badly. So he used his .38 Smith and Wesson revolver.[20]

In the Southwest, settlers encountered Indian hostility aroused by the Spanish conquistadors of an earlier day. While

[19] William Ralganal Benson, "The Facts of the Stone and Kelsey Massacre in Lake County," manuscript, Bancroft Library, University of California, Berkeley; *The History of Napa and Lake Counties.*

[20] MacLeod, *op. cit.*, 487.

the Spaniards had improved the lot of the Indians by bringing in horses, cattle, and sheep, they often had treated the tribesmen cruelly and had exploited their labor and their resources. Later invaders from the East, instead of removing this enmity, sometimes pushed its roots deeper.

There, as elsewhere, many a massacre by the Indians could be traced to treachery by the whites. The Apaches, who, under Victorio, Geronimo, and others, terrorized Arizona and New Mexico for fifty-one years, might have been relatively peaceful wards except for a succession of killings that led them to distrust the white man's word. In 1835 two white traders arrived at an Apache camp. While the women were preparing gifts for the visitors, the latter killed the friendly Apache chief by shooting him in the back. At the same time, they slaughtered a score of women and children and wounded as many others by attacking the camp with a hidden trench mortar loaded with shrapnel. The six warriors in the camp escaped, but they did not forget what they had seen.

In January, 1864, another Apache chief, whose people were suffering from hunger, took thirty-five of his warriors and went to the whites under a flag of truce to make peace. The Apaches would quit taking ponies and cattle from the settlers, he said, if the newcomers would cease killing the Apaches' deer and taking their corn land. With his men seated about the campfire of the whites, he pleaded for peace. But as he talked, a signal from the leader of the whites set off a volley of rifle shots from these and their Indian allies. The unsuspecting Apaches died without a chance to defend themselves. Only one escaped from this massacre of the Bloody Basins, but the story he told stirred other Apaches to vengeance.

Still the whites thirsted for Apache blood. In April, 1871, after a group of Pinal Apaches from the mountains had killed a white man and driven off four horses and six head of cattle, Tucson citizens decided to wipe out a camp of peaceful Aravaipa Apaches who had not been involved in the raid. Six white volunteers and forty-eight Mexicans were issued guns and ammunition by the Adjutant General of Arizona and were joined by ninety-two Papago Indians, enemies of the Apaches, armed with clubs. The 146 raiders attacked the Aravaipa village before daybreak and butchered 118 Aravaipas, 110 of them women and children. They carried off as captives 27 children. After President Ulysses S. Grant threatened to place Arizona under martial law, the leaders of the raid were tried but were promptly acquitted by a local jury.[21]

To the north, Cheyennes and other tribesmen were slaughtered with equal abandon by white raiders. In Colorado, relations between the early settlers and the Indians were strained in the spring and summer of 1864. Alarmed at the intrusion and hostility of the whites, Indian marauders had stolen horses and cattle, interrupted and destroyed the mails. They had attacked the caravans of emigrants and traders, plundering the wagons, driving off the horses and mules, and killing some of the whites. All supply roads between the Missouri River and Denver were cut off. The people of that city were infuriated when bodies of the four members of the Huntgate family, mutilated and scalped, were drawn through the streets in an ox-wagon and placed on display.

Because the Civil War had made Colorado's military defense inadequate, punitive steps were taken by territorial troops. In June, Governor John Evans called on friendly Indians to camp near the forts so they would not be wiped out in the war of extermination. In August, he advised the whites to hunt down the Indians and kill every hostile warrior they encountered. In November, Colonel J. M. Chivington, in civil life a Methodist preacher, decided to crush the Indians by slaughtering a band of friendly Cheyennes, who, conforming with instructions, had made their camp on Sand Creek near Fort Lyon. He publicly stated that his policy was to kill and scalp all, big and little, since "nits make lice."

Chivington commanded a regiment of hundred-days men, the Third Colorado Cavalry, recently raised by authorization of the War Department. At Fort Lyon he picked up some regular United States troops and had with him more than nine hundred men and several howitzers when he approached the Indian

[21] Thomas Edwin Farish, *History of Arizona;* Woodworth Clum, *Apache Agent.*

camp. This camp of Cheyennes and some Arapahoes contained about two hundred warriors and five hundred women and children.

The soldiers struck between dawn and sunrise on the morning of November 29, taking the Indians by surprise. Thinking the attackers had made a mistake, the aged Chief White Antelope rushed out to stop them; but he was shot down. Chief Black Kettle ran up on the pole in front of his lodge a large American flag and under it a small white flag, as he had been advised to do to show that the camp was friendly. But appeals and flags were disregarded. With howitzers, rifles, and knives, the soldiers butchered the Indians, regardless of sex or age. The braves defended themselves ably but were no match for the more numerous and better-equipped whites.

Screams of the women and children for mercy were of no avail. One youngster, just old enough to walk, was shot at by three soldiers in succession until he was killed. A lieutenant shot and scalped three women and five children who had been captured by soldiers and were being conducted to the whites' camp. Many of the bodies of the Indian dead, estimated at 150 to 500, were horribly mutilated by the soldiers; and more than a hundred scalps were taken. Chivington reported that night that he had had nine men killed and thirty-eight wounded.

Back in Denver, Chivington and his men were acclaimed as heroes, and one newspaper asserted that they had covered themselves with glory. At a theatrical performance the Indian scalps were exhibited between acts, and the soldiers were vigorously applauded. Only later came unfavorable reaction from other parts of the country. A Congressional committee, after listening to much testimony, concluded that Chivington "deliberately planned and executed a foul and dastardly massacre, which would have disgraced the veriest savage among those who were the victims of his cruelty" and asserted, "It is difficult to believe that beings in the form of men, and disgracing the uniform of United States soldiers and officers, could commit or countenance the commission of such acts of cruelty and barbarity."

A similar verdict followed from a commission named by

Congress, with General W. T. Sherman as one of its members. This group reported that the Sand Creek massacre "scarcely has its parallel among the records of Indian barbarity. Fleeing women, holding up their hands and praying for mercy, were brutally shot down; infants were killed and scalped in derision; men were tortured and mutilated in a way which would put to shame the savage ingenuity of interior Africa." General Nelson A. Miles called the massacre "perhaps the foulest and most unjustifiable crime in the annals of America."[22]

This slaughter aroused the northern Indians to new hostilities against the whites. The Cheyennes—joined by the Sioux, the Iowas, the Comanches, and the Apaches—swooped down upon the outer settlements to burn, plunder, and butcher. In the spring of 1865 the government had to withdraw eight thousand troops from the Civil War in a futile effort to subdue the enraged tribesmen. This campaign took the lives of hundreds of soldiers and cost taxpayers more than ten million dollars—nearly a million for each Indian killed.[23]

Despite treaties signed in October, 1865, the fighting continued and spread. Nebraska Indians, alarmed at the disappearance of their game and determined to keep the approaching railroads out of their hunting grounds, attacked settlements and stagecoach lines, and tore down telegraph wires. On the Cimarron, a band of Cheyennes drove off cattle of the stockmen. In retaliation, General W. S. Hancock led a punitive expedition from Fort Leavenworth. On April 19, 1867, he burned a village of nearly three hundred lodges on Pawnee Fork and captured nearly a thousand buffalo robes.

The Cheyennes and Sioux driven from this village, their

[22] "Massacre of the Cheyenne Indians," in Report of the Joint Committee on the Conduct of the War, 38 Cong., 2 sess. 1865; *Condition of the Indian Tribes,* report of the joint special committee appointed under the joint resolution of March 3, 1865; Report of the Secretary of War, communicating evidence taken by a military commission ordered to inquire into the Sand Creek Massacre, 39 Cong., 2 sess., *Exec. Doc. 26;* Report of the Indian Peace Commissioners, 40 Cong., 2 sess., *Exec. Doc.* 97 (1868); J. P. Dunn, *Massacres of the Mountains,* 396–446; George Bird Grinnell, *The Fighting Cheyennes;* 159–73; Stanley Vestal, *Warpath and Council Fire,* 63–78.

[23] Grant Foreman, *A History of Oklahoma,* 154.

agents said, were peaceful people who had detached themselves from those making depredations. Once inflamed, however, they began raiding Kansas emigrant trains, railway work crews, and passenger stations. Disaster overtook the roving tribesmen again on the cold morning of November 27, 1868, when they were living peaceably in a camp of more than six hundred lodges on the Washita. Approaching over snow-covered ground, Lieutenant Colonel George A. Custer and his troops made a surprise attack and a much criticized massacre, killing 103 warriors and a number of women and children.[24]

In Washington the official policy toward the Indians generally was well-intentioned; but often it suffered from lack of information, from misrepresentation and pressure by those who coveted the Indian lands, and from poor administration in the field. Thomas Jefferson had wanted to move the eastern tribes to the Louisiana Territory; and early in 1825, in the administration of James Monroe, the Secretary of War, John C. Calhoun, recommended that the Indians be moved beyond the Missouri River. He assumed that this western land, though it abounded in game for the Indians, never would be desired by white settlers.

Following the adoption of this plan, many tribes were uprooted and sent west. Often such moves brought severe hardship, as in the case of the relatively civilized Cherokees, who were driven from Georgia to what became northeastern Oklahoma. As soon as Indian lands were desired by white settlers, some excuse would be found to violate or revise treaties; either the tribes would be moved farther west or their reservations would be restricted.

Often the relations between the frontier settlers and the Indians were made worse instead of better by the activities of Indian agents. These men were appointed in Washington on a basis of political spoils. Some of the agents were honest and capable; but so many were not that the term "Indian agent" came to be synonymous with grafter. Often the agent, who knew he would be turned out when there was a change in administra-

[24] *Ibid.*, 154–59; Vestal, *Warpath and Council Fire*, 152–63.

tion, pocketed half or more of the annuity money intended for the Indians and sold the annuity goods to conniving traders. Thus it was possible for an Indian agent on a salary of $1,500 a year to save $40,000 in four years. Thousands of cattle which agents bought with federal money, ostensibly as food for the Indians, never reached the tribal camps.[25]

Almost equally blundering was the army in its dealings with the western Indians. In reviewing this warfare, Major Eben Swift thus summarized the prevailing policy: "Civilization approached the American Indian with a Bible in one hand and a paper treaty in the other, a bludgeon in her sleeve, and a barrel of whiskey in her wagon, not to mention the blight that goeth unto the third and fourth generation. The task of the soldier was to punish the Indian when he applied his crude ideas of justice or revenge and to force him to obey when he could not be cajoled or scared."[26]

Instead of acting as a police force to keep the Indians in line and to ferret out individual offenders, army officers often avenged an Indian raid by swooping down upon a camp and slaughtering as many as possible, with no attempt to distinguish the guilty from the innocent. While some officers tried to befriend the Indians, others followed a policy like that of Colonel Thomas Moonlight, who was put in command of Fort Laramie in 1865. A few weeks after his arrival two Sioux warriors came to the fort, bringing a white woman and her baby whom they had ransomed from Indian captors. Instead of rewarding these friendly men, Moonlight had them hanged by chains and left their bodies dangling for months from a gallows on the bluff.[27] This attitude, in many instances, led normally friendly Indians

[25] Frederic L. Paxson, *History of the American Frontier, 1763–1893,* 503–504; Everett Dick, *Vanguards of the Frontier,* 101–22; Flora Warren Seymour, *Indian Agents of the Old Frontier.* Mrs. Seymour shows the Indian agent in a more favorable light.

[26] Martin F. Schmitt, editor, *General George Crook, His Autobiography, xiii.*

[27] Colonel Thomas Moonlight, report, War of the Rebellion records, Series 101, p. 276; Cheyenne *Sun,* December 9, 1886; Grinnell, op. cit., 181; LeRoy R. Hafen and Francis Marion Young, *Fort Laramie and the Pageant of the West,* 332–33. Moonlight later became territorial governor of Wyoming.

to join hostile bands and prolonged the period of Indian violence against the whites.

Clashes like that on the Little Big Horn in 1876, in which Custer and his men were annihilated, might have been prevented if a more sensible policy had been followed in getting the warriors back on their reservations.[28] "I know of no Indian war," said Charles Erskine Scott Wood, "that could not have been avoided by a little common humanity of frontiersmen, honesty of the Indian Ring in Washington, and common sense by the commissions sent out."[29]

Not until 1880 did the sufferings of the Indians and the frauds practiced against them shift white sentiment to the side of tolerance and justice. For years the tribes had been robbed and removed and their lands invaded. There were notorious scandals in the Indian service in the administration of President Grant: a sergeant reported in 1869 that contractors avoided scales "as they would the plague"; a House committee found Grant's first Indian commissioner guilty of "irregularities, neglect, and incompetency"; rancid flour and rotten beef were issued to the Oglala Sioux in 1875. Finally the exposure of federal corruption, the threat to invade the Indian Territory, and the disastrous removal of the Poncas in 1877 turned public opinion toward a fairer Indian policy.[30]

The Indians, for their part, had begun to realize that they no longer could resist the tide of white settlement. "Nobody wants peace more than I do," said Cochise, the aged Apache leader. "I have killed ten white men for every Indian I have lost, but still the white men are no fewer; and my tribe is growing smaller and smaller. It will disappear from the face of the earth if we do not have a good peace soon."[31]

As peace gradually settled on the Indian frontier, even the fierce Geronimo was tamed. He took to selling post cards and trinkets at expositions and was cheered as a hero in Theodore Roosevelt's inaugural parade. Long before that, the outlying

28 Paxson, *op. cit.*, 504.

29 Quoted by Stanley Vestal in *Sitting Bull*, 96.

30 Loring Benson Priest, *Uncle Sam's Stepchildren*, 66–80.

31 Flora Warren Seymour, *The Story of the Red Man*, 311.

farmer and ranchman had quit fearing Indian scalpers and merely dreaded the visits of bronze beggars and petty thieves. Many of the blanketed tribesmen still had agile fingers for food and loose articles. Settlers had a saying that an Indian would steal the tires from a man's wagon while it was being driven at a trot.[32]

In time the whites discovered that most of the Indians were as willing to repay kindness as to avenge wrong. In Matagorda County, in southern Texas, the early settlers made friends readily with the Karankawas. In a hot, dry summer, the wife of the chief heard that the daughter of one of the settlers was sick. She immediately sent some of the Indians to a well three miles away to bring a jug of fresh water to speed the girl's recovery.[33]

Northern Texas provided a similar instance. In the cabin village of Hardscrabble—later Lancaster—the settlers were frantic when they heard that a band of hostile warriors was approaching. They waited anxiously, with rifles in their hands, as the bearded Roderick Rawlins rode off across Ten Mile Creek to meet the visitors. But the chief, after looking closely at Rawlins, recognized him as the one who, after an earlier fight, had given him medicine instead of killing him. The Indians camped by the creek and gave the settlers no trouble.[34]

Finally, even military officers discovered that not all red men were devils. General George Crook, one of the army's more successful commanders in the West, found that the Indians generally responded to decent treatment. In addressing the West Point graduates of 1884, he concluded that "with all his faults, and he has many, the American Indian is not half as black as he has been painted. He is cruel in war, treacherous at times, and not over cleanly. But so were our forefathers. His nature, however, is responsive to treatment which assures him that it is based upon justice, truth, honesty, and common sense. It is not impossible that, with a fair and square system of dealing with him, the American Indian would make a better citizen than many

[32] Everett Dick, *The Sod-House Frontier, 1854–1890*, 166.

[33] John C. Marr in *Matagorda County Tribune,* August 23, 1945.

[34] Kenneth Foree in Dallas *Morning News,* June 5, 1945.

AN INDIAN FORAY
Harper's Weekly, May 10, 1873

Denver Library Western Collection

THE BATTLE OF THE WASHITA
Custer directed the massacre

Denver Library Western Collection

who neglect the duties and abuse the privileges of that proud title."[35]

Tomahawk justice had run its course. In the era of early settlement, vengeful retaliation between the hostile races had provided hair-raising incidents that would be related and pictured for generations. These had come at a high and usually needless cost in blood and sorrow on both sides. Pacification of the Indians was the first step in bringing order and law to the western frontier. It left many other steps to be taken before the whites could attain peace among themselves.

[35] Schmitt, *op. cit.*, *xiv*.

2. Regulators and Moderators

The feud arose from retaliation, which, since the first law of life is self-preservation, became the first law of man.

—WILLIAM SEAGLE, *The Quest for Law*

IN a street in the sleepy village of Shelbyville, near the eastern edge of the Republic of Texas, Joseph G. Goodbread was sitting on a weather-beaten hitching-rack one day in 1840, when the dogwood and sweet gum were beginning to show their fall colors. Goodbread was talking with a friend, who was idly marking in the dust with a stick.

Their conversation was interrupted by a ruffian who rode up on a fine Kentucky mare. The intruder had a rifle in his hand and fire in his eye. He was Charles W. Jackson, who had been the captain of a small steamboat on the Mississippi and Red rivers and who had escaped to Texas after being arrested for shooting one of his passengers. Jackson recently had tried for a seat in the Texas Congress but had been defeated.

Raising his weapon, Jackson coolly told Goodbread that he intended to shoot him. The astonished Goodbread tried to pacify his assailant. He said he thought the difficulty they had had earlier was settled amicably and assured Jackson that he held no ill will against him.

"Besides," he added, "I'm unarmed."

"So much the better," said Jackson, who then took deliberate aim and shot his victim through the heart, killing him almost instantly.[1]

[1] Ephraim M. Daggett, "Recollections of the War of the Moderators and Regulators." This manuscript by one of the Regulators is in the Texas collection of the late Dr. William E. Howard of Dallas; a transcript is in

Unwittingly Jackson had provided the incident that was to set off one of the western frontier's most devastating feuds—a conflict in which men on both sides, seeking justice through retaliation, gave rein to the most savage instincts.

Vengeance, the most common motive in the clashes between early settlers and Indians, intensified many of the quarrels among whites and converted some of them into bloody vendettas. Where statutory law was weakly enforced, some men felt impelled to seek justice of a sort by repaying wrongs in kind. Often this brought counteraction from the other side. As relatives and friends took up the cause, several of these feuds continued for years and became local wars before they were suppressed.

In the trouble in eastern Texas, Jackson had been embittered against Goodbread by Alfred George, who was running for sheriff of Shelby County. In 1839, George had sold Goodbread a Negro and had been paid in certificates for more than forty thousand acres of land. Both men knew that the certificates were bogus. The commissioners of that and near-by counties had been issuing these fraudulent papers in wholesale lots, and the faked ones passed for almost as much value as the genuine.

In 1840 the Republic had taken notice of these land frauds. In July of that year Shelby County was visited by a traveling board which weeded out the bogus certificates and, incidentally, invalidated those which Goodbread had traded to George for the Negro. George then demanded compensation from Goodbread; and then, fearing that Goodbread might dispose of the Negro, he induced the black man to run off and stay in the woods, where he supplied him with food.

Irked at this conduct, Goodbread aired the whole transaction, possibly aiming to defeat George's political campaign. George's next move was to enlist the services of Jackson, telling him falsely that Goodbread, instead of forgetting an earlier

the University of Texas library. Daggett, born in Canada in 1810, settled in Shelby County in the spring of 1840. He later served as an officer in the war with Mexico. Following the war, he moved to the site of Fort Worth and became one of the founders of the town established there in 1849.

difficulty, which had been patched up, had threatened to shoot Jackson down, as he would a dog, the next time he met him. Jackson, though surprised at this, agreed to put Goodbread out of the way.

After killing Goodbread, Jackson went to a local justice of the peace, Jonas Phelps, and made a two-hundred-dollar bond to appear at the next term of the district court. Later, after finding that he had been indicted for murder, Jackson became alarmed and obtained a change of venue to the Panola district of Harrison County, which adjoined on the north. After granting this change, Judge Thomas Johnson ordered George, who had been elected sheriff, to keep Jackson in jail without bond. The sheriff replied that the jail was in disrepair and was insecure. The best he could do, he said, would be to keep the prisoner under guard. But as soon as court was adjourned and the judge was gone, he turned Jackson loose.

Since the Panola court would not open for months, Jackson began taking steps to make sure of his acquittal. To be certain that he would have friends in the courtroom and, in the meantime, to wipe out or drive away any friends of Goodbread who might testify against him or make trouble for him, he organized a company of armed men. He called it the Shelby Guards, but most people referred to the group as Regulators. Ostensibly he used these rough, reckless fellows to suppress horse thieving and cattle rustling; and some honest men joined them because of their professed purpose. Actually they formed a guard for their leader and inflicted terroristic vengeance on persons he suspected of being his enemies.

Under the guise of vigilantes bent on putting down crime, Jackson's Regulators horsewhipped Squire Humphries, who was accused of horse theft, and drove other men out of the county. In the winter they decided to attack several of the slain Goodbread's friends who lived along McFadden Creek in the northern part of the county. First they went to the home of James Strickland, better known as Tiger Jim. On finding that he was away, they left a guard about the house and went to the cabin of two brothers, William (Buckskin Bill) and Bailey McFadden. When they learned that the brothers, too, were absent, they burned the McFadden and Strickland homes and their contents, refusing to allow the women and children to save even blankets to protect themselves from the cold.[2]

When Jackson finally was brought to trial in Pulaski, on July 15, 1841, Sheriff George had twenty of Jackson's followers, armed with double-barreled shotguns, pistols, and knives, guard the prisoner. The courtroom was crowded with other armed men, most of them Jackson's friends. More loitered outside, at the edge of a corn field.

When Judge John M. Hansford fined the sheriff for bringing the defendant into court armed, Jackson removed his weapons and placed them on the judge's bench. Then he took off his coat and his shoes, sat down in front of the judge, and demanded trial.[3]

After spending most of the day in picking a jury, Judge Hansford adjourned court for the night, instructing the sheriff to keep the prisoner in close custody, and left town. The next morning the judge failed to appear. Someone reported that he had gone to Marshall, saying that he did not intend to try Jackson with a mob of 150 of the latter's men in or surrounding the courthouse. The judge had also left the court clerk a note stating that he no longer would act as judge unless he could have a special force for protection. For the sheriff of Harrison County he had left an order which read:

> Being unwilling to risk my person in the courthouse any longer where I see myself surrounded by bravos and hired assassins, and no longer left free to preside as an impartial judge at this special term of court called for the trial of Charles W. Jackson, I order you to adjourn the court tomorrow at eight o'clock by proclamation without delay. From you at the regular term I shall expect

[2] Levi Henderson Ashcroft, "The History of the War Between the Regulators and Moderators of Shelby County." This book-length, unpublished manuscript was written in Tyler, Texas, in the early eighteen fifties. Dr. Ashcroft, a physician and lawyer, was born in North Carolina in 1803. He came to Texas in 1838 and lived in Shelbyville during the troubles there. Transcripts of his history are in the Texas State Library and the libraries of the University of Texas and Southern Methodist University.

[3] Daggett, *op. cit.*

the prisoner. You will secure the prisoner and keep him safely until then, by causing him to be securely ironed and keeping a strong guard until delivered by due course of the law.[4]

On hearing this, Jackson's attorney demanded that the trial proceed without the judge. The prosecuting attorney refused to introduce his witnesses, but the attorney for defense made a speech to the jury on the right of self-defense. After this plea the jurors voted to acquit Jackson, and the sheriff set him free. Judge Hansford, however, had not escaped trouble for long. Before the Shelby County disorders ended, he was mysteriously shot and killed.

Jackson's next move was to begin the lucrative work of capturing Texans who were wanted in Louisiana for stealing Negro slaves. He and his men delivered seven of these culprits to the proper Louisiana officers and collected rewards of several hundred dollars on each. One of the seven was the judge of the probate court of Harrison County, who later was convicted and sentenced to seven years in prison.

But retribution was on the way. The men whose homes were burned, along with other friends of Goodbread who were outraged at the farcical acquittal of Jackson, formed an opposition group of armed men. They called themselves the Moderators and put in command Edward Merchant, a man of determined character who had fled from Alabama after killing a man there. Most of the Moderators were from the northern part of the county. Despite their professed aims of preserving order and upholding the established courts, their first objective was to kill Jackson.

Thus began the war of the Regulators and the Moderators, one of the bloodiest vendettas of the rampaging frontier. For more than three years the fighting smoldered and flamed. It took many lives, kept the eastern section of Texas in continual turmoil, scared away respectable settlers, and caused others to leave. With the country thinly populated and the Republic's law enforcement weak, these roving bands of feudists killed

[4] Records of court proceedings of Harrison County, Minute Book A, 64; The *Red-Lander*, July 22, 1841.

and burned to bring vengeance on their foes. They treated the opposition forces with little, if any, more consideration than they would have given to painted savages.

One basic reason for the trouble was that many of the men who settled this section had emigrated for reasons similar to those of Jackson and Merchant. The area was at the edge of a formerly disputed strip which for years had been regarded as neutral ground and governed by neither Spain nor the United States. In 1831 a Texas settler, W. B. Dewees, had written: "It is nothing uncommon for us to inquire of a man why he ran away from the States. Few persons feel insulted by such a question. They generally answer for some crime or other which they have committed. If they deny having committed any crime or say they did not run away, they are generally looked upon suspiciously."[5]

Others gave like reports. Judge John Summerfield, who, under the pen name of A. W. Arrington, wrote a novel on the war of the Regulators and the Moderators, remarked in his preface that this section, like others on the frontier, had been "settled by a strange mixture of heterogeneous elements—by the enterprising and the virtuous seeking to improve their condition and by the vicious of different grades who desired to escape from the trammels or the terrors of the law."[6]

In Shelby County the Moderators were not long in catching up with Jackson. Eight of them ambushed him in the northern part of the county as he was returning from Logansport, on the Louisiana side of the Sabine River. The assailants were Buckskin Bill and Bailey McFadden and their younger brother Rufus, aged fourteen, Tiger Jim and Henry G. Strickland, Thomas Boatright, James Bledsoe, and Squire Humphries. Jackson was accompanied by an unoffending young German, Sidney Lauer, who had been a grocer in Shelbyville for several years.

From a thicket of undergrowth along the road, the hidden men poured a volley of buckshot into Jackson, who was struck

[5] W. B. Dewees, *Letters From Texas,* 135.

[6] A. W. Arrington, *The Rangers and Regulators of the Tanaha, viii.*

in the head and died instantly.[7] Humphries, remembering the whipping he had received at Jackson's hands, kicked the body and remarked, "We have finished the old fool now. The buzzards will have a feast tonight. Keep mum, boys, and we'll get rid of the whole gang."[8] Lauer, shot by accident because he happened to be in the way of the gunmen, was taken to a near-by farmhouse, where he died the next day.

While few persons in Shelby County regretted the death of Jackson, the killing of Lauer aroused indignation. Many concluded that the Moderators were little, if any, better than the Regulators they opposed. The latter group soon found a new leader in tall young Charles W. Moorman, a former Mississippian familiarly known as Watt Moorman, who had come to Texas in preference to facing a forgery charge.[9] A restless fellow who could not stick to any business, Moorman excelled in marksmanship, played billiards and tenpins, and dabbled in verse. He had many friends and had no scruples against riding their horses, spending their money, or wearing their clothes.[10] Under happier circumstances he might have become a leader in some useful field.

Moorman led a picked detachment of Regulators in search of the killers of Jackson and Lauer. The pursuers rode fast horses and covered long distances. Moorman carried a hunter's horn to summon his men and to signal them to advance or to retreat. Soon the Regulators caught Squire Humphries and exacted from him a confession that implicated the three McFaddens in the slaying of Jackson and Lauer. Enraged at this treason, Tiger Jim Strickland and Buckskin Bill McFadden called at the home of Benjamin McClure, a cousin of Humphries. When McClure opened his door, they shot him, then remounted their horses and headed southwestward, through pine forests, toward Montgomery County.[11]

[7] Ashcroft, *op. cit.*

[8] Quoted from an early issue of the *Cherokee Standard*, Rusk, Texas, date not given, in the Galveston *News*, July 28, 1907.

[9] Ashcroft, *op. cit.*

[10] Daggett, *op. cit.*

[11] Quoted from an early issue of the *Cherokee Standard*, date not given, in the Galveston *News*, July 28, 1907.

Quickly the Regulators took up the trail. With them was John W. Middleton, a deputy sheriff sympathetic with their faction. Moorman and his men ranged through the woods and across the rolling prairies of several counties to the west and southwest. One night they encountered Tiger Jim encamped twenty-five miles north of Crockett. They fired on him, wounding him in the shoulder; but he escaped in the darkness by lying on the side of his fleet horse.

Later the Moorman party found some of the Moderators at a house about a mile south of Montgomery. Quick on the draw, they killed James Bledsoe and captured the three McFaddens. On the way home with their captives, they encountered a hostile crowd of settlers in the village of Crockett but escaped without casualties.

Back in Shelbyville the Regulators tried their prisoners before a crowd of townspeople gathered at the courthouse on October 9, 1841. At the conclusion of the testimony, the citizens gave their verdict—174 for hanging and none against. Then the two older McFaddens were taken about a mile east of town and hanged from the same tree. The boy, Rufus, because of his youth and his promise to reform, was let off with twenty licks of a blackjack and ordered to leave town.[12]

Despite the one-sided vote for hanging the McFaddens, responsible people in Shelby and adjoining counties were turning against both the warring factions. Within two weeks of the double hanging, the *Red-Lander*, a newspaper published at San Augustine, observed:

> Both parties are doubtless culpable and liable to censure. With each party are associated many worthy and excellent citizens, and with them are also some of the most reckless desperadoes and daring outlaws on earth. It is ever the case when a portion of a community resorts to a summary process or to the lynch code for the redress of grievances. The most despicable loafers in a community

[12] The *Red-Lander*, October 14, 1841; John W. Middleton, *History of the Regulators and Moderators and the Shelby County War in 1841 and 1842 in the Republic of Texas*, 16–17, pamphlet by a deputy sheriff of Shelby County who sympathized with and aided the Regulators.

are the first to join the mob and are the most energetic in inflicting punishments on persons who are generally less obnoxious to society than the loafing vagabonds who would fain work a reformation in their morals.[13]

Colonel Alexander Horton, who knew many of the feudists, wrote a decade later: "Nearly all of the men engaged in this deadly feud were small farmers, recent immigrants to Texas; most of them had been dragged into this thing by unscrupulous men. A large majority of them were good men, honest and true, but they had fallen upon evil times."[14]

Law-abiding citizens of Shelby County, who occupied a neutral but precarious position between the Regulators and the Moderators, were worried. A group of them applied on October 16 to Judge G. W. Terrell of their district for aid to support their demoralized county officers and to protect lives and property. Sheriff George, fearing for his life, had fled to Nacogdoches, where he remained for several months, leaving his deputy to carry on his duties.

Judge Terrell acted promptly. He appointed Colonel Alexander Horton marshal of the district, with authority to order into the field such forces as might be required to disperse the roving bands and to restore order. Colonel Horton quickly organized a militia of three hundred. Before long he had in every part of the country armed men ready for duty.

On the evening of the eighteenth, while Colonel Horton was still busy with his preparations, a formidable force of about seventy Moderators advanced into San Augustine County, adjoining Shelby on the south. The invaders passed through the town of San Augustine and encamped a short distance away, in the woods on the Ayish Bayou. Their action greatly alarmed the residents, who were all the more excited when they heard that a body of 250 Regulators was on the way to give battle to the Moderators.

In the evening, while San Augustine people established

[13] The *Red-Lander,* October 21, 1841.

[14] Alexander Horton, "Early History of San Augustine," manuscript of a series of articles which appeared in a San Augustine newspaper, 1884–89, quoted by George Louis Crockett in *Two Centuries in East Texas,* 198.

pickets about their town and brought out rusty guns, boarding pikes, axes, and hatchets, Colonel Horton with three lieutenants went to the camp of the Moderators in an effort to prevent a fight. Later in the night he headed in the opposite direction to meet the approaching Regulators, whom he found encamped five miles from town. The Regulators had denounced Judge Terrell's writ as illegal, but the next morning both they and the Moderators were induced to return home without a battle.[15]

This truce diminished the violent activities of the two factions for a time. But Shelbyville was still an armed camp, dominated by the Regulators; and Moorman and some of his gunmen continued to make forays into the country. Across the Sabine in Louisiana, they caught up with one of the original Moderators, Thomas Boatright, who, along with Squire Humphries, had been accused of stealing horses early in 1840. Boatright, who had lost his shoes, coat, and hat, in a sudden flight from Shelby County, was picking cotton on the Ferguson plantation in De Soto Parish to replenish his clothing. The Regulators captured him in the field and took him back to the Texas side, near the Watson ferry. As they hesitated to kill him in cold blood without a pretext, they worked out a stratagem. A Regulator who had a law license pretended to befriend the prisoner, called him over toward a cane brake, and told him to run. Boatright started to sprint for safety but quickly fell dead with his back full of buckshot.[16]

Moorman, who was indicted for the Boatright killing but avoided trial, continued to hunt down the Moderators. He failed to get the Strickland brothers, but other hands were reaching for them. Tiger Jim was killed in a gun fight in Louisiana, and Henry had a gun smashed through his skull when he went berserk in a grocery. In Shelbyville, Moorman's intimidating influence was so strong that many men who would have preferred to stand aloof joined the Regulators from fear of being punished as Moderators. Moorman seemed impervious to assassins' bullets; an impetuous young teacher fired at him from ambush but succeeded only in wounding him.

15 The *Red-Lander,* October 21, 1841.
16 Ashcroft, *op. cit.*

The high-handed methods used by Moorman and his Regulators were shown in a note they left on one citizen's door. It read:

Shelby County, January 4th, 1842.

Mr. West:

Sir:—Not finding you at home, this means of notifying you to leave our county by the 14th inst. was necessarily adopted. If, sir, after the prescribed time, you are found within the limits of our county, you will be dealt with according to Lynch. This certainly cannot be comfortable. Nevertheless, you must and shall go, as the undersigned and others will convince you on a failure to comply with the requisitions.

By order of the Shelby Guards.

C. W. Moorman, Col. Commandant.
B. F. Hooper.
W. Cook.
Charles B. Daggett.[17]

The terror caused by this feud had an adverse effect on farming and business. In the issue of January 17, 1842, the *Red-Lander* asserted that "land is now worth only ten cents an acre in Shelby County, where formerly it was valued at more than twenty times that sum; and the tide of emigration has completely turned from that county, which is shunned by the emigrant as another Sodom."

To some degree the feud spread to adjoining counties. One of its more striking episodes occurred early in 1842 at Potter's Point on Ferry or Soda Lake, later known as Caddo Lake, in Red River County, later Marion County. Colonel Robert Potter, a signer of the Texas Declaration of Independence and the first secretary of the navy of the Republic of Texas, had built his home on this point. Potter was serving his second term in the Texas Senate. He was a Moderator and had incurred the enmity of a neighbor, Captain William P. Rose, who headed a band of

[17] The *Red-Lander,* January 17, 1842, reprinted in the Houston *Morning Star,* February 5, and the Houston *Telegraph and Register,* February 9.

Harrison County Regulators. On November 15, 1841, President Mirabeau B. Lamar had offered a reward of five hundred dollars for the capture of Rose, who was wanted in connection with several killings.

On February 28, 1842, following the adjournment of the Texas Congress, Colonel Potter arrived back in eastern Texas, determined to capture Rose. He gathered about twenty men and went to Rose's home, but Rose hid under a pile of brush and escaped notice. In retaliation, Rose and his armed band surrounded the Potter home before dawn on March 2 and captured two members of the household as they crossed the yard to get corn to be ground for breakfast. When Potter went out to face his assailants, he was fired upon and ran down the hill to the lake. Leaning his rifle against a cypress on the bank, he dived into the chilly water. But his pursuers were close at his heels. As the colonel rose to the surface for air, one of them shot him in the head with his own weapon.[18]

When the district court met in Shelbyville in the spring of 1842, Moorman and his men mounted a small cannon on cart wheels and pointed it at the courthouse; but Judge William B. Ochiltree was not intimidated. He ordered the sheriff to remove the artillery piece and to arrest anyone who interfered with him. The district attorney, Royal T. Wheeler, presented to the grand jury the names of a dozen or more men who had taken part in the hanging of the McFaddens. As most of the jurors had had a hand in this hanging and excused themselves for that reason, they returned no indictment.[19] While the court was in session, Moorman beat an old man over the head with a club.

[18] Harriet A. Ames, "The History of Harriet A. Ames During the Early Days of Texas", manuscript, of which the University of Texas library has a transcript; New Orleans *Daily Picayune*, March 19, 1842; A. W. Arrington, *Desperadoes of the Southwest;* John H. McLean, "Bob Potter and Old Rose," *Texas Methodist Historical Quarterly*, Vol. II, No. 1 (July, 1910), 1–11; John H. McLean, *Reminiscences*, 15–21; Louis Wiltz Kemp, *The Signers of the Texas Declaration of Independence*, 258–77. McLean, a Methodist preacher, defends Rose against Potter. He attributes Potter's enmity to Rose's support of another candidate for the Senate and asserts that Potter, by misrepresentation, induced President Lamar to offer the reward for Rose's capture.

[19] Ashcroft, *op. cit.*

Dripping with blood, the victim rushed into the courthouse for protection; but no one dared to arrest the Regulator chief.[20]

Watt Moorman resigned his command in midsummer, and the Regulators met in Shelbyville on July 9 to elect a successor. They chose H. W. K. Myrick,[21] but Moorman continued to be the effective leader and soon was back in full control.

Between forays, Moorman found time for romance. He courted and married Helen Mar Daggett, the comely and popular daughter of a respectable farmer who sympathized with the Regulators and the sister of two active Regulators, Charles B. and Ephraim M. Daggett. As Moorman was hardly the domestic type, the treatment he gave his bride soon brought a separation. She returned to her father's home but never fully lost her affection for the bold clan leader or her interest in the Regulators.

The retaliatory raids and killings continued. One Regulator, Henry Runnels, accused another, Samuel Hall, of stealing his hogs; but the latter indignantly denied the charge. Both men went about armed, and before long a farm hand who had worked for Runnels shot and killed Hall. The killer escaped; but later one of Hall's brothers, Joseph, caught him in Arkansas, took him over the line into the Cherokee Nation, and hanged him.

Partisans of the murdered Hall also hired two gunmen to kill Runnels. The pair carried out this task on a lonely road while Runnels was on his way to Shreveport with a load of cotton. The Regulators caught one of the gunmen and hanged him from a scaffold they had prepared in advance in Shelbyville's public square, fifty feet from the courthouse. Later the Regulators went after James Hall. They killed him while he and his brother John were plowing corn on the former's farm, six miles below Shelbyville.

These and other bold killings led to a revival of the Modera-

[20] Oran M. Roberts, "The Shelby War, or the Regulators and Moderators," *Texas Magazine*, III (August, 1897), 51. Roberts, who settled in San Augustine in 1841, was a lawyer whose work took him to Shelbyville when court was in session there. As district attorney he was present at the 1844 meeting with President Houston which preceded the issuance of the proclamation to end the Shelby County War. Roberts was Governor of Texas, 1879–83.

[21] The *Red-Lander*, November 10, 1842.

tors with a new name, new leadership, and higher aims. In a secret meeting at Bells Springs, six miles from Shelbyville, outraged citizens, including neutrals and former Moderators, organized a company of Reformers and put Colonel James F. Cravens in command. Although usually referred to as Moderators, this new group aimed to end bloodshed and to support the established law-enforcement agencies rather than to obtain direct vengeance for its members.

In an effort to make peace, leaders of the two factions met at Camp Graham Springs. Moorman, who still designated himself colonel commandant of the Shelby Guards, agreed that, if Cravens' men would retire to their homes and lay down their arms as peaceful citizens, no good citizen in Shelby County would be molested. Yet the ink was barely dry on this pact when Moorman himself shot and killed a man at a Baptist revival meeting at the Masonic Hall in San Augustine. His victim was John M. Bradley, a prominent citizen who was accused of harboring Moderators and who was suspected of implication in the killing of Runnels.

The feud continued to have a depressing effect on Shelby County. Colonel Alexander Horton, who was there throughout the trouble, wrote later:

> Men quit their homes and banded together for safety. Want of confidence and suspicion seemed to be contagious. A reign of terror and dread of impending evil spread themselves like a nightmare over the land. The farms were left untilled, growing in weeds. Men barred their doors at night, nor would they open them unless at the call of a well-known voice. Men were shot from ambush, prisoners were hanged, others were driven from their homes. The most foolish and extravagant infatuation seemed to have seized upon all alike.[22]

Of this period, a Shelbyville citizen wrote to a friend in Charleston: "Civil war, with all its horror, has been raging in this community. The citizens of the county are about equally divided into two parties, the Regulators and Moderators. It is

22 Horton, quoted by Crockett, *op. cit.*, 198.

no uncommon sight to see brothers opposed to each other. Every man's interest in this county is seriously affected."[23]

With his mounted band of one hundred armed men, Moorman continued to terrorize several counties. By the middle of 1844, he began to acquire thirst for still greater power. The Republic of Texas, established in 1836, had been growing weaker. Its money was almost worthless, its political factions were at each other's throats, and its puny military force was a faint shadow of the small but victorious band at San Jacinto. Sam Houston had returned to the presidency but faced many difficulties. Why should not a strong man like Moorman overturn the government by force and even usurp the seat of the popular Houston?

No one knows just what went on in Moorman's mind, but he formed a provisional committee and was believed by some to be making preparations to take over the government of Texas, reserving for himself the post of commander of the Republic's military forces. His committee met secretly at the home of Matthew Brinson on July 28, 1844, with a hundred of Moorman's Regulators acting as guards. After its organizational work was done, Moorman handed the committee a list of twenty-five citizens of Shelby County, who he said had disturbed the peace or opposed the Regulators. He asked, and obtained, approval for notifying them to leave the county within fifteen days or suffer death. The list included several of the county's leaders, such as Sheriff A. Llewellyn and his deputy, Colonel James F. Cravens.[24]

On the next day the Regulators set out confidently to serve personal notices to the proscribed men. But some of the messengers, on looking into the muzzles of loaded pistols, lost interest quickly. Moorman had to satisfy himself by posting the list on the courthouse door. This warning stirred the town but had an effect opposite to that intended. So many men enlisted under Cravens' leadership against the Regulators that Moorman sent to San Augustine County for help. Then he retired to

[23] Letter, dater September 22, 1844, published in the *National Intelligencer,* October 31, and the New Orleans *Daily Picayune,* November 1.

[24] Ashcroft, *op. cit.*

WATT MOORMAN
His horn summoned the Regulators

Mrs. Will Lake, Fort Worth

the Beauchamp farm on the Buena Vista road, three miles west of Shelbyville. With eighty men, he occupied a fenced half-acre that contained a log cabin and a supply of planks that his men used in making a barricade.

Both sides gathered forces quickly. Colonel Cravens prepared to attack the Regulators but was at a disadvantage because he had no artillery and no cover for his men. Firing went on for several hours on August 5, and both parties suffered from lack of water. In this Battle of the Cow Pens, one Moderator was killed and several men on each side were wounded. Moorman was not at the fort during this fighting, as he had gone after recruits.

That night, while the Moderators were encamped on a creek in the timber, two miles away, the Regulators abandoned their fort. In the darkness they went to Hilliard's Spring, near Flat Fork Creek, fifteen miles distant. On their way they met Moorman with thirty recruits. At the spring they found one hundred men from Harrison County and the Panola area. They immediately began felling pines to build fortifications.

Cravens and his men followed the Regulators. On the morning of August 9, they reached a log church about two miles from Hilliard's Spring, where they stopped to await promised supplies. By this time Cravens had about 165 men, armed with whatever weapons they happened to own. Soon the Moderators saw a woman riding toward their camp. By looking closely they discovered that she was Watt Moorman's wife. The visitor called for Colonel Cravens and complained that she had been shot at by some of his men along the road. Cravens apologized for the lack of chivalry, and she rode off. As she left, the Regulators began firing on the Moderators, who discovered that Mrs. Moorman's visit had been only a ruse to distract their attention.

Cravens occupied high ground, lightly wooded. Making use of this advantage, he sent a detachment to hide in the bed of a small creek below his main position. There his men soon made a surprise attack on an approaching company of Regulators from Harrison County, commanded by Captain George Davidson. In this skirmish Davidson was killed. Two other Regulators suffered wounds from which they died later, and others received lesser injuries. At this outcome, the Harrison County men retreated precipitately to the shelter of the woods.

The church hill battle continued for several hours, but in a desultory manner. Most of the firing was done from behind trees. With no uniforms worn on either side, the fighters sometimes had difficulty in distinguishing friends from enemies. There was a great variety of garb, although most of the feudists wore jeans and broad-brimmed wool hats. Unable to induce his followers to renew the assault, Moorman blew a retreat blast on his hunting horn. At this the Regulators retired in considerable disorder to Hilliard's Spring. After attending their dead and wounded, they left in the night. Later they took a new stand at a Methodist camping ground three miles south of Shelbyville, where they began building defenses.[25]

Before much more fighting could take place, however, the feudists learned that Sam Houston had sent a large militia force on their trail. The President, accompanied by General Thomas J. Rusk, had come to San Augustine in mid-August, at the insistence of local citizens. As he sat on a pile of firewood and whittled a stick of white pine, Houston listened to Judge Ochiltree and others. Then he issued a proclamation calling attention to the state of anarchy in Shelby County, where parties were "arrayed against each other in hostile attitude, contrary to law and order." To end these hostilities and to re-establish order, he commanded all citizens engaged therein to lay down their arms and retire to their homes.[26]

President Houston's call for militiamen brought six hundred volunteers from San Augustine, Sabine, Nacogdoches, and Rusk counties. These were placed under the command of Colonel Travis G. Broocks of San Augustine. At the same time, Colonel Alexander Horton, who had become marshal of the Republic, was given orders to arrest ten of the leading men of each party and bring them to President Houston. On the arrival of the

[25] *Ibid.*

[26] "Proclamations of the Presidents", Republic of Texas, Texas State Library, Austin; Amelia W. Williams and Eugene C. Barker, editors, *The Writings of Sam Houston,* IV, 361–62; the *Red-Lander,* August 17, 1844; Roberts, *op. cit.,* 56.

militia force, Cravens ordered his men to lay down their arms; but Moorman dispersed his Regulators. Before long, however, the militiamen captured the belligerent chief, disarmed him, and took him—along with others—to the President. When Judge Ochiltree convened court in Shelbyville, Sam Houston appeared there and gave the feudists a fatherly talk.

This meeting ended the Shelby County War, a tragic conflict in which frontiersmen sought justice on a basis of barbaric vengeance. Watt Moorman was tried for the murder of Bradley but was acquitted on the plea that Bradley had threatened his life. Feeling lost without his following, Moorman wandered from place to place. After a few years, he quarreled with a Logansport doctor, Robert Burns, and boasted that he would kill him before sundown. But when they met, the doctor reached his trigger first, and the former clan leader fell dead in a Logansport street.[27]

In Shelby and adjoining counties, where an estimated fifty men had died in the fighting between Regulators and Moderators in the four years since the killing of Joseph Goodbread, factional feeling gradually died down. There were only a few sporadic outbreaks after the battles of August, 1844. Admission of Texas to the United States brought a stronger government, new immigration pushed the frontier farther west, and leaders of the opposing groups signed a peace pact. In this they agreed to drop the designations of Regulators and Moderators, to forgive and forget, and to discountenance any attempt to revive the unfortunate strife. In 1846, Shelby County men, who a few years earlier had been deadly enemies, rode off together, even though in two separate companies, to fight the Mexicans.

The recriminations of these early Texas feudists had proved as futile as the tomahawk justice inflicted by and against the red men. They had failed to pacify the frontier. Instead, they had impeded settlement and had delayed the effective operation of lawful courts. Yet elsewhere on the fringe of white habitation there still were many impetuous men who believed that a personal wrong called for direct retaliation.

[27] Undated letter from the clerk of the court at Mansfield, Louisiana, to Sam Asbury, in Asbury papers, University of Texas library.

3. Feudist Guns

The typical feud is not lawlessness. It is an appeal to a law which is felt to be a reasonable substitute for legal redress which cannot be obtained—sometimes to a law higher or more valid than those on the statute books.

—C. L. Sonnichsen, *"I'll Die Before I'll Run"*

As dusk settled over the farm of the elderly Pitkin Taylor in southern Texas one summer evening, five armed men crept stealthily along the corn rows toward the house. One of the intruders had a cowbell which he rang at intervals, while another noisily crushed stalks of corn. Soon Taylor heard the bell and went to drive out the cow he supposed had wandered into the corn field. As he came within range, six-shooters blazed and the old man fell with a mortal wound. Another Taylor had been put out of the way.[1]

Many such incidents spotted the Sutton-Taylor vendetta, longest and bloodiest of the frontier feuds in Texas. These conflicts were most common in the decade that followed the Civil War. Many families had been uprooted from their old homes and forced to make a new start. Some were willing to forget the past, but others carried westward unhealed wounds of the conflict and nursed bitterness in their hearts. Often tempers were short and insults were magnified. In the absence of other punishment, many felt called upon to avenge wrongs to themselves or to their kin. Nearly always their actions evoked counter-vengeance, as in the earlier conflict of the Regulators and the Moderators. Often well-intentioned efforts to bring order

[1] San Antonio *Light,* June 29, 1913; Jack Hays Day, *The Sutton-Taylor Feud* (pamphlet by a Taylor kinsman), 14–15.

through informal regulatory action started feuds that took many lives.

In Missouri and elsewhere, remnants of William C. Quantrill's band of guerrillas and bushwhackers continued to prowl and to carry vengeance to their foes. Kansas, Arkansas, and the Indian Territory nourished vendettas that went on for years. Little Lake Valley in California was the scene of a feud between the Coates and Frost families in 1865. This bitterness was the result of a fist fight between two schoolboys and culminated in a gun battle in which six men were killed.

The feuds of this period were most numerous and most serious in those parts of the frontier which suffered the injustices of Reconstruction. The Sutton-Taylor strife began in the summer of 1866 and lasted about fifteen years. It was an outgrowth of disputes over longhorn cattle in an era in which the ranges were unfenced and the branding of calves of doubtful ownership was a profitable venture. The feud might have died down quickly, had it not been intensified and prolonged by oppressive measures of the carpetbaggers. Since the state government was one that honest men could not respect and minor political offenses were made an excuse for terrorism on the part of state troops, many Texans decided to inflict their own penalties on persons who had insulted them, made off with their cattle, or killed their relatives.

Early in the Reconstruction period, members of the Taylor family incurred the wrath of carpetbag officials by punishing a Negro for some offense. Rather than submit to the troops sent after them, they became fugitives. In one place or another they hid, taking food and horses where they could. Charles Taylor, with several others, was arrested in the summer of 1866 by a party of farmers and ranchmen from DeWitt County who were out looking for horse thieves. Taylor made a dash for freedom but was shot and killed.

The DeWitt County party was led by young William Sutton, whose family already had had trouble with the Taylors over cattle. A few months later Buck Taylor encountered Sutton in a Clinton saloon and threatened to shoot him. Instead, Sutton killed Taylor and one of his friends, Dick Chisholm. With two Taylors dead, their kinsmen swore vengeance against Sutton and his partisans. While some of the elders advised caution, the hot-blooded younger Taylors were determined to punish the Sutton faction and to even the score of dead.

Both families had good records until their feud made them deadly enemies. At the head of one clan was Creed Taylor, nearing sixty years of age, an early settler and a veteran of many forays against Indians and Mexicans. The Taylor family had several branches and many marriage connections. The other side was led by six-foot William Sutton, only twenty years old when the feud began. Sutton was no carpetbagger but came to regard the Taylors as outlaws and sided with the troopers who hounded them.

On the rolling prairies and in the post-oak thickets, the feud sputtered and crackled. Before long two more Taylors were killed and Sutton received a bullet wound while sitting in a saloon in Cuero. John Wesley Hardin, one of the most heartless gunmen in the state and an in-law of the Taylors, shot down one of their foes in Cuero. On several occasions, open battles between armed bands of the two factions were narrowly averted.[2]

The feud flamed high on the morning of August 26, 1870, when armed horsemen of the Sutton faction took in tow Henry and William Kelly, brothers who lived on adjoining farms in DeWitt County. The visitors said they were going to take the Kellys to Hallettsville, thirty-five miles distant. Henry's wife, suspecting foul play, followed in a buggy along a woods trail. She reported that from an elevation she saw the riders halted in an open space. William had dismounted and was cutting tobacco to fill his pipe. As he struck a match to light the pipe, one of his captors shot him. At the same time, another member of the Sutton faction shot Henry, who fell from his horse. The assassins then fired into the bodies, and gun smoke obscured their departure through the brush.[3] Later they were acquitted on their plea that the Kellys had been shot while trying to escape.

[2] [Victor M. Rose], *The Texas Vendetta, or the Sutton-Taylor Feud;* John Wesley Hardin, *The Life of John Wesley Hardin.*

Feudists on both sides had reason to fear shots in the back. Near Tomlinson Creek, between Helena and Yorktown, Taylor men ambushed and killed two of the Sutton faction in the spring of 1873. A few days later, retribution overtook reckless Jack Helm. He had been one of the commanders of the state troops sent against the Taylors but had been dismissed. Wes Hardin and Jim Taylor, a son of the slain Pitkin Taylor, found Helm working in a blacksmith shop in the country.

"You're the man I'm after," said Jim; and before Helm could get his gun, he shot him dead. Then the visitors calmly remounted and rode off.[4]

Soon afterward, three of the Taylor faction were locked in the DeWitt County jail on a charge of cattle theft. Before they could be tried, Sutton partisans broke into the jail, took the prisoners out, and hanged them from a tree in the cemetery. At this, armed feudists began to gather in Clinton, ready for battle. Bloodshed seemed likely, but Judge Henry Clay Pleasants induced the glowering men to go home.

Leaders of the two factions signed a peace pact in May, 1873, but its effect did not last long. Before the end of the year, a Taylor man was slain in front of his store at Thomaston. In the following spring, William Sutton went to Cuero to arrange for sending a herd of cattle to Kansas. Feudists on both sides assembled there in armed groups, each cautiously watching the other for the first sign of attack. This maneuvering went on for two days. Merchants closed their stores, and townspeople remained fearful behind closed doors. Finally good sense prevailed, and the men on both sides agreed to return home without a clash.

Soon afterward, Bill Sutton, who several times had barely dodged whistling bullets and twice had had his neck imperiled in murder trials, decided to quit. A quieter countryside might be better for the baby he and his young wife were expecting. After starting his cattle on the trail to Kansas, he prepared to

[3] Sworn statements made by Mrs. Henry Kelly and others on October 15, 1870, published in the Austin *Daily Republican,* November 1, 1870, and reprinted in [Rose], *op. cit.*

[4] Hardin, *op .cit.,* 81–82; Day, *op. cit.,* 18.

take a ship for New Orleans. With his wife and a friend, Gabriel W. Slaughter, he went to the Gulf port of Indianola. On March 11, a few minutes after the three had walked up the gangplank, they were followed by Jim and Bill Taylor.

Sutton saw them first.

"Hell's in the door, Gabe!" he shouted. "Here comes Jim Taylor."

Both the hunted men reached for their guns, but were too late. The two Taylors fired, and Sutton and Slaughter fell dead. The assassins returned quickly to the wharf, mounted the fast horses they had tied there, and galloped out of town.[5]

Reuben Brown of Cuero became head of the Sutton faction —but not for long. While playing cards in the back room of a saloon, he was riddled with lead from Colts in the hands of three masked men. For a while thereafter the feud abated. In the next two years the Taylor faction was subdued, and partisans of the Suttons became peace officers. But cattle thefts continued, along with occasional shootings.[6] Then, on the night of September 19, 1876, conflict burst out anew at the country home of Dr. Philip Brazell.

Dr. Brazell, a former member of the Georgia Legislature, was a respected, law-abiding country physician of DeWitt County. He had remained aloof from the Sutton-Taylor feud and had treated gunshot wounds of men on each side. The Brazells were asleep in their rural cabin when members of the Sutton faction arrived, between ten and eleven at night. Calls of the visitors and the barking of dogs woke members of the family, who were ordered from the outside to light a lamp. The callers, who said they were looking for a fugitive, told the family to dress and come out of the house.

The night riders took with them to the near-by woods Dr. Brazell, his eldest son, George, and two younger sons, Theodore, eighteen, and Sylvanus, seventeen. Mrs. Brazell, a grown daughter, and the younger children were left at the house. About ten minutes later, as the clock struck eleven, Mrs. Brazell heard

[5] [Rose], *op. cit.,* 52; Hardin, *op. cit.,* 86–87; [George H. French, compiler], *Indianola Scrapbook,* 85–91.

[6] [Rose], *op. cit.*

shooting. The feudists had shot the doctor through the body and one leg and had put a bullet between George's eyes. Both died at once. The younger sons, who witnessed the killings and recognized the assassins, escaped to a neighbor's house, where they remained until morning.[7]

The unprovoked Brazell murders aroused the law-abiding people of DeWitt County as no earlier crime had done. When the district court met in December, Lieutenant Lee Hall and six of his Texas Rangers were on hand to summon and protect witnesses, a task with which the sheriff could not be trusted. Although survivors of the Brazell family had feared to reveal the names of the killers at the coroner's inquest, the grand jury had evidence that led it to indict seven men, two of whom were deputy sheriffs. With the warrants in his pocket, Lieutenant Hall and sixteen Rangers set out from Clinton in a cold drizzle on the evening of December 20 to find the indicted men. They came upon all of them, with a group of people, dancing at a wedding party at a farm home near Cuero.

After having his men surround the house, Hall stepped unarmed into the doorway. As those inside recognized him, the music stopped. Women screamed, and men reached for their guns.

"Do you want anyone here, Hall?" asked the bridegroom, one of the indicted deputies.

"Yes, I want seven men," he answered, naming the questioner and six others.

"How many men you got?" asked the other deputy.

"Seventeen, counting myself," Hall replied calmly.

"Well, we've got seventy. I guess we'll have to fight it out."

"That's the talk!" shouted the lieutenant. He gave the feudists three minutes to get out their women and children and ordered his men to shoot to kill. But before the three minutes were up, the men inside decided they did not want to fight and allowed Hall and his men to take their guns. The party then continued, with the Rangers rotating at guard duty and taking

[7] *Cases Argued and Adjudged in the Court of Appeals of the State of Texas,* VIII, 254–310.

part in the festivities. At daybreak the Rangers returned to Clinton with their seven prisoners.[8]

Despite threatening letters, Judge Pleasants refused bail. Because of the terrorism prevailing in DeWitt County, he sent them to another county for trial. Three of them were convicted in April, 1878, but in the following year the Court of Appeals reversed the judgment. The higher court held that the indictment was faulty and that illegal and inadmissible evidence had been allowed to go to the jury over the objections of the defendants.[9] In 1891 a new indictment was obtained. Later one of the assassins, David Augustine, was convicted and sentenced to twenty-five years in prison. His sentence was confirmed in 1899, nearly twenty-three years after the double murder; but he was pardoned before he could be taken to prison. By this time the flames of the tragic Sutton-Taylor conflict had long since subsided.

This and other feuds were evidences of growing pains in the settlement of the West. Cattlemen were pushing into the unoccupied plains to profit from the increased demand for beef. From behind, they were being crowded by homesteaders looking for free farm land. Often statutory law and effective courts were slow in catching up with this westward tide. In such a situation, many of the pioneers continued to try their cases with six-shooters and Winchesters.

While feuds broke out elsewhere on the western frontier, they seemed especially bitter among the trigger-fingered Texans. When the Sutton-Taylor vendetta was at its height, one almost as deadly began between the Horrell and Higgins families and their partisans a few counties to the northwest. Again Reconstruction imposed irritations and insults, converting a difficult situation for cattlemen into an explosive one.

The outbreak came early in 1873 at Lampasas, a frontier cow town in the hill country northwest of Austin. In the un-

[8] N. A. Jennings, *A Texas Ranger*, 281–88; Frank Bushick, *Glamorous Days*, 235–36; Dora Neill Raymond, *Captain Lee Hall of Texas*, 70–72.

[9] *Cases Argued and Adjudged in the Court of Appeals of the State of Texas*, VIII, 254–310.

fenced pastures, where scrub oaks and cedars provided cover, cattle stealing had become serious. A local company of Minute Men, formed to cope with Indian raiders, had proved ineffective against the white rustlers. After the sheriff had been killed while trying to make an arrest, the Adjutant General, F. L. Britton, sent a detachment of the unpopular state police—the Reconstruction substitute for the Texas Rangers—to Lampasas to restore order and security. Captain Thomas Williams took with him seven men, one of them a Negro. On his way the Captain had recourse to a jug and indiscreetly boasted that he was "going to clean out those damned Horrell boys."

When the state policemen arrived in Lampasas, past midday, they dismounted and tied their horses to the live oaks that made a clump of green in the center of town. In looking about, Captain Williams recognized Bill Bowen, a brother-in-law of Merritt Horrell. He noticed that Bowen wore a pistol as he entered Jerry Scott's Gem Saloon at the northwest corner of the square.

Williams told the Negro to watch the horses, stationed three of his men outside the saloon, and entered with the other three. As most of the unoccupied men were attending an exciting trial elsewhere in town, the saloon at that hour had only about fifteen patrons. Some were drinking, and others playing billiards; one was sawing a fiddle, and another picking at a banjo.

Once inside the saloon, Captain Williams turned to Bill Bowen, who still had on his six-shooter.

"I see you're wearing a pistol," he said. "I arrest you."

Then Martin Horrell spoke up. "You haven't done anything, Bill. You don't have to be arrested if you don't want to."

This remark was a signal for gunfire that began almost simultaneously from both sides. Williams fired at Mart Horrell, wounding him seriously. Return fire filled the saloon with smoke. When it cleared, Captain Williams and one of his men, T. M. Daniels, lay dead on the floor. One of the other policemen, Wesley Cherry, was killed outside the door. Another, Andrew Melville, received a mortal wound as he ran down the street toward the Huling Hotel. The uniformed Negro leaped on his horse and made a John Gilpin ride back to Austin, sixty-seven miles away.[10]

After carrying the wounded Mart to their mother's home, not far from the saloon, Tom and Merritt Horrell, along with Bill Bowen and several others, left town hastily. When the Adjutant General arrived with a new detachment of policemen, he arrested Allen Whitecraft, James Grizell, Jerry Scott, and the disabled Mart, but was unable to find any of the other Horrells.[11]

The policemen took the prisoners to the jail at Georgetown, in near-by Williamson County. Mart Horrell's wife followed and nursed him in his cell. As soon as he was able to ride again, she informed his brothers; and soon afterward, a group of horsemen arrived with Winchesters and a sledge hammer. The jail door gave way, and the prisoners walked out.[12]

Back in Lampasas County, the Horrells decided to sell their herds and move to New Mexico. Accompanied by Bill and Tom Bowen, John Dixon, Ben Turner, and several other men, they headed northwestward through Russell Gap. After delivering their surplus cattle in Coleman County, they trailed out across the plains to Lincoln County, New Mexico, and settled on the upper Hondo River, west of Roswell.

There they found that peace was still a jump ahead. New Mexico had its own cattle troubles, and relations between the Mexicans and the Anglo-American settlers were tense. Disputes of the Horrell clan with the Mexicans over water rights led to a gun battle in Lincoln. When the smoke lifted, Ben Horrell and several others were dead.

In retaliation, the Horrells rode into Lincoln and shot up a Mexican *fiesta,* killing four men. The Mexicans complained to the governor about the Horrells, and the latter decided to end the trouble by moving back to Texas. On their way to Roswell, they were ambushed and lost Ben Turner, a brother-in-law, who

[10] James B. Gillett, *Six Years With the Texas Rangers* (revised edition), 73–74.

[11] San Antonio *Herald,* March 25, 1873.

[12] Gillett, *op. cit.,* 75.

[13] C. L. Sonnichsen, "I'll Die Before I'll Run: A History of Feuding in Texas," manuscript.

had been with them in the fight in which Captain Williams was killed.[13]

The Horrells together with their in-laws and friends returned to the wooded Lampasas hills late in February, 1874. But again the peace they sought proved elusive. On the last day of that month the sheriff was hunting them with a posse of fifty men—about five times as many as were in the Horrell party. On March 5 the two groups met. The sheriff's minute men fired on the Horrells. But the hunted men, apparently determined on a peaceful existence, refused to shoot back. Rufus Overstreet and Jerry Scott were captured, the latter with a bullet hole through his lung. Merritt Horrell escaped with a slight wound, and a bystander was shot in the abdomen.[14]

In the following September, Merritt Horrell and Bill Bowen surrendered on the charge of having killed the state policemen. They made bonds of ten thousand dollars each and returned to their cattle raising.[15] In October, 1876, they were tried and acquitted.[16] At that time the Horrells were living on Sulphur Creek, in the northern edge of Burnet County, about ten miles southeast of Lampasas.

Acquittal on the 1873 charge, instead of ending their troubles, was a prelude to worse ones for the Horrells. Their former friends and neighbors, the Higgins family, who still ranched on the Lampasas River northeast of town, re-entered their affairs to brew a tragic feud. A misunderstanding arose; and John Pinckney Calhoun Higgins, better known as "Pink," accused Merritt Horrell, youngest of the brothers, of tampering with his stock. After more words, the fiery Pink announced that he was going to kill every one of the Horrells if they did not let his cattle alone.

Soon afterward, on January 22, 1877, Merritt Horrell was sitting in a chair in a back room of the Gem Saloon, warming himself by the fire. The cozy atmosphere changed suddenly

[14] Lampasas *Dispatch,* March 19, 1874, republished in Dallas *Daily Herald,* March 25.

[15] Austin *Daily Statesman,* September 20, 1874, citing the Lampasas *Dispatch.*

[16] Austin *Weekly Statesman,* October 12, 1876.

when Pink Higgins entered the room with a gun in his hand. Pink poured four bullets into Merritt, two of them after he had fallen to the floor. Merritt died within a few seconds, not far from the spot where Captain Williams had expired four years earlier. Then Pink rode hurriedly out of town. Mart and Tom Horrell and a sheriff's posse took his trail but failed to locate him.[17]

Violence broke out once more on the morning of March 26. As Tom and Mart Horrell made their way to town, they were wounded by shots from ambushers in the brush along a creek. Tom chased off the attackers but was unable to hit them. Soon afterward the re-established Texas Rangers, failing to obtain co-operation from the sheriff, took the trail of the gunmen.[18] Late in April, Pink Higgins and Bob Mitchell surrendered to the Rangers and were freed on bonds of ten thousand dollars each.[19]

Even this did not end the feud. On the night of June 11, someone broke into the courthouse and carried off the files on all pending cases.[20] On the fourteenth the Horrell and Higgins factions engaged in a gun battle in the streets of Lampasas—the shooting lasting for several hours and sending many persons rushing for shelter. Finally neutral citizens induced the feudists to leave town. In this latest outbreak, Frank Mitchell, who had no part in the quarrel, was killed by a wild shot; and Bill Wren, a friend of Pink Higgins, was wounded.[21]

The Horrells returned home on July 7. For several weeks Lampasas people lived in fear of another clash. As local officers seemed helpless, Major John B. Jones, of the Texas Rangers, decided it was time to intercede.[22] Jones was acquainted with both factions. On the night of July 27, he sent Sergeant N. O. Reynolds with a detachment of Rangers to bring in the Horrells. Against the advice of the sheriff, Reynolds set out for the Horrell

[17] Galveston *News,* January 30, 1877.

[18] Gillett, *op. cit.,* 77; Sonnichsen, "I'll Die Before I'll Run," MS.

[19] Sonnichsen, *Ibid.*

[20] Galveston *News,* June 15, 1877.

[21] Austin *Weekly Statesman,* June 21, July 5, 1877.

[22] Major John B. Jones, letter to William Steele, Adjutant General, July 10, 1877, Adjutant General's papers, Austin.

ranch, with Bill Wren as a guide. A mile away, Wren pointed to a light in the Horrell cabin and announced he would go no farther, "No, not for a million dollars!"

The Rangers surrounded the Horrell home and waited quietly until just before dawn. Then they tiptoed into the room where the brothers and their friends were sleeping. When Reynolds called to Mart Horrell, each feudist awoke to find himself looking into the muzzle of a cocked Winchester in the hands of a Ranger. Mart said they would not surrender, and Tom declared it would be better to die fighting. But when Reynolds promised to guard them in his camp instead of turning them over to the sheriff to be mobbed, they decided to give up. After surrendering their guns, they mounted their horses and rode into Lampasas under guard.[23]

Within a day or two, Major Jones rounded up Pink Higgins, Bob Mitchell, and Bill Wren from the other side. Then he began discussing peace terms separately with the two groups. On July 30, he witnessed a peace proposal addressed to Pink and his two associates and signed by Tom, Sam, and Mart Horrell. The Horrells offered to cease their strife, to bury the bitter past forever, and to abstain from insults and injuries if the Higgins faction would make a similar pledge. On August 2, Higgins, Mitchell, and Wren signed a conciliatory reply, witnessed by Jones.[24]

Unlike most pacts to end feuds, this one was scrupulously observed. Yet Mart and Tom Horrell did not long enjoy the peace they had found. On the night of May 28, 1878, an old bachelor who kept a store on Hog Creek, thirty miles west of Waco, was killed and his place looted. Various persons were accused of participation or complicity in this crime. Among those arrested was Bill Crabtree, a blustering desperado from McLennan County. Crabtree, taken in the latter part of August, turned state's evidence and implicated the two Horrells. Mart

[23] Austin *Weekly Statesman*, August 2, 1877; Gillett, *op. cit.*, 78–79. Wren's relatives, whose account differs from Gillett's, said that Wren went all the way to the house with the Rangers.

[24] Letters from Horrell and Higgins factions, July 30 and August 2, 1877, Adjutant General's papers, Austin.

and Tom were arrested early in September and lodged in the jail at Meridian. While the brothers were undergoing an examining trial, Crabtree was released on September 28 and on that night was shot dead at the edge of town. The Horrells remained in jail. On the night of Sunday, December 15, more than one hundred horsemen rode into Meridian. The visitors broke up a church service by firing their guns and kept the townspeople away while about fifty masked men from their ranks entered the jail. Forcing another prisoner to hold a light, the intruders riddled the Horrells with lead.[25]

With the Horrells out of the way, Pink Higgins found his old haunts tame. He drifted northwestward to Kent County and became a range rider on the vast Spur Ranch. There his daring and his marksmanship were put to frequent use in protecting the grazing herds from brand-burners. Meanwhile, ranchers in Lampasas County breathed easier. The surging frontier had pushed on, leaving the green hills almost as peaceful as the steers that fattened on their grasses.

For much of Texas, that was a trying period. Although the state had thrown off its Reconstruction yoke early in 1874, it was still beset with economic troubles. Some relief was beginning to be felt as great herds of longhorns were trailed to Kansas markets and as railroads penetrated the range country. But crime was still rampant. In the spring of 1878, when the final chapter of the Horrell tragedy was being enacted, Sam Bass was robbing trains in northern Texas, and in many sections horse thieves and cattle rustlers were a constant menace.

While bullets were still flying in Lampasas, a similar but shorter-lived feud broke out in Mason, two counties to the southwest. In this rolling to hilly range land, splotched with stunted oak, mesquite, and cedar, more trouble had started from cattle stealing. On June 25, 1874, Judge Wilson Hey of Mason County wrote to Governor Richard Coke, telling of the rustling and asking that Texas Rangers be sent. Major John B. Jones went to investigate; and on August 17, he wrote to Captain

25 Galveston *News*, December 17, 1878; J. B. Cranfill, *Dr. J. B. Cranfill's Chronicle*, 221–24.

C. R. Perry at Menardville, "I find the people here a good deal excited in regard to the cow thieves and rumors coming in now of more depredations of the same kind."[26]

Most of the settlers of Mason County were of German ancestry and were hard-working, law-abiding farmers and stockmen. For the cattle stealing, they blamed outlaws from surrounding counties. The relative prosperity which the Mason County stockmen had achieved through their industry and thrift had excited envy in some quarters. In addition, a few hotheads still wanted to punish them for the lack of enthusiasm they had shown for the Confederate cause a decade earlier. Depletion of the herds continued through the following winter.[27]

The smoldering Mason County War burst into violence early in March, 1875. Many of the stockmen had decided that the only way to protect their cattle was to take the law into their own hands. Sheriff John Clark had arrested five men on charges of cattle rustling and had lodged them in the jail at Mason. But the suspected men did not find safety in their cells. A crowd of thirty to forty men gathered at the jail door and demanded that John Worley, the deputy sheriff in charge, surrender the prisoners without delay.

On learning what was afoot, Sheriff Clark went to look for Lieutenant Dan W. Roberts of the Texas Rangers, who happened to be in Mason to buy grain for his camp. Clark, finding Roberts asleep in a hotel room, woke him and told him of the predicament. Then the two officers, with James Trainer, hastened to the scene. Men from the crowd ordered them to halt and told them they would not be hurt if they kept their distance. The three backed off to the courthouse, about thirty steps from the jail. Then the sheriff rushed upstairs and, aiming his rifle through a window toward the crowd, threatened to kill the first man who touched the jail door.

At this move, about ten of the men in front of the jail walked

26 Letters of Judge Hey and Major Jones, Adjutant General's papers, Austin.

27 Austin *Daily Statesman*, October 17, November 14, 1875; Kathryn Burford Eilers, "A History of Mason County," M. A. thesis, University of Texas.

past Roberts and Trainer and went up to talk with the sheriff. They said they meant no harm to him or to the county but were going to have the prisoners at any cost. After that, Roberts and Trainer watched from a distance while the sheriff went for help. While he was gone, the crowd battered down the jail door, removed the five alleged rustlers, and headed south with them, down the Fredericksburg road.

Soon the sheriff returned to Roberts and Trainer, bringing five or six men. Then all of them hastened in pursuit—Clark on horseback, the others afoot. They had gone only half a mile when they saw the crowd ahead of them and began firing. The vigilantes, their work interrupted, began shooting the prisoners they had not yet hanged. One had his brains shot out, but the other—a tenderfoot who had been hired as a cook by the accused rustlers—jerked the noose from his neck, leaped over a fence, and escaped by running across a plowed field. As the crowd scattered, the sheriff and his helpers cut down the three men they found hanging to a limb. One of them was still warm and his neck not broken. Roberts ran to a near-by branch, brought water in his hat, and—with this and rubbing—revived the victim, although he still had a glassy stare and was unable to talk until the next morning.[28]

Violence recurred two months later. Tim Williamson, a reputable stockman in charge of Charles Lemburg's herds, had been arrested on a charge of cattle theft and had easily made bond. When John Worley came to take him to court, Williamson went with him readily. On their way to Mason, they saw a party of masked and armed men riding in their direction. With a presentiment of what this meant, Williamson begged the deputy to allow him to try to escape. Instead, Worley deliberately shot his prisoner's horse in the loin, leaving Williamson unmounted as well as unarmed. In a few moments, he lay dying beside his horse.

Mason County was aroused over the killing of Williamson, for he had many friends and few could believe him guilty of

[28] San Antonio *Herald*, August 30, 1875; Austin *Daily Statesman*, October 17, 1875; Dan W. Roberts, *Rangers and Sovereignty*, 87–90; Thomas W. Gamel, *The Life of Thomas W. Gamel*, 20–21.

rustling. Particularly incensed was his close friend Scott Cooley, a former Texas Ranger, who had been farming near Menardville. Cooley had worked for Williamson and twice had gone up the Kansas cattle trail with him. When Cooley had been stricken with typhoid fever, Williamson's wife had nursed him. On hearing of the cold-blooded killing, Cooley saddled his pony and rode into Mason, heavily armed. As he was not known there, he remained for several days without arousing suspicion—long enough to learn the names of the masked men who had killed his friend. Then Cooley set out on a mission of vengeance. In this he soon had the help of other friends of Williamson—George Gladden of Loyal Valley, John Ringgold, and the two Beard brothers, John and Moses, from Blanco County.

Late in July, Cooley and his friends, disguised as Indians, came upon a party of Willow Creek men out looking for strayed livestock. They fired on these cattlemen, killing Henry Doell and wounding another man. Next, Cooley went after John Worley. At the foot of Weber Hill he found the deputy helping Doc Harkey, a neighbor, dig a well. After dismounting and asking for a drink, he asked the man turning the windlass if his name was John Worley. On receiving an affirmative reply, he whipped out his pistol and shot him, killing him instantly and causing Harkey to plunge to the bottom of the well. Cooley then removed Worley's scalp, put it in his pocket, remounted, and galloped off. Soon afterward another man on Cooley's list, young Charles Bader, was waylaid and killed.

These killings chilled the blood of Mason County people. Women were afraid to go out at night, and men slept with pistols under their pillows. As in other feuds, some who wanted to keep out of trouble were virtually forced to take sides. Late in September, Major Jones headed for Mason with a company of Rangers; but before he arrived, more blood was shed. On hearing that Scott Cooley's band was prowling on the Llano River, twelve miles south of Mason, Sheriff Clark had climbed into his buggy and driven to Keller's store near Cold Springs, taking along Peter Bader and others. There the sheriff's party had encountered some of Cooley's men. In the ensuing clash, Mose Beard was mortally wounded, and George Gladden caught nine bullets but survived. Soon afterward the Cooley party killed, in the presence of his family, a man they suspected of having led them into a trap at Keller's.[29]

Major Jones and his Rangers, on their way to Mason, reached Keller's store on the Llano soon after the fight there. As they rode up, they saw fifteen to twenty men, bristling with Winchesters, carbines, and six-shooters, pop out from behind a wall. These were the sheriff and his posse, who were on the lookout for further trouble. They had heard a rumor that a band of thirty of Cooley's men was coming "to burn out the Dutch." The Rangers camped overnight at Cold Springs without incident. When they arrived at Mason, they learned that a prominent resident, Daniel Hoerster, had just been shot from his horse and killed in one of the streets.

Major Jones was told that fifteen men had been killed in the feud and that two rival bands of about thirty heavily armed men each were roaming over the country, each expecting an attack from the other. The presence of forty Rangers quieted the people, but for two weeks their scouting for Scott Cooley and his men brought no result. Most of the Rangers knew the country, but they also knew Cooley—and liked him. Some of them were said to have met their former associate at night on the outskirts of Mason and told him they did not care if he killed every one of the men responsible for Tim Williamson's death.

At this, Jones made a speech to the Rangers. He reminded them of their oath and pointed out that Cooley's war of vengeance was a defiance of law. He offered an honorable discharge to any sympathizers of Cooley who did not wish to pursue him. Three Rangers took discharges, and about a dozen others were transferred to different posts. After this purge, the Rangers began to get results. George Gladden, who had recovered from his bullet wounds and had killed Peter Bader in Llano County, was caught and later was sentenced to prison. John Ringgold was jailed in Lampasas but escaped. John Beard

[29] Austin *Daily Statesman*, July 31, August 22, October 17, 22, 1875; San Antonio *Herald*, August 30, September 20, 1875; Roberts, Dan W., *op. cit.*, 87; Gillett, *op. cit.*, 46–47; Gamel, *op. cit.*, 29–31.

left the state. Sheriff Clark, realizing the difficulties and dangers that might lie ahead for him, resigned and departed. Cooley returned to Blanco County, where his friends shielded him, and soon afterward he died. Mason County, after two years of turmoil, returned to its former status as quiet cow country.[30]

In regions where population was spread thin, where land titles and cattle brands were often in dispute, where roads were poor and courts were far away, it was easy for feuds to arise. Once blood was shed, it was hard to reason with the wronged frontiersmen and to prevent retaliation. Impatient men did not want to leave retribution to the next world; they insisted on inflicting it themselves—and without avoidable delay.

Before Mason County was fully pacified, another Texas feud broke out over the salt deposits at the foot of the Guadalupe Mountains, 110 miles east of El Paso. For many years, people from both sides of the Río Grande had been coming there to take salt without payment. In 1877, Charles H. Howard of El Paso, a political schemer who had won election as a district judge, set out to get personal possession of these deposits. When Judge Howard tried to levy tribute on persons who came for salt, he was seized by an infuriated crowd. His captors released him only after he had agreed in writing to resign his judgeship, to relinquish to the public his claim to the salt deposits, to make a twelve-thousand-dollar bond, and leave El Paso County forever.

Howard left for Mesilla, New Mexico, but came back quickly with a double-barreled shotgun and, on October 10, killed a political opponent, Louis Cardis. Again the judge escaped to Mesilla. As stern-faced Mexicans were coming across the border and threatening Howard's bondsmen, Major Jones was sent to restore order. He recruited a new company of Rangers and left them, with an untried lieutenant, to handle the situation.

When Howard returned to Texas in December, the Mexicans quickly took up his trail. Their first victim was one of Howard's

30 Major John B. Jones, reports to William Steele, Adjutant General, September 28, 30, October 28, 1875, Adjutant General's papers, Austin; Austin *Daily Statesman,* November 18, 1875.

bondsmen. They stabbed him in the heart, scalped him, and left his body in a gunny sack in the sand hills. The judge had a Ranger escort, with the inexperienced lieutenant in charge, but was besieged nonetheless. Finally, to save the lives of the Rangers, Howard surrendered. He and two of his friends were shot by the Mexican mob, and Howard's body was hacked and mutilated. After the bodies were dragged half a mile and dumped into an old well, the salt carts resumed their tedious journeys.[31]

As if not to be outdone by Texas, New Mexico burst out a few months later with a full-dress feud in Lincoln County. Since the summer of 1876, trouble had been brewing there between John S. Chisum and the nesters and small cowmen. These lesser stockmen resented Chisum's monopoly of the ranges and stole his cattle on many occasions. The Lincoln County War, however, was mainly an outgrowth of business jealousy. Lawrence G. Murphy, James J. Dolan, and John H. Riley ran a store in frontier Lincoln and dealt in horses and cattle. On the side, they served as a "fence" for stock thieves. These merchants were resentful when, in the spring of 1877, an Englishman, John H. Tunstall, settled in Lincoln and opened a mercantile and banking business.

Tunstall had as a partner a local lawyer, Alexander A. McSween, who had arrived two years earlier; and the firm obtained part of its financial backing from John S. Chisum. The proprietors of the older store, in addition to resenting competition, were angered when McSween refused to defend some of their associates who had been caught red-handed stealing cattle on Chisum's Pecos River range. Instead, McSween accepted a retainer from Chisum to prosecute the rustlers, and obtained their conviction. More than that, he showed that Murphy, Dolan, and Riley were in collusion with the thieves.

Murphy decided to strike back. On February 18, 1878, he summoned the sheriff, who usually did his bidding, and handed him a bogus writ of attachment for a herd of horses in Tunstall's

[31] *El Paso Troubles in Texas,* 45 Cong., 2 sess., *House Exec. Doc. 93,* Serial No. 1809, 53; Gillett, *op. cit.,* 136–41; Walter Prescott Webb, *The Texas Rangers,* 343–67.

possession. The sheriff passed the writ on to a deputy, who set out with a posse made daring by Murphy's liquor. They rode to Tunstall's Río Feliz ranch, only to find the owner absent. But on their way back to town, they encountered him, unarmed, and killed him without warning.

McSween, who assumed that the sheriff would take no action, obtained warrants and special constables. Then he organized a posse that included William H. Bonney (Billy the Kid), a drifter cow hand who had been working for Tunstall at the time of the latter's death. This party captured two of Tunstall's killers. While the prisoners were being taken to Lincoln, a member of the posse was killed. At that, the captives tried to escape, but were shot down by the Kid. These shootings intensified the feud. Across the ranges, gunfire answered gunfire. Many other victims, including McSween, fell to feudists' bullets before the bloody Lincoln County War came to an end.[32]

By this time, frontier conditions in the Southwest were giving way to more orderly procedures; but Texas had one more cruel feud. This was the political war between the Jaybirds and the Woodpeckers in Fort Bend County. In this county, near the Gulf Coast, the Negroes outnumbered the whites. Early in 1888, the Democrats began planning to oust the few remaining carpetbaggers and to end the county's corrupt misrule. They organized a Young Men's Democratic Club and called a mass meeting to be held on July 7 at Richmond, the county seat.

Response came quickly. The July gathering was preceded by a gala parade and was attended by more than two hundred men. As the movement gained momentum, the Young Democrats adopted gaudy uniforms and wore them to their meetings. Their attire led someone to refer to them as Jaybirds—Jaybirds trying to get the Woodpeckers out of their holes. The names caught on and were accepted by partisans on both sides.

But the feud did not stop with name-calling. After some Democrats began soliciting votes from Negroes, violence broke out. On the evening of August 11, as he and his family were

[32] Pat F. Garrett, *The Authentic Life of Billy the Kid* (revised edition), 51–73; George W. Coe, *Frontier Fighter,* 18–134; Miguel Antonio Otero, *The Real Billy the Kid,* 27–74.

seated about their parlor table reading the Bible by lamplight, J. M. Shamblin, a white planter living on the Brazos River, was mortally wounded with buckshot. "Hell in the neck for all misleaders," said the death note left by the assassin. The killer was a Negro tenant, later legally hanged.

Soon came another shot in the darkness. This time the victim was Henry H. Frost of Richmond. On the evening of September 3, as he was walking home from his store just after dark, he was shot and wounded. This shooting filled the town with armed men. A mass meeting of the Jaybirds on the fourth brought out four hundred. The Jaybirds ordered five Negroes to leave the county within ten hours and declared that they would hold the Republican leaders responsible if any more assassinations occurred.

Such measures were not effective for long. The Republicans decided not to put a ticket in the county race; but the Democrats—as often happened in Texas—split into two rival factions. Some of those who had stuck to the Cleveland and Thurman Club and others who had been Jaybirds but had been disappointed in failing to get nominations joined together to form an independent Democratic ticket and to seek Negro support. This group inherited the Woodpecker name. The Woodpeckers blamed the Jaybirds—the lily-white faction—for the killing of a Negro and the wounding of another at a church on October 12.

The November election, which the Woodpeckers won, failed to end the bad feeling between the two factions. Bitterness was especially strong between Kyle Terry, the Woodpecker elected tax assessor, and Ed Gibson, the Jaybird he had defeated. In June, 1899, while both were in Wharton to attend a trial, Terry shot and killed Gibson. Out on bond while awaiting trial, Terry went to Galveston. There, in February, 1890, he was killed by an attacking party that included Volney Gibson, a brother of his victim.

Meanwhile, although Rangers had come to restore order, the two Fort Bend County factions were still looking for trouble. On August 16, 1889, they engaged in a street battle in Richmond. When the firing ceased and the smoke lifted, Sheriff Tom Garvey and his uncle, Jake Blakely, a former county treasurer, lay dead, as did a young Negro girl who happened to get in the way. Henry H. Frost was wounded—mortally this time. Soon after this battle, Sergeant Ira Aten of the Rangers was made sheriff. Early in September, the Woodpeckers either resigned or were removed from office and were replaced by Jaybirds. With the nickname retained, the Jaybird organization was still in strong control of the county government half a century later.[33]

These and other frontier feuds did not start from any desire of men to kill their neighbors. They arose from conditions which the participants—usually respected citizens before the trouble broke out—regarded as intolerable and as incapable of remedy by lawful means. Often the feud began with an effort at informal regulation. This action begat vengeance and counter-vengeance and led to a jungle-like war of extermination. Usually the feud died out when effective statutory law caught up with the frontier. The readiness of pioneer settlers to right their own wrongs took many lives, but at times it may have been a deterrent to crime. As C. L. Sonnichsen, historian of Texas feuds, remarked, "You think twice about killing a man if you know that his brother will be on your trail with a Winchester right after the funeral."[34]

[33] Sergeant Ira Aten, letter to Captain L. P. Sieker, dated Richmond, Texas, September 3, 1889, Adjutant General's papers, Austin; Dallas *Morning News,* March 21, 1896; Jesse A. Ziegler, *Wave of the Gulf,* 152–58; Clarence R. Wharton, *History of Fort Bend County,* 192–215.

[34] Sonnichsen, "I'll Die Before I'll Run," MS.

4. Bad Blood in Arizona

To avenge the death of a kinsman was for long more than a right. It was a religious duty.
—William A. Robson, *Civilisation and the Growth of Law*

SHIELDED on the north by the towering Mogollons, central Arizona's Tonto Basin was fine grazing land. Pleasant Valley, the cowmen called it in the middle eighteen eighties, when there was grass enough for every herd. With no white settlement within seventy miles, it was a quiet valley, too, until smoldering enmity between two families, the Grahams and the Tewksburys, blazed into one of the West's fiercest feuds. This vendetta made every trail unsafe and caused more than a score of men to die in their boots.

In the more remote ranges, the frontiersman always had to be prepared to defend his life with his six-shooter. A ready gun, nimble fingers, and a steady hand were the first requisites for longevity. He never knew when he might be ambushed by an Indian scalper, a Mexican brigand, or a white desperado. Yet these dangers seemed mild when some bitter quarrel set neighbor against neighbor, each trying to avenge his wrongs in the other's blood. While the seeking of justice through retaliation was hardly a prevailing practice, it spotted the frontier with searing feuds. In most of the West these feuds had given way to orderly conduct when one of the worst of them all converted Pleasant Valley into an inferno of death.

Boston-born John D. Tewksbury, who built his cabin on Cherry Creek about 1880, was an amiable, elderly man who never quarreled with anyone. He had gone to California in the gold rush, and had married an Indian woman there, by whom he had three sons, Edwin, John, and James. After his wife's death, he went to Globe, Arizona, where he married a woman of English birth before settling in the Tonto Basin. Tewksbury's few cattle and hogs and the wild game of the valley provided the family with meat. Other needs were met with wages earned by the three grown, half-Indian sons who worked for neighboring cattlemen.

Thomas H. and John Graham also reached Arizona by way of California. Born on a farm near Boone, Iowa, these brothers were as honest and peaceful as Tewksbury. They settled in Pleasant Valley in the fall of 1882 and built their cabin about ten miles northwest of the Tewksburys' dwelling. Their much younger half-brother, William, came to live with them. Like the Tewksbury sons, the Grahams hired out occasionally to neighboring ranchmen, including James Stinson.

The younger Tewksburys and the Grahams apparently got along well with each other until the spring of 1884, when they had trouble over cattle. Unfenced ranges and careless branding left many animals of uncertain ownership. Misunderstandings were easy, even when there was no intention to steal. One early account said that the Tewksburys and the Grahams, while working for Stinson as cow hands, joined to put their own brand on some of the boss' stock. They quarreled, it continued, when one of the Grahams registered the partnership brand in his own name and refused to admit the Tewksburys' claim to joint ownership.[1] Stinson later supported this account by saying that his cattle began disappearing and that soon the Grahams and the Tewksburys were fighting over them.[2]

First the Grahams and then the Tewksburys were charged in court with stealing cattle, only to have the cases dismissed. But their troubles with each other became worse. As the feud deepened, the Grahams acquired as partisans another family of cowmen, the five sons of Mark Blevans—John, Charles, Hamp-

[1] Joseph Fish, "History of Arizona," MS, Arizona State Historian, Phoenix; Will C. Barnes, "The Pleasant Valley War of 1887," Part I, *Arizona Historical Review*, Vol. IV, No. 3 (October, 1931), 10.

[2] Earle R. Forrest, *Arizona's Dark and Bloody Ground*, 39, citing an interview with Stinson in the *Arizona Republican*, Phoenix, November, 1930. Forrest's excellent book is the most detailed and best documented history of this feud.

ton, Sam, and Andy. Andy, the son of Mark by an earlier marriage, was known in Arizona as Andy Cooper. Wanted in the Indian Territory for selling whiskey and in Texas for a killing, he made his father's ranch on Canyon Creek the headquarters for a band of cattle rustlers.

In 1886, Ed Tewksbury shot and wounded Jim Stinson's range foreman, who had accused him of stealing horses. Then, in the fall of that year, serious trouble broke out. At Flagstaff, far to the north, the leading sheepmen of that section, A. A. and P. P. Daggs, had more woolies than they could feed for the winter. Knowing they would have to reduce their flocks unless they could find more winter range, they looked longingly at Pleasant Valley. The cattlemen in the valley banned sheep, with the rim of the Mogollons as a deadline; but the Daggs brothers knew of the simmering feud between the Tewksburys and the Grahams and decided to try to turn it to their advantage. They summoned John, Jim, and Ed Tewksbury and the Tewksburys' friend, William Jacobs, and made a proposition that promised not only money but an opportunity to get even with the Grahams.

That fall the cowmen in Pleasant Valley could hardly believe their eyes when they saw great flocks of sheep tumbling over the rim of the Mogollons. The woolies swarmed down the trails into the forbidden territory and began devouring the luxuriant bunch grass the cattlemen had counted on for their herds. The half-Indian Tewksburys had been threatening to bring in sheep, but the other cowmen thought they were only bluffing. Now, many who would have preferred to keep out of the feud felt obliged to support the Grahams in defending their ranges against the invaders.

Quickly the Pleasant Valley cattlemen gathered at the Graham ranch to decide on strategy. Hot-headed Andy Blevans advocated immediate slaughter of all the sheep and their herders, but Tom Graham insisted that milder methods be tried first. Night bullets that just missed the herders as they sat before their campfires would scare them away, he thought. His advice prevailed, but the Daggs brothers and the Tewksburys were not so easily dissuaded. After a few months, the more impetuous cowmen no longer could be held in check. They began killing the sheep at night, shooting some and driving others off bluffs or into creeks. And early in February, 1887, someone killed and beheaded a Navajo herder.[3]

By spring so many sheep had been killed that the Daggs brothers withdrew their flocks from the prohibited Tonto Basin. The Tewksburys had suffered defeat in the first round of their feud, but they were not giving up. They would bide their time. Pleasant Valley remained quiet until one day late in July when Mark Blevans–Old Man Blevans to his neighbors–rode out from his ranch in the morning and failed to come back. Like the elder Tewksbury, Mark Blevans was not involved in the feud; but his sons were in the midst of it. Andy, in addition, was under indictment on a charge of cattle rustling in Apache County.

For several weeks the Blevans sons and some of their friends, including several young cow hands from the Hash Knife Ranch beyond the Mogollons, scouted the surrounding country. They were looking for the missing man and, in the view of the Tewksburys, looking for trouble.

They found the latter on August 10. Hampton Blevans was out that day with seven companions, including three men from the Hash Knife outfit–Tom Tucker, Bob Gillespie, and John Paine, a fighting Texan. Paine had been brought to Arizona by the Hash Knife's owners, the Aztec Land and Cattle Company, to keep sheep off the cattle ranges. About noon the scouting party drew up at the old Middleton ranch, which the Tewksbury brothers recently had occupied. In front of the fence that surrounded the cabin they stopped their horses. Staying in their saddles, they called out to see whether anyone was at home. In answer, Jim Tewksbury appeared at the open door. John Paine inquired whether the cowmen could get dinner there. Even in the hospitable West, Jim may have thought this a strange question, coming from men who had been trying for months to drive him and his brothers out of Pleasant Valley.

[3] *Hoofs and Horns*, Prescott, February 10, 1887; *Arizona Silver Belt*, Globe, February 12, 1887; Barnes, "The Pleasant Valley War of 1887," Part I, *Arizona Historical Review*, Vol. IV, No. 3 (October, 1931) 32.

"No, sir," he replied, "we don't keep a hotel here."

"Is Mr. Belknap here?" asked Tom Tucker.

"No, sir," Tewksbury answered, "he just rode off."

"Well, boys," Tucker told his fellow cowpunchers, "we'll go on down to Vosberg's and get some dinner."

What happened next became a matter of controversy. Tucker said that the visitors wheeled their horses and started to leave. The men inside the cabin said that Blevans and Paine reached for their guns. At any rate, Jim Tewksbury's Winchester blazed from the doorway, and the horses jumped. Blevans pitched to the ground with a bullet through his brain. Paine fired at Tewksbury, but the wily Jim dodged behind the door in time. Then Paine's horse, struck by a bullet, crashed upon him. As the Texan jerked himself out and started to run for shelter, he was cut down and fell lifeless in the dust beside the body of Blevans. Tucker caught a bullet in his lungs, and one of the others received flesh wounds; but both stuck to their saddles.

This battle was over in a few seconds, leaving two dead. The six surviving visitors galloped away to the Graham ranch to treat their wounds and to find recruits for renewing the feud.[4]

Now the war was on in earnest. Tom Graham still wanted to avoid further violence but was overruled. The Tewksburys fled to a fortified stronghold in the mountains, where partisans of the Grahams besieged them and tried to starve them out. Returning with water from a spring one dark night, Jim Tewksbury was trailed by one of the besieging cow hands. He gave this fellow a shot in the thigh that caused him to bleed to death. About that time Sheriff William Mulvenon of Yavapai County left Prescott with a posse to look for the slayers of Hampton Blevans and John Paine but failed to find them.[5]

While this posse was still scouring the hills, William Graham, twenty-two years old and the youngest member of his family, was marked for feudist vengeance. As he was riding along a lonely trail three and one-half miles from his home, he was ambushed by James D. Houck, a sheepman from Apache County who had a deputy sheriff's badge. Houck was prowling alone

[4] Saint Johns *Herald*, August 18, 1887; Forrest, *op. cit.*, 58–73.

[5] Flagstaff *Champion*, August 24, September 3, 1887.

as a partisan of the Tewksburys. When Billy Graham came along, the deputy ordered him to surrender, and the young cowman answered with a shot. Houck fired back, inflicting a wound from which Graham died at his home the next day.[6]

No longer was there any holding back by Tom or John Graham. Both were out now for Tewksbury blood. They did not have long to wait. On the early morning of September 2, the two surviving Grahams, the remaining Blevans brothers, and other foes of the Tewksburys surrounded the latter's reoccupied cabin. The attackers blocked every means of escape. Outside they caught the younger John Tewksbury and William Jacobs, who were looking for horses. Andy Blevans shot them and left their bodies on the ground in view of the cabin.

The battle continued for hours. The Grahams and their allies poured lead into the cabin from every side, but the fighters inside kept themselves shielded. Meanwhile, enough bullets were coming from windows of the Tewksbury home to keep the besiegers behind trees, outbuildings, or other shelters. Finally, as hogs approached the two bodies and began rooting at them, the cabin door was flung open and a woman screamed: "I can't stand it! I must bury them. They'll have to kill me to stop me."

The white-faced woman stepped out, with a shovel in her hand. She was the newly widowed Mrs. John Tewksbury. Defying the bullets and walking straight ahead, she went to the bodies. While her baby wailed in the cabin and the guns of the feudists were temporarily silenced, she drove off the hogs. Then she dug two shallow graves and buried her husband and his friend.

After Mrs. Tewksbury returned to the cabin, the guns began barking again. But the Graham and Blevans brothers were unable to account for any more of their foes that day. Late in the afternoon, John Meadows, a justice of the peace from Payson, appeared with a posse. He dispersed the raiders, restored order on the ranch, and exhumed the bodies for an inquest. But the feudists vanished before he could arrest anyone.[7]

[6] Coconino *Sun*, September 17, 1887; Saint Johns *Herald*, September 29, 1887; Forrest, *op. cit.*, 74–93.

[7] Coconino *Sun*, September 10, 1887; Flagstaff *Champion*, September

The breathing spell that followed the battle at the Tewksbury ranch lasted for only two days. The setting for the next round was the dusty cow town of Holbrook, about seventy miles northeast of Pleasant Valley. Andy Blevans, whose stepmother lived there, rode into Holbrook on the morning of September 4. In a saloon he boasted of having killed John Tewksbury and William Jacobs two days earlier. Andy knew that a warrant had been issued for his arrest on a charge of having stolen Navajo ponies, but he did not think any officer would dare try to take him in tow.

That afternoon another horseman rode into Holbrook. This was the new sheriff of Apache County, Commodore Perry Owens, who was rounding up jurors for the next term of court. A former Texas trail driver, Owens had been elected to clean out the cattle rustlers. His flamboyant cowboy outfit, the long hair over his shoulders, and his habit of wearing his Colt on his left side, butt forward, made some citizens uncertain whether they had picked the right man. They found out in Holbrook that day.

When the sheriff heard that Andy Blevans—known there as Andy Cooper—was in town, he said he intended to arrest him. Meanwhile, Andy, who had seen Owens, decided that he might be needed back in Pleasant Valley and had his horse brought from the livery stable so that he could depart at once. The sheriff, Winchester in hand, noticed Andy saddling his horse in front of the Blevans' frame cottage. Andy, despite his boasting that morning, went into the house hastily when he saw the officer approaching.

As Sheriff Owens walked up to the house, he saw a man eyeing him from the doorway. When he drew near, someone slammed the door. Stepping on the porch, he glanced through a window and saw three other men. Then he called for Andy to come out. Ignoring the sheriff's order, Andy went into another room. There, with his six-shooter ready for action, he faced the

---

10, 1887; *Arizona Silver Belt*, October 1, 1887; Will C. Barnes, "The Pleasant Valley War of 1887," Part II, *Arizona Historical Review*, January, 1932, 30; Joe T. McKinney, "Reminiscences," *Arizona Historical Review*, July, 1932, 145; *ibid.*, October, 1932, 202; Forrest, *op. cit.*, 94–106.

SHERIFF COMMODORE P. OWENS
He made every bullet count

Forrest Collection, Arizona Pioneers' Historical Society

officer through an open door. At the same time, John Blevans pointed a gun at Owens from another door. Caught in a potential cross-fire, the sheriff was in an unenviable position but kept his nerve and looked Andy coolly in the eyes.

The rustler, on the other hand, failed to shoot when he had the advantage. Hesitating, he asked the sheriff what he wanted, as if he did not know.

"I want you," Owens told him calmly.

"What do you want with me?"

"I have a warrant for you."

"What warrant?" asked Andy, stalling for time.

"The same warrant for horse stealing I told you about some time ago," replied the sheriff.

"Wait, an' I'll see about it."

"No, I'll not wait. You must come at once."

"I won't go."

With that, the shooting began. Andy's shot went wide of its mark, but the sheriff's gave the rustler a mortal wound. Meanwhile, John Blevans fired from the side door, narrowly missing Owens but hitting Andy's horse tied in front of the house. The sheriff then turned his Winchester on John, who quickly staggered back with a wound in his shoulder. The sheriff's next assailant was Mose Roberts, a brother-in-law of the Blevans boys. Mose dashed out of the house with a six-shooter, but Owens beat him to the draw and sent him running back with a fatal shot.

The remaining male in the house was Sam Houston Blevans, a youth of sixteen. Refused the use of John's gun, he grabbed that of the expiring Andy, pulled away from his mother's clutches, and dashed out. He was just in time to get a bullet in his heart and stagger back into his mother's arms.

Sheriff Owens, his smoking Winchester still in his hand, was unscratched. In a minute's time he had left three men dying and another wounded. Never again would anyone question his courage, coolness, or marksmanship. The coroner's jury found that he had acted in the discharge of his duty. In agreement, the Saint Johns *Herald* noted: "Too much credit cannot be given to Sheriff Owens. It required more than ordinary courage for a man to go single-handed to a house where it was known that there were four desperate men inside and to demand the surrender of one of them."[8]

In Pleasant Valley the feud raged on. With the Blevans men so nearly wiped out, the Grahams lost some of their numerical advantage. But, since their youngest brother had been killed, they unrelentingly carried on their private war against the Tewksburys. On September 17, some of the Graham faction made an early morning raid on the Tewksbury ranch on Cherry Creek but failed to surprise their foes. Two of the attackers were wounded, and one of these, Harry Middleton, died two days later at the Graham ranch.

Again an arm of the law reached into the basin. The continued killings brought another invasion by Sheriff Mulvenon, whose bailiwick included most of Pleasant Valley. Bested in his first attempt to round up the feudists, he had decided to make another try. After raising a posse, he went into the disputed territory in an effort to arrest the leaders. Possibly influenced by two Tewksbury partisans, George A. Newton and Jim Houck, who had joined his party, the sheriff went after the Grahams first.

On September 21, before daylight, the Mulvenon posse took possession of the Perkins store, a stone building put up several years earlier for defense against the Apaches. The store was within view of the Graham's cabin and that of Al Rose. The men hid their horses, and some posted themselves behind the stone walls of a home that the owner of the store, Charles E. Perkins, was building near by. In an effort to decoy the Grahams into an ambush, six members of the posse rode leisurely past the two cabins and then tied their mounts in front of the store. Soon afterward John Graham and Charles Blevans rode cautiously toward the store and circled it.

As the two feudists approached the half-completed home, Sheriff Mulvenon stepped from behind a wall, a double-barreled shotgun in his hand.

[8] Saint Johns *Herald*, September 9, 1887; Coconino *Sun*, September 10, 1887; Ward R. Adams, *History of Arizona*, 102–33; Forrest, *op. cit.*, 107–34; Will C. Barnes, *Apaches and Longhorns*, 144–52.

"Boys, you know me," he said, "I have a warrant for your arrest. Put up your hands!"

Graham and Blevans instantly wheeled their mounts and reached for their six-shooters. But they were too late. Charges from Mulvenon's shotgun and the rifles of his hidden men quickly felled the two horsemen. Blevans was dead, and Graham was dying.

Next Mulvenon surrounded the two ranch homes, a move which, made earlier, might have achieved more success in catching the feudists alive. Al Rose surrendered when he saw the odds against him, but Tom Graham had slipped away. Later the posse went to the cabin of the Tewksburys, who apparently had been informed of the sheriff's purpose. The two remaining Tewksbury brothers and five of their friends surrendered without a fight. At Payson the prisoners were brought before John Meadows, justice of the peace. Meadows discharged Rose and a Mexican, since there was no evidence against them. The Tewksburys and their partisans he sent to Prescott. There they made bonds to appear before the next grand jury and later were set free to return home.[9]

From this point on, the Tonto Basin war became a bit less bloody. Yet the situation remained tense, and everyone living in the disputed area took precautions against surprise attack. Frederick R. Burnham, a youth who lived in Pleasant Valley at the time but did not take sides in the feud, wrote many years later in his autobiography:

Even the little children absorbed the fear around them and showed pathetic furtiveness. I recall a day when three of us, all heavily armed, rode up to a cabin on Tonto Creek and saw a little girl, about five years old, carrying a white pitcher of water from the spring to the house. When the child sighted us, she gave a scream, dropped the pitcher, and ran—not to the house, as a child ordinarily would, but to the creek bottom, shouting at the top of

[9] Coconino *Sun*, September 24, 1887; Saint Johns *Herald*, September 29, 1887; *Arizona Silver Belt*, October 1, 1887; Joe T. McKinney, "Reminiscences," Part III, *Arizona Historical Review*, October, 1932, 199–201; Forrest, *op. cit.*, 135–50.

her voice, "Daddy! Here they come to kill you." She already understood that her own presence in the cabin might deter her father from shooting the enemy. Fortunately Daddy was not an impulsive man and was not disposed to fire until quite satisfied it was against a foe. But the little girl refused to come out of hiding until her mother's voice called, with just the right ring of assurance.[10]

Tom Graham, thirty-three years of age, was the only one of the three brothers left. Of his friends, the Blevans family, five of the six men were dead, and the other was in jail. Tom, living alone, let his thoughts turn again to the seventeen-year-old girl he had met in Phoenix and had planned to marry. Taking advantage of a lull in the fighting, while the Tewksbury brothers were still in jail at Prescott, Tom arranged for the wedding and invited his relatives from Iowa. On October 8, he married Anne Melton at her parents' home near Tempe, just east of Phoenix.

Tom's father, who had come for the wedding, begged the bridegroom to bring his young wife and return to Iowa with him; but Tom refused. Four days after the wedding, Tom went to Phoenix and asked the sheriff of Maricopa County whether a warrant had been issued there for his arrest. He was told that Maricopa County had no warrant for him, but on the eighteenth he was arrested there by Sheriff Mulvenon of Yavapai County. The next day Mulvenon took him to Prescott, where he made a bond of three thousand dollars and was released. The Tewksbury brothers, set free a few days earlier, had gone to Holbrook to replenish their store of ammunition.[11]

Tom Graham and his bride had not been back in their ranch cabin long before tragedy struck the neighborhood again. Early in November, Al Rose, one of Graham's closest friends and strongest supporters, was encamped with two companions near the Houdon ranch, where the Jump-off trail crossed Spring Creek, nine miles southwest of Pleasant Valley. Early in the morning, while the others were getting breakfast, Rose went out to look for the saddle horses they had left hobbled to graze during the night. A few minutes later he was shot from ambush

[10] Frederick R. Burnham, *Scouting on Two Continents*, 25–26.

[11] Phoenix *Herald*, October 13, 18, 1887; Forrest, *op. cit.*, 151–62.

by a party of Tewksbury men. His comrades heard two shots and rushed out to find him lying dead in the grass.[12]

A few weeks later the law made its feeble voice heard again. When the court opened at Prescott early in December, the men of the two factions who were under charges encamped separately near the O K corral and store. They refused to speak to their foes but avoided any open clash. The grand jury indicted the two Tewksburys and their associates for the killing of Hampton Blevans at the Middleton ranch on August 10, but took no action against Tom Graham. The Tewksburys went on trial in the district court in June, 1888. Since no one dared risk his life by testifying against them, their case was dismissed for lack of evidence.[13]

Defensive vigilance of the Graham and Tewksbury factions made bloodshed less frequent, but August, 1888, brought a new outbreak. Although this violent incident was only indirectly a part of the feud, it was perpetrated by associates of the Tewksburys and was instigated by Jim Houck, who still used his deputy's badge as a shield for undercover feudist activities. Its victims were three men who were not partisans of either side. They were James W. Stott, a young New Englander who had established a cattle ranch at Bear Spring, in the Mogollons, and who made the mistake of buying some stolen horses with blotched brands; Billy Wilson, a wandering prospector who had stopped at this ranch on the preceding day; and Jim Scott, a young cow hand from Weatherford, Texas, who worked for the Hash Knife and happened to be at the Stott ranch at the wrong time.

Early on the morning of August 11, about a dozen horsemen led by Jim Houck stopped at the Stott cabin. They had fictitious warrants for the men they found there, and took Stott, Wilson, and Scott for a one-way walk. They left the fourth occupant of the ranch house, a young consumptive who had been staying with Stott for several months. Suspicious of foul play, the in-

[12] Prescott *Courier,* November 7, 1887; Joe T. McKinney, "Reminiscences," Part II, *Arizona Historical Review,* July, 1932, 144; Forrest, *op. cit.,* 173–74.

[13] Forrest, *op. cit.,* 160–70.

valid went out before noon and found the three bodies hanging from the limb of a tree along the trail. Houck reported that a body of masked men had taken the prisoners from his posse. Suspicion pointed to Houck, who had threatened to run his sheep on the Stott ranch and who later boasted of his part in the lynching; but lack of evidence saved him from arrest.[14]

Later that year the deadliest gunman among the feudists, Jim Tewksbury, was removed from the scene. Jim suffered from tuberculosis and, on December 4, died at the home of his sister in Globe.[15] His passing left only one of the principals on each side of the feud. Of the three Tewksbury brothers, only Edwin was left. Of the three Grahams, there was only Tom; and his wife was trying to persuade him to leave the dangers of Pleasant Valley. Al Rose was gone, and so were all the Blevans men except the one who was in prison.

By this time the flames that had seared the basin had subsided. Tom Graham and Ed Tewksbury seemed willing to drop the feud that had cost so many lives, but neither could fully control his trigger-fingered partisans. The vendetta smoldered but refused to die. Finally, in the summer of 1889, when an addition to his family was expected, Tom Graham gave in to his wife's entreaties. He turned his cattle over to his partner, S. W. Young, and, with his wife, went to live on a quiet farm near Tempe. Some people thought the feud had ended, especially since—even with the last Graham gone—Ed Tewksbury dared drive no more sheep over the rim of the Mogollons.[16]

Such optimism, however, proved premature. The next man to disappear was a partisan of the Tewksburys. He was George A. Newton, a jeweler in Globe who operated a cattle ranch in Pleasant Valley. Any cattleman taking the side of the Tewksburys as he did was likely to be a special object of attack, but he looked out well for his defense. That is, he did until one day in September, 1891, when he saddled his horse in Globe and

[14] Phoenix *Herald,* August 16, 23, 1888; Flagstaff *Champion,* August 18, 1888; Joe T. McKinney, "Reminiscences," Part III, *Arizona Historical Review,* October, 1932, 202–203; Forrest, *op. cit.,* 189–210.

[15] Phoenix *Herald,* December 6, 1888.

[16] Will C. Barnes, "The Pleasant Valley War of 1887," Part I, *Arizona Historical Review,* No. 3, October, 1931, 20; Forrest, *op. cit.,* 216–21.

started for his ranch, sixty-five miles away. He had ridden this trail many times, but this time he disappeared. Except for the pack horse he had led, no trace of him was found.[17]

For three years Tom Graham lived peacefully on his farm near Tempe. In June, 1892, he returned to Pleasant Valley with an old friend to get his share of the cattle from his partner. He went unarmed, shook hands with some of his former enemies, and drove his cattle out with no sign of molestation. It looked as if the Tonto Basin war really had ended.

Again such hope was unwarranted. On the following August 2, as Graham was driving a four-horse team with a wagonload of grain from his farm to Tempe, two horsemen lay in wait for him in a mesquite thicket near the Double Butte school. As the wagon passed, these men lifted their guns. One of them shot Graham in the back. Both Graham and the three children who witnessed the firing identified the assassins as Ed Tewksbury and John Rhodes. Graham died that afternoon.[18]

Rhodes and Tewksbury were arrested. Rhodes refused to talk, even after the hoofprints of one of the assassin's horses were shown to match those of his own mount. Tewksbury—still wearing a red hatband like that which witnesses had noticed on one of the killers—repeatedly asserted that he was innocent. At a hearing on the charge against Rhodes before a justice of the peace in Tempe, the young widow of Tom Graham drew her late husband's six-shooter from her umbrella. Pointing it at Rhodes, she pulled the trigger. But the gun failed to go off. The justice discharged Rhodes, much to the disgust of Tempe citizens, who held a meeting and adopted a resolution condemning the action.[19]

Ed Tewksbury was jailed in Tucson, then taken to Phoenix. Because of public feeling against him there, his trial was shifted

[17] Barnes, "The Pleasant Valley War of 1887," Part II, *Arizona Historical Review,* No. 4, January, 1932, 40; Forrest, *op. cit.,* 211–15.

[18] Barnes, "The Pleasant Valley War of 1887," Part I, *Arizona Historical Review,* No. 3, October, 1931, 21–28; Forrest, *op. cit.,* 221–33.

[19] Tucson *Star,* August 13, 20, 1892; Tempe *News,* August 20, 1892; Phoenix *Gazette,* August 20, 1892; Barnes, "The Pleasant Valley War of 1887," Part I, *Arizona Historical Review,* October, No. 3, 1931, 25–27; Forrest, *op. cit.,* 233–49.

to Tucson. There it opened on December 14, 1893. With money obtained from some unknown source, Tewksbury engaged the Territory's ablest lawyers for his defense. After a trial that involved more than seventy-five witnesses, he was found guilty on December 23, whereupon his lawyers appealed on technicalities for a new trial.

Tewksbury's second trial began January 2, 1895, and on the tenth his fate went to a jury which disagreed. On February 6, he was released on bail, after having spent two and one-half years behind bars; and on March 12, 1896, the charge against him was dismissed. Ed returned to Pleasant Valley, where his father had died; but he did not stay long. He moved to Globe, where he became a peace officer. Soon his health was impaired by tuberculosis contracted while he was in jail, and died there on April 4, 1904.[20]

Even the embers were cooling. Except for the shooting of Horace Philley, a cow hand killed in Reno Pass soon afterward, Tom Graham's death was the last act of bloodshed in the feud that had raged in the Tonto Basin. As new settlers came into the valley and barbed-wire fences crossed the ranges, hostility ceased. The feud's bitterness remained only in the fading memories of some of the pioneer ranchmen. In time, when the tragic drama could be reviewed without reviving hostile feelings, it gave occasion for holding a yearly rodeo on what had been the Graham ranch.

Story and legend kept the feud from being forgotten. The conflict provided plots and incidents for two novels, Zane Grey's *To the Last Man* and Dane Coolidge's *The Man Killers.* Finally the facts of the vendetta were painstakingly pieced together by Earle R. Forrest for his book, *Arizona's Dark and Bloody Ground.* Even before that, nearly everyone in Pleasant Valley could look back without rising anger to the era in which, to many, vengeance seemed to be the only means by which they could obtain justice.

By the time the Grahams and the Tewksburys were gone, feuding was out of fashion in the West. Yet this did not mean that violence was abandoned as a means of settling disputes.

[20] Forrest, *op. cit.,* 250–76.

Rivalry for grass and water was still strong. The clashing interests of sheep and cattle, which played only an incidental part in the Tonto Basin war, had begun to draw gunfire and blood in many localities. As fighting over personal grudges gave way to conflicts between competing economic groups, the ranges still rumbled with battle.

WAR ON THE RANGES

5. Rivals for Grass

> The lion might lie down with the lamb, but never the steer with the sheep. The cowboy might marry a squaw, but he deigned not to associate with the shepherd. If you want to provoke him to shooting, call him a sheepherder.—CLARA M. LOVE, "History of the Cattle Industry in the Southwest"

ON the cattle ranges of the western frontier the appearance of a sheep wagon on the horizon was a call to war. To the cowman the white canvas of the sheepman's wagon had the effect of a red flag on a bull. Arms toughened in roping and branding reached for long rifles. The intruder must be driven off. The fact that the pasturage he sought was on public land made no difference. The cattlemen were there first, and they were not going to be "sheeped out." They could not afford to have alien flocks devour their grass and pollute their streams.

To the cattlemen, the sheepman was the pariah of the plains, an interloper who deserved no quarter. Even the hired cow hand, with his polished boots, sleek horse, and fancy trappings, was by comparison an aristocrat of the range. He looked down upon the shabby sheepherder, who was usually afoot, in a wagon, or on a burro. On encountering a herder in town, some cow hands would bleat derisively in imitation of a sheep. Especially unpopular was the drifter sheepman, who wandered far from home, lived in his wagon all summer, and sometimes twisted together the lower wires of a fence to allow his flock to graze in a cattleman's privately owned pasture.

In Texas, as elsewhere on the frontier, cattlemen seldom referred to sheepmen without an uncomplimentary epithet. M.

W. Hickman said that in Runnels County, he was brought up to hate sheepmen. A sheepherder, he added, "was too low for a decent man's notice." Pomp Cutbirth, who grew up in Callahan County, said that there a sheepherder was regarded as "lower down than a thief. He was just too low down for any use."[1]

The early cattleman's low regard for sheepmen and mutton was aptly summarized by Emerson Hough:

> The concensus of opinion was that no man engaged in walking sheep could be a decent citizen. He was a low-down, miserable being, whom it was correct to terrify or kill. A popular contempt was entertained for "sheep meat," and anyone addicted to the habit of eating it was considered of degenerate tendency. The little cow-town hotel at times served this meat, but the waiter girls had scorn in their voices when they called to the cook through the kitchen window for a "plate of sheep."[2]

The typical conflicts between cattlemen and sheepmen were not feuds. They did not stem from personal or family quarrels and the retaliation to which such quarrels often led, but were, essentially, expressions of economic rivalry between groups competing for the limited grass and water the plains afforded. Even the cow hand's social contempt for the sheepherder failed to hide his concern over a rival who might push him off the range. Each side used trickery and sometimes force to gain the partisan ends it regarded as justice.

Except in the states and territories bordering on Mexico, the cattlemen generally had squatters' rights on the ranges and therefore regarded the sheepmen as intruders. When the sheepmen pointed out that the pastures their flocks grazed upon were public ranges, to which they had as much right as the cowmen, the latter sought to bolster their position by charging the woolies with various kinds of damage.

1 T. R. Havins, "Sheepmen-Cattlemen Antagonisms on the Texas Frontier," *West Texas Historical Association Year Book*, Vol. XVIII (October, 1942), 12, citing interviews with the men named, Big Lake, Texas.

2 Emerson Hough, *The Story of the Cowboy*, 301–302.

Hostile cattlemen attributed to the flocks a whole catalog of crimes. The sheep killed the grass, they said, by nibbling it close to the ground and trampling the roots with their sharp hoofs. The cowmen regarded a "sheeped-off" range as virtually ruined. Moreover, they complained of the odor the sheep left on the land they grazed upon and in the streams and pools from which they drank. This scent, remaining for hours after the flocks had gone, was distasteful to horses and even more distasteful to cattle, both of which often refused to graze after the sheep or even to drink after them unless extremely thirsty. The cattlemen also asserted that the browsing woolies destroyed young trees in the public forests.[3]

In Oregon the cattlemen's view was thus espoused in 1899 by the Eugene *Guard*:

> At one grazing a band of sheep will almost totally destroy a range of thousands of acres. I saw miles and miles of land as bare as a fire-swept prairie. Such land is utterly useless for grazing, as the sheep's sharp hoofs kill the roots of the grass and it takes several years for it to grow again. The cattlemen, therefore, must find new ranges, which is not an easy matter, even in interior Oregon. They would not object if the grass were only cropped, but it makes them bitter to see fine ranges entirely destroyed.

The Portland *Oregonian* branded this statement as an absurd exaggeration. It pointed out that "there are ranges which have been grazed by sheep every season for many years and which nevertheless yield a fine forage crop annually. Under careful administration, a country may be ranged by sheep indefinitely, but they must not be allowed to remain upon it after the surface grass is eaten off."[4]

This reasoned defense did not convince many. John Muir ranted against sheep as "hoofed locusts."[5] Others sought to strengthen the case against the flocks by quoting the prophet Ezekiel: "Woe be to the shepherds of Israel! Seemeth it a small

[3] Philip Ashton Rollins, *The Cowboy* (revised edition), 36–38.
[4] Portland *Oregonian*, July 15, 1899.
[5] William Frederick Bade, *Life and Letters of John Muir,* I, 201.

thing unto you to have eaten up the good pasture, but ye must tread down with your feet the residue of your pasture? And to have drunk of the deep waters, but ye must foul the residue with your feet?"[6]

Outraged cowmen found many ways to terrorize the sheepmen. To drive off their rivals, bands of armed, and often masked, night riders burned the sheep camps, threatened the owners and herders, and occasionally killed a few of them. Cattle raisers destroyed the flocks by clubbing, shooting, dynamiting, burning, poisoning, and stampeding them over cliffs—a practice sometimes called rim-rocking. On occasion they drove sheep from water holes, causing them to die of thirst. Sheepmen in the West suffered hundreds of violent attacks as their flocks invaded public lands which the cattlemen claimed for their exclusive use.

The lonely herder in his isolated camp was an easy victim for organized raids. He was almost helpless when a dozen or more horsemen swooped down upon his camp in the dead of night, with guns popping. Often he could only look on as the attackers wrecked his wagons and slaughtered his woolies. Sometimes a herder died defending his flock and filled a mountain grave. But always there were more flocks and more herders. The fleecy tide could not be held back.

The plains of central and western Texas were the settings for many such raids, but few of the raids were fatal to herders. Violence by the cattlemen against the sheep and their keepers began there soon after the Civil War. Charles Hanna, who brought the first sheep into Brown County in 1869 and built a rock corral to hold his flock at night, lost all of his woolies because of the animosity of neighboring cattlemen. When he went to his corral one morning to turn his sheep out on the range, he found every one of the three hundred with its throat cut.[7]

A decade later, as more sheep were brought in, such incidents became common, but even in those early days some cow-

[6] Ezekiel 34: 2, 18.

[7] Havins, *op. cit.*, 18, citing an interview with Brooke Smith, Brownwood, Texas.

men and sheepmen got along peaceably. Charles Goodnight, who had large cattle interests in the Texas Panhandle and in New Mexico, was one person who respected the sheepmen's rights. He had had one costly experience. In the winter of 1875–76, sheep owned by the governor of New Mexico had drifted to the range his cattle had been using. While Goodnight was in Colorado, one of his cow hands, the Irish Dave McCormick, warned the herders to remove their flocks. When they refused, McCormick, with the aid of a Mexican *vaquero,* Panchito, drove the sheep into the Canadian River, where four to five hundred were drowned or perished in the quicksand. Later, in a court at Las Vegas, Goodnight had to pay the damages. In 1876, Goodnight made an oral agreement with the sheepmen concerning the division of the ranges. Except for brief violations by two sheep outfits, this pact was kept for many years.[8]

In the rolling hills of the San Saba country, troubles were frequent. Late in 1879, young Peter Bertrand, whose father had lived in Texas for more than fifty years and bore the scars of many Indian arrows, was warned by intruding cattlemen to move his sheep from the water hole they had been using on the creek. When he refused, one of the cowmen set his dog on the sheep. Soon afterward, Bertrand moved his flock down the creek and established quarters for the winter, but his move failed to satisfy the cowmen. One night they fired a volley of bullets into the pen, killing a number of his sheep, and stopped the attack only when Bertrand returned their fire with a double-barreled shotgun.[9]

Other clashes followed soon. On the night of January 22, 1880, on Fall Creek prairie in San Saba County, thirteen hundred sheep were resting quietly in two pens. These sheep were part of the Ramsay brothers' seven thousand head which grazed in the southern part of that county and over the line in Llano County. Their rest ended suddenly as horses' hoofbeats split the winter air. A band of cattlemen rode up to the pens and began shooting the woolies, throwing them into a panic. Some of the men dismounted, took out big knives, and began slitting

[8] J. Evetts Haley, *Charles Goodnight, Cowman and Plainsman,* 279–89.
[9] Galveston *News,* December 25, 1879.

throats. When they left, 240 of the sheep were dead and many more were wounded, with blood streaking their wool. Those able to run were scattered in all directions. The herder, in his camp near the pens, was roused by the firing but—alone, unmounted, and unarmed—could not defend his charges. This was the sixth outrage of its kind in the San Saba country in two months.[10]

Often Texas cow hands, to get a bit of excitement or to throw a scare into the sheepherders, would ride into a sheep camp at night and practice their marksmanship by using the pots, kettles, and other equipment as targets. Sometimes they would dump all the food and force the herders to go hungry. Some of the sheepmen fought back, but not always effectively. In a few instances, cow hands on the sheep ranges heard bullets whizzing by their ears and retired to safer territory.

One pioneer Texas sheepman, C. C. Doty, established his rights by calling a cowman's bluff. The cowman, who claimed all the range below the South Concho River ordered Doty to leave within three days and threatened him with hanging if he failed to go. On the third day, the cowman was back with two of his hands, all three bristling with guns.

"Why haven't you moved?" the cattle raiser demanded.

"I like this country, and I've decided to stay," Doty answered calmly.

At this unexpected reply the three turned and rode off. Doty sent to Austin for information and learned from the Land Office that the swaggering cattleman owned only a small fraction of the range he claimed, which was what Doty had suspected. When the bully tried his tactics on another sheepman, shooting his water barrels full of holes, Doty warned him that if he made any more trouble there would be fifty thousand sheep on the range in three months. This prospect was enough to make the blusterer change his mind.[11]

In 1883 there were many depredations against sheepmen

[10] San Saba *News*, January 31, 1880. Republished in the Austin *Daily Statesman*, February 6, and the Galveston *News*, February 7.

[11] Roy Holt, "C. C. Doty, West Texas Pioneer," *Sheep and Goat Raiser*, November, 1941.

in Texas, some of them linked with the drought and the fence-cutting troubles of that year. Several Brown County sheepmen were ordered to leave the county after having their homes and sheeppens burned, their flocks fired upon, and some of their sheep killed.[12] One sheepman who moved out of Brown County with a thousand woolies ran into similar discouragement in Shackelford County, two counties northwest. Raiders who galloped into his camp one night in August fired their pistols into his herd and cut the throats of twenty sheep.[13]

In the same month several sheepmen were ordered to leave Hamilton County but refused to go. One night eight masked men went into the pen where Ed Pendleton's flock was quartered, about a mile from his house. After binding the herder and threatening his life, they opened the gates and began killing and maiming the sheep. When they had killed eighty-eight and wounded fifty, they scattered the others. Then they untied the herder and told him he would be killed if he left the place before morning.

A few days later a dozen sheepmen assembled at Carlton to discuss their grievances. They found the meeting hall in possession of about one hundred hostile men, who ordered them to leave. After some discussion, the majority of the larger group agreed that the sheepmen and their property should be protected; but only a few of them were willing to sign the sheepmen's petition asking the governor for protection.[14]

In the next few years cattlemen in many Texas counties ordered sheepmen to leave, and in some cases they used violence in trying to enforce their edicts. In 1884, near Laredo, neighboring cowmen cast hostile eyes on the Callighan ranch, which ran more than forty thousand sheep. When the Mexican herders ignored orders to depart, one of them was slain. The sheriff and his posse captured four of the killers. The leader died before he could be brought to trial, but the others were punished.[15]

Similar clashes, with varying outcomes, took place on other

[12] Galveston *News,* January 15, 1884.

[13] Albany *Echo,* August 25, 1883.

[14] Waco *Examiner,* August 26, 1883.

[15] *American Hereford Journal,* January 1, 1945.

Texas ranges. In Stonewall County a prominent cowman scattered a flock of sheep, shot many of them, beat the young herder with a rope, and threatened to kill him if he did not take away the rest of his sheep. In Pecos County, near Fort Stockton, a drunken cow hand scattered a flock of woolies, drove some into bogs, caught one of the Mexican herders, and beat him with a lariat. But the herder's Anglo boss appeared in time to shoot the cow hand's horse, disarm and tie him, and beat him with his own rope. In the mountains of Jeff Davis County an argument over deadlines led to a gun fight in which a sheepman killed a Mexican *vaquero* and beat a cow hand with a rifle. Texas Rangers caught the sheepman, who later was tried and convicted.

Any sheepman who took his flocks on a long drive ran heavy risks. One pioneer Texas breeder who discovered this was Arthur G. Anderson. On the Hat A Ranch which he established in Pecos County in 1888, Anderson ran thirty to forty thousand head. He used to buy California stock to improve his sheep. While trailing home his second bunch of California woolies from the railroad at Alpine, he was arrested near Fort Davis and ordered to pay a fine. Knowing that such a fine was unlawful, he refused.

Since this "mile-high" frontier cow town had no jail, Anderson was placed in a dry cistern under the courthouse floor. Every day he was taken out and given a chance to pay the fine, but still he refused. After a week of this treatment, the cowmen released him on a five-hundred-dollar bond that called for his appearance in court later. Anderson finally got together the California sheep the cowmen had scattered over a wide area and trailed them home, forfeiting his bond.[16]

In some of the mountain states, conflicts between cattlemen and sheepmen were more numerous and more violent. In New Mexico in 1884, Arcadio Sais was grazing seven hundred sheep on the Carrizozo range on a contract from Dionisio Chávez. On

[16] Arthur G. Harral, "Arthur G. Anderson, Pioneer Sheep Breeder of Texas," *Southwestern Sheep and Goat Raiser* (now *Sheep and Goat Raiser*), November, 1935.

the night of June 10, after Sais had bedded down his sheep for the night, a neighboring cowman and four of his hands stampeded the flock. Riding into the panicked sheep, they killed them with six-shooters and did not leave until all of them were dead. Nearly a year later a stockman who brought 750 sheep to his ranch on Little Creek in Lincoln County was warned by cattlemen to remove the woolies from the range. He refused to do so, and a few days later one of his herders was fired upon.[17]

Arizona had frequent clashes of the same kind. In 1881 an Arizona ranchman, D. A. Sanford, acquired thirteen thousand sheep and sent John Cady to look after them. Cady, who had been working with cattle, found that the neighboring cowmen, his former friends, were suddenly hostile. They advised him to take Sanford's sheep off the range if he wanted to avoid trouble. He told them to mind their own business, but soon he began to find some of his sheep killed and others driven away. His herders were shot at, and several times Cady himself narrowly escaped death in the three years before Sanford decided to go out of the sheep business.[18]

In the San Francisco Mountain country of Arizona, the cattlemen's hatred for sheepmen ran high in 1884. To discourage and drive off the sheepherders and their flocks, cowmen corralled more than a hundred wild range horses, tied rawhides to the tails of some of them, strapped cowbells to the necks of others, and drove them one night into the midst of ten bands of sheep bedded down near each other. To speed the horses, the cowmen let out wild yells and fired their six-shooters. The 25,000 terrified woolies ran in all directions, and many were killed or injured. It took the herders a week to gather the remaining sheep and to separate the individual flocks.

Other Arizona sheepmen had similar troubles that year. On the Little Colorado range, cattlemen raided a sheep camp, tied the herders to trees, and drove more than four thousand sheep into the river where it was boggy and full of quicksand. Hun-

[17] *Golden Era,* White Oaks, New Mexico, June 18, 1885; *Lincoln County Leader,* June 6, August 1, 1885; William A. Keleher, *The Fabulous Frontier,* 95–96.

[18] John Henry Cady, *Arizona's Yesterday,* 98–101.

dreds of sheep were mired and died, and others were scattered over a wide area. Then the raiders wrecked the camp, killed the pack animals, and turned the herders loose.[19]

In 1887 the driving of sheep into the forbidden Tonto Basin played a part in the bloody Graham-Tewksbury feud. Although so many of these woolies were killed that the others were withdrawn, the sheepmen were not the losers in all such clashes. On the Little Colorado River, west of Holbrook, a sheepherder bested some cattlemen in the late eighties. The cowmen caught the herder butchering a beef in a cedar thicket. After whipping him with their ropes, they took out a knife and marked each of his ears with an overbit. Then they turned him loose and told him to leave the country. In two years he was back, with long hair covering his mutilated ears—and with a smart lawyer. Rather than face criminal charges and civil suits, the cowmen paid ten thousand dollars.[20]

Meanwhile, sheep were being moved into the ranges of states to the north. In 1869, Colorado was reported to have two million woolies and only one million cattle.[21] As the better pastures became filled, antagonisms arose. In the southern part of the state the sheep ranch of John T. Collier was invaded by a band of cattlemen on the night of March 9, 1874. The marauders entered the corral and killed all of his fine imported Merino bucks, which were valued at one thousand dollars apiece.[22] The autumn of that year brought trouble in Bent County, in the southeastern section of the state. Jeremiah Booth, who had about 2,900 woolies on his ranch, found 234 of his graded Cotswolds poisoned, and at the same time he was warned to leave within ten days.[23]

Early in 1882, dissension spread into central Colorado. Sheepmen in the northern part of El Paso County, within view of Pike's Peak, began receiving anonymous letters warning them to move out. A year later, on January 6, 1883, a group of masked

19 William MacLeod Raine and Will C. Barnes, *Cattle,* 251–54.

20 Barnes, *Apaches and Longhorns,* 127–29.

21 Annual Report of the General Land Office, 1869, 153.

22 Austin *Daily Statesman,* March 24, 1874, quoting the Cimarron *News.*

23 Las Animas *Leader,* October 9, 1874.

men rode up to one of the sheep ranches and brutally beat the herder, leaving him unconscious. Then they set fire to the cabins and corrals and began shooting the woolies. The sheep not killed were driven off into the plains.[24]

Another outrage took place in 1884 in southern Colorado. In the San Luis Valley, cow hands wrecked the fine home and ranch headquarters of Teofilo Trujillo while he and his family were away. They smashed the seven stained-glass windows of the house, burned the ranch buildings, and shot or clubbed more than half the sheep, in plain view of the herders.[25]

Conflicts between cattlemen and sheepmen arose later in northwestern Colorado. Sheep had been brought into Río Blanco County in 1883, a year ahead of the cattle. There was no trouble at first; but in the early nineties, so many Utah sheepmen began sending in large flocks that the Río Blanco ranges became crowded, and some of the cattlemen resorted to violence. They clubbed to death one band of sheep, shot every one of a band of more than two hundred rams on Miller Creek, drove over Book Cliff another flock of about one thousand woolies, and tied one sheepman to a tree and whipped him. In 1894 the offending sheepmen agreed to leave the county.[26]

Yet trouble continued, mainly between the cattlemen of northwestern Colorado and the sheepmen of southern Wyoming. Special targets of the cowmen were the three Edwards brothers, Welshmen, who had settled at Rock Springs, Wyoming, in the late eighties. The sheepmen insisted upon driving their flocks across the state line for summer pasturage in the Colorado mountains, where they devoured thick growths of bluestem grass that the cattlemen wanted to save as winter sustenance for their herds. As early as 1891 this seasonal movement of Wyoming sheep had begun to alarm the cowmen of Moffat and Routt counties.

Violent action broke out three years later in Garfield County,

[24] *Daily New Mexican,* Santa Fé, January 14, 1883, Denver dispatch citing a report from Colorado Springs.

[25] C. E. Gibson, Jr., "The Original Settler at Medano Springs," manuscript in the library of the State Historical Society of Colorado, Denver.

[26] Ed P. Wilber, "Reminiscences of the Meeker Country," *Colorado Magazine,* Vol. XXIII, No. 6 (November, 1946), 275–77.

local sheep being the victims. On September 10, 1894, while the sheepmen were in Grand Junction, fifty miles to the southwest, raiders killed 3,800 woolies, by stampeding them over a bluff into Parachute Creek, and shot one of the herders, leaving him wounded on a mountain trail.[27]

In the following year, Routt County cowmen gathered at Steamboat Springs and Hayden and issued warnings for Wyoming sheepmen to keep their flocks out of the Bear River Valley. They mobilized armed forces to enforce their edict.[28] Few serious clashes occurred that year, but friction continued for more than a decade. Some of the sheepmen agreed to deadlines but did not always observe them; hence outbreaks of violence were frequent. In one of these, on November 10, 1899, a score of masked cowmen attacked a sheep camp on the lower Snake River, forty miles northwest of Craig. After capturing the Mexican herder and demolishing his wagon, they used the spokes to club the sheep. When they left, 940 sheep were dead and 50 were crippled.[29]

The turn of the century brought new outbreaks. In 1900, cattlemen patrolled the Colorado-Utah line for fifty miles to keep out sheepmen and their flocks. Some of the Colorado sheep raisers retaliated by poisoning springs and stampeding cattle; nevertheless, many of them suffered heavy losses. Usually there was no compensation, but in one instance the Prairie Cattle Company, whose cow hands had killed four thousand of Jesús Ma Perea's sheep, agreed to pay for this damage.[30]

Trouble recurred in southern Colorado in 1900 when mounted cow hands in Huerfano County slaughtered about five hundred woolies. They clubbed and trampled about half of them and drove the others over a thousand-foot cliff. Their

[27] Craig *Courier*, September 14, 1894; Edward Norris Wentworth, "Sheep Wars of the Nineties in Northwest Colorado," *The Brand Book*, Vol. II, No. 7 (July, 1946).

[28] Cheyenne *Leader*, May 23, 28, June 8, 12, 1895; Craig *Courier*, July 12, September 14, 1895.

[29] Craig *Courier*, November 18, 1899; Denver *Post*, November 21, 1899; Denver *Times*, November 21, December 2, 1899; *Rocky Mountain News*, Denver, November 22, 1899.

[30] Ora Brooks Peake, *The Colorado Range Cattle Industry*, 90.

job completed, they rode into Sharpsdale and celebrated by shooting up the town.[31] Such raids were seldom repaid in kind; however, in March, 1901, in western Colorado, Delta County sheepmen killed eighty of John Lamb's cattle.[32]

Occasional raids continued in western and northwestern Colorado for several years. In July, 1902, fourteen masked cowmen shot and stabbed about two-thirds of a flock of one thousand Angora goats on Piñon Mesa, ten miles south of Grand Junction.[33] In 1906, raiders shot and killed two hundred woolies grazing in the Dominguez Canyon, eighteen miles west of Delta. Three years later, in Garfield County, twenty miles from Atchee, only a single, wounded sheep survived the brutal slaughter of a flock of about 1,500. Most of the woolies were clubbed; some were smothered by throwing a tarpaulin over them.

On the ranges still farther north, sheep kept moving in, despite the sometimes militant opposition of the cattlemen. Even the scattering of saltpeter or blue vitriol on the ranges, which meant certain death to the woolies, failed to check the invasion. Sheep outnumbered cattle in Montana in 1881 and in Wyoming a decade later. In 1902 the latter state had nearly seven times as many sheep as cattle.[34] But this shift in numerical strength by no means diminished the antagonism of the cattlemen.

In the Dakota Badlands, a Frenchman, young Antoine de Vallombrosa, Marquis de Mores, established a vast ranch on the Little Missouri in 1883. Soon he was grazing fourteen thousand sheep along with his cattle. But his introduction of sheep so enraged neighboring cattlemen that they poisoned his woolies by the hundreds.[35]

Idaho had repeated clashes between cattlemen and sheepmen in the middle nineties. In February, 1896, two sheepherders encamped in Shoshone Basin were shot to death in their wagon. Their sheep were scattered over the range; and their dogs, left

[31] Denver *Times*, September 16, 1900.
[32] *Rocky Mountain News*, March 24, 1901.
[33] Denver *Times*, July 7, 1902.
[34] Ernest Staples Osgood, *The Day of the Cattleman*, 189, 230.
[35] Bruce Nelson, *Land of the Dacotahs*, 192–202.

tied to the wagon, were nearly starved when found, days later. Jack Davis, a Nevada gunman who had been hired by a big cattle company in Idaho, had been threatening sheepmen and had wounded several. He was seen in the vicinity of the sheep camp shortly before the killing but disappeared before the bodies were found. Months later he was arrested in Arizona and brought back for trial. In the following year he was convicted and sentenced to be hanged; but influential cattlemen obtained stays, a commutation to life imprisonment, and finally a pardon.[36]

Montana, with fewer clashes of this kind than some of the other mountain states, had a serious one in December, 1900. At Otter, in Custer County, eleven men stampeded and killed a whole band of three thousand head of sheep belonging to R. R. Selway, the largest sheep owner in eastern Montana.[37]

The mountain valleys of Wyoming were the scenes of many armed conflicts. After sheepmen had taken their flocks across a deadline set by the cattlemen, the latter attacked the camps and destroyed sheep worth twenty thousand dollars. A few weeks later, near Rock Springs, cow hands slaughtered nearly twelve thousand sheep. Those not shot or clubbed to death were driven over a precipice. In other instances, poison was scattered over the sheep ranges. Near Laramie and Cheyenne, several flocks were driven into the hills, where coyotes and mountain lions devoured them. One prominent sheep raiser, Griffith W. Edwards, was tied to a tree while his flocks were slaughtered before his eyes.[38]

At the beginning of 1887, southeastern Wyoming was the site of an attack on helpless sheep with the most cruel of all weapons—fire. On finding 2,600 sheep in the corrals of Charles Herbert near Tie Siding, attackers killed a few and then set fire to the wool of the others. As the terrified animals could not get out, most of them died from burns or suffocation.[39]

[36] Cornelius J. Brosnan, *History of the State of Idaho* (revised edition), 240–41; Charles Shirley Walgamott, *Six Decades Back*, 169–77.

[37] Denver *Republican*, December 30, 1900.

[38] Raine and Barnes, *op. cit.*, 252–53.

[39] *Carbon County Journal*, January 8, 1887.

As in Colorado, the bitterness in Wyoming carried over into the new century. Early in February, 1902, a flockmaster on No Water Creek, near Thermopolis, was shot and killed.[40] In central Wyoming, in July of that year, masked raiders killed several thousand sheep and their herders.[41]

In the same season, in the western part of the state, sheepmen began taking their flocks up the Green River and westward. They crossed the Bridger Mountains into lush ranges the cattlemen claimed. After several herders were whipped with lariats by masked men and sent back across the mountains, the sheepmen joined forces. With armed guards, they took about ten thousand woolies, in four bands, into the forbidden territory. To counter this move, the cattlemen met in the frontier town of Pinedale and formed a band of masked raiders. At night they visited the four sheep camps. In the darkness they overpowered the herders, blindfolded them, and tied them to trees. Then they spent the remainder of the night clubbing and shooting the sheep. In each camp they killed about two thousand. At dawn they burned the wagons and camp equipment and released the sheepmen with warnings to take the shortest route home.[42]

In the Big Horn Basin of northern Wyoming, feeling was especially bitter. There, in February, 1903, a band of masked cattlemen swooped down upon a large sheep camp. They killed the herders, slaughtered many of the sheep, and scattered the others.[43] In the spring of 1904, an assassin shot and killed Lincoln A. Morrison without warning at his sheep camp near Kirby Creek.[44] A year later, mounted raiders rim-rocked a large band of woolies and burned the camp.[45]

By this time similar troubles had broken out in eastern

[40] Denver *Post,* February 15, 1902.

[41] Charles Moreau Harger, "Sheep and Shepherds of the West," *Outlook,* Vol. LXXII, No. 12 (November 22, 1902).

[42] Denver *Republican,* March 30, 1902; Raine and Barnes, *op. cit.,* 264–66.

[43] Thermopolis *Record,* February 6, 1903; Harold E. Briggs, *Frontiers of the Northwest,* 335.

[44] Thermopolis *Record,* June 2, 1904.

[45] Cody *Enterprise,* August 24, 1905.

Oregon. In 1897, cattlemen established a deadline against sheep around the headwaters of the South Fork of the John Day River. The sheepmen generally respected this ban, though the land was public; but soon the cattlemen became more officious. On June 1, 1899, cowmen in southwestern Grant County sent anonymous letters to sheepmen in adjoining Crook County. These letters warned the wool growers not to summer their flocks at the head of the South Fork of Beaver Creek or on Clear Creek or Warm Springs Creek.[46] The Portland *Oregonian* condemned as grossly criminal the cattlemen's resort to arms to keep sheepmen from federal land.[47] But the cattle raisers paid no heed; they were determined to keep out the woolies.

The next four years brought sporadic gun battles in which the Grant County cowmen destroyed thousands of sheep. One sheepman near Heppner lost four hundred head in September, 1902. A newspaper correspondent wrote that "no Grant County jury would convict a Grant County man for shooting a sheepherder pasturing outside sheep in a Grant County range. Those who do not take a hand in the fight stand ready to protect those who, with gun in hand, go out on the range."[48]

Cattlemen organized in bands of sheep shooters in Crook, Grant, and Lake Counties. These raiders were estimated to have slaughtered in 1904 6,000 sheep valued at twenty thousand dollars. Yet, in spite of rewards offered for their conviction, not one man was even indicted by a grand jury. On February 3 of that year, five masked men raided a camp of 3,000 sheep near Christmas Lake. They tied the herders while they shot or clubbed to death more than 2,500 sheep. Cattlemen who killed sheep near Silver Lake were blamed for the death of Creed Conn on March 4, 1904, a merchant who knew too much of the raid to suit them. On April 29, in the same county, nine raiders killed more than 2,200 sheep of a flock of 2,700.[49]

Month after month the slaughter continued. On June 13,

[46] Portland *Oregonian,* July 10, 1899.

[47] *Ibid.,* July 15, 1899.

[48] *Ibid.,* September 19, 1902.

[49] *Ibid.,* December 12, 1904, April 23, 1905; Raine and Barnes, *op. cit.,* 258–61.

near Mill Creek, masked men shot to death sixty-five head belonging to Allie Jones. A month later, on the night of July 14, six men with Winchesters raided the camp of Miles Lee on Old Baldy Mountain, fifteen miles south of Baker. The herder, G. W. Brooks, was alone, as the camp tender had gone into town for supplies. When the raiders began firing into the band of 2,300 sheep scattered about the camp, Brooks seized his rifle and rushed out. From behind trees, he fired eleven shots. Unable to reach more ammunition, he was forced to flee.[50]

On the afternoon of August 19, after learning that the herder was alone and unarmed, Crook County cattlemen with blackened faces raided the camp of Morrow and Keenan on Willow Creek. First, they bound and gagged the herder. Then, kneeling to avoid wasted shots, they began slaughtering the sheep, killing about half the flock of two thousand thoroughbreds. Some of the others, without a herder for two days, were killed by coyotes. "That sheepman will never get within miles of our range again," boasted one of the shooters.[51]

Winter brought little diminution of the killing. Near Paulina, in eastern Crook County, mounted cattlemen with Winchesters and six-shooters raided F. M. Smith's flock, killing about five hundred woolies. This may have been the raid referred to by the corresponding secretary of the Crook County Sheep Shooters Association, who boasted that its members had celebrated New Year's Day by slaughtering "five hundred sheep belonging to a gentleman who had violated our laws." A few days later the same anonymous secretary claimed that the association had killed eight to ten thousand sheep in the preceding shooting season. He forecast a bigger showing for the season ahead.[52]

This prediction was not borne out, although sporadic raids continued. On April 13, 1905, nine masked men rode into the sheep camp of Klum and McKendree in southeastern Klamath County, just above the California border. After covering the lone herder with their rifles, they trussed him so that he could

[50] *Crook County Journal,* June 16, 30, July 7, 21, 1904; Portland *Oregonian,* July 16, 1904.

[51] Portland *Oregonian,* December 12, 1904, April 23, 1905.

[52] *Ibid.,* January 3, 1905; Raine and Barnes, *op. cit.,* 259–60.

not move and covered his head with a sack. Then they began the slaughter of the sheep, killing more than a hundred and scattering others to become prey for coyotes. This done, the raiders went to the sheep camp of Dave Elder, to the east, where they burned everything of value.[53]

These and earlier raids led the Portland *Oregonian* to refer to the southeastern section of the state as "darkest Oregon." This newspaper remarked that "no homeseeker who comes to the state with the intention of remaining here will care to settle in a district where murder goes unpunished simply because local public sentiment is in favor of the murderer.[54] Finally, in November, 1906, a peaceful allotment of public range lands for 1907 marked a virtual cessation of this Oregon strife.

While the conflict in the mountain pastures of Oregon ran its course, trouble continued in Wyoming. In the summer of 1905, Louis A. Gantz had seven thousand sheep in a camp on Shell Creek, in the Big Horn Basin, about forty miles from the town of Basin. On the night of August 24, ten masked men rode into his camp and shot or clubbed to death about four thousand sheep. The raiders also killed a team of horses and burned the camp, destroying wagons, equipment, grain, and provisions. They tied two dogs to the wagon wheels and let them burn to death. The attackers tried to justify their action by claiming that the flock, headed for summer pasture, had dawdled on its way through the cattle ranges and had eaten all the grass. Gantz, who lost about forty thousand dollars in this foray, knew he could gain nothing by trying to prosecute the attackers in a Wyoming court.[55]

The flocks pushed on across the plains and into the high valleys, but opposition persisted. In 1907, dynamite was used—in addition to rifles and clubs—to destroy a band of sheep on Trapper Creek that cattlemen said had grazed on their ranges.[56]

[53] Portland *Oregonian,* April 23, 1905.

[54] *Ibid.,* April 28, 1905.

[55] *Natrona County Tribune,* Casper, August 25, 1905; Alfred James Mokler, *History of Natrona County, Wyoming, 1888–1922,* 364–65.

[56] Lovell *Chronicle,* May 4, 1907; Denver *Republican,* May 27, 1910.

A year later, bands of night riders, armed and masked, terrorized the upper Wind River country, burning sheep camps and killing the woolies.[57]

Outbreaks of violence in Wyoming were becoming less frequent, but those which occurred brought tragic results. In the spring of 1908, J. W. Blake of Lander had a drop band on leased land inside the Shoshone Indian Reservation, which should have been a safe place. His sheep were in charge of Robert Meigh and two assistants. One rainy night about midnight the herders, who were sleeping on the wet ground, were wakened by a volley of shots. Mounted raiders ordered them to get into their boots and hasten to their wagons. One herder found his boots frozen, but incentive shots from a six-shooter enabled him to get them on quickly anyway. The cattlemen tried to burn the wagons but found them too wet. Then they chopped the wheel spokes on one side of each and turned the wagons over.

At dawn the attackers, with warning shots, ordered the three herders to hasten home. The trio started off but hid near by. With the herders gone, the visitors began slaughtering the sheep. When Meigh and his companions returned, they found 350 sheep dead or wounded. Orphaned lambs were looking for their mothers or bleating piteously beside their bodies. Ewes, brooding over their dead offspring, refused to leave. Finally the sheepmen patched together one wagon and took the remaining sheep to town. There they learned that Blake had just died. Meigh, who succeeded him, issued six-shooters to his men.[58]

In the same year, western Colorado witnessed an incident which suggested that resort to violence was beginning to abate. Sheepmen who wintered their flocks in southern Utah were barred that fall by the scarcity of water and feed from the circuitous route they usually followed—to avoid the deadlines fixed by cattlemen—in getting their animals back from summer pasturage high in the Colorado mountains. In desperation, they hired and armed more than one hundred guards, massed their flocks closely, and drove them through the forbidden territory.

[57] *Big Horn County Rustler,* May 22, 1908.

[58] *Natrona County Tribune,* April 6, May 20, 1908.

The cattlemen, realizing the plight of their traditional rivals, did not molest the flocks or their guards.[59]

The following spring brought one of the bloodiest outrages in range history which aroused public sentiment against such violence. This was the infamous Tensleep raid, in the troubled Big Horn Basin of Wyoming. On the night of April 2, 1909, two sheepmen, Joseph Allemand and Joseph Emge, made camp on the north side of Spring Creek, near Tensleep. They had with them a herder, Jules Lazair, and about five thousand sheep. Across the creek, in another wagon, were two more herders, Pierre Cafferal and Charles Helmer. They were in sheep country but had passed across a forbidden cattle range to get there.

That night, while all five men were asleep, about a score of armed and masked raiders attacked the camp. First they aroused Cafferal and Helmer, took them aside, and held them under guard. Next they fired a volley into the wagon on the north side of the creek, killing Emge and Lazair. A few minutes later, as one of the raiders piled brush against the wagon to kindle a fire, Allemand staggered out. He was ordered to throw up his hands and did so.

Allemand's surrender, however, failed to satisfy one of the raiders. Herbert Brink fired at the sheepman and killed him while his arms were still raised. "It's a hell of a time of night to come out with your hands up," he shouted as Allemand fell. The attackers poured kerosene on the two sheep wagons, the supply wagon, and the buckboard, and burned them. For good measure, they slaughtered several dogs and twenty-five sheep.

Cut telephone wires kept news of this raid from reaching the county seat until the next day. Sheriff Felix Alston hurried to the scene with a posse. In looking for evidence, he noticed that one man's tracks showed a boot heel turned and run over on one side. This clue led to the arrest of Brink, who came the next day to view the bodies. Other suspects were arrested soon. Rewards totaling $5,000 were posted by the sheepmen. Several

[59] Raine and Barnes, *op. cit.*, 261–62; Wentworth, "Sheep Wars of the Nineties in Northwest Colorado," *The Brand Book*, Vol. II, No. 7 (July, 1946), 19–20.

Assassins Raid Camp

One of the Bloodiest Affairs in Many Years in the Range History of Wyoming

THREE MEN KILLED AT NIGHT

ARMED MOB LEAVES AWFUL TRAIL OF DESOLATION AND DEATH

Another tragedy of the range has been enacted, and more blood marks the trail of "civilization."

Last Friday night a band of fifteen or twenty armed men attacked the sheep camp of Joe Allemand and Joe Emge on Spring creek, a small stream that empties into Nowood above Tensleep. Allemand, Emge and a herder named Lazair were sleeping in a wagon on a high point on one side of the creek and two of the herders were in a wagon on the other side. The latter two were taken captive first and were marched a few hundred yards away, where they were held under guard until the tragedy was over and then ordered to move on and not look back. The wires had been cut so that no word was received at Basin until next day.

After taking the two herders captive the mob opened fire on the wagon in which the other men were sleeping. Allemand got out but was found a short distance away with a bullet hole in his left side and one in his neck. The wagon was riddled with holes and Emge and Lazair were probably killed at the first volley. When the mob was satisfied the men were dead they approached the wagon and set it on fire, first saturating it with coal oil. The other wagon was also burned, as well as a supply wagon and a buckboard, and several sheep dogs and about twenty-five head of sheep were killed.

Sheriff Alston and a deputy and County Attorney Metz went to the scene of the assassination immediately on receipt of the news. The sight that greeted them was almost too horrible for belief. The bodies lay where they fell, those of Emge and Lazair in the charred ruins of the wagon, burned almost beyond recognition. An automatic revolver and rifle lay under Emge's body and a rifle on top of the body of Lazair. Near the creek was a stone on which was a bunch of bloody black hair and little pools of blood were near at hand, which leads to the belief that at least one of the raiders was wounded, and this may lead to their discovery.

Three was a sensational report yesterday morning that the sheriff and a deputy had been killed by the raiders, but this was wholly unfounded. The officers are not making public what they find in the way of incriminating evidence. $2,500 reward has been offered for the conviction of the assassins, and it is thought the state will add considerable more.

Allemand and Emge were both old timers in the basin and both were highly respected. Allemand has been in the sheep business for many years, while Emge had recently sold his cattle and bought sheep. Lazair was a citizen of France, and this may put an international aspect on the affair and cause the United States to take a hand in bringing the perpetrators of the outrage to justice.

A large delegation of Masons from Basin, where Allemand held membership in the order, went up to Spring creek and held ritualistic services over his remains.

REPORT ON A RAID
Thermopolis *Record*, April 10, 1909

Wyoming State Library

county associations offered $1,000 each, and the National Wool Growers Association announced that it would back the prosecution with $20,000.

On May 6 the grand jury indicted Brink and six others. Later four of the men confessed to participation in the raid and pleaded guilty. In the consequent trial, which ended on November 13, Brink was sentenced to hang for murder but later his penalty was commuted to life imprisonment. Two of the men were given twenty to twenty-six years for second-degree murder, and two others three to five years for arson. Charges against the other two men were dismissed.[60] The Tensleep raid, coming when Wyoming was estimated to be producing more wool and mutton than any other state,[61] climaxed the range war between sheepmen and cattlemen and was the last major resort to violence there.

Colorado, however, continued to have occasional raids, even though, in most of the West, frontier conditions had long since vanished. In the winter of 1915, while George Wolly was in Denver, cattlemen wiped out his whole flock on his homestead south of Craig.[62] In 1917 nearly two thousand sheep belonging to John Campbell were killed in a gulch near Crested Butte. The attackers tied the herder and threw him into the gulch before killing his flock.[63] Three years later an armed conflict was reported from the Gunnison National Forest.[64] After that, the range war virtually ceased; yet in 1920 armed cowmen killed 150 sheep at Morapos, while others drove 1,200 over a cliff on

[60] Indictment and trial records in Tensleep case, district court, Fifth Judicial District, Big Horn County, Wyoming, 1909; *Big Horn County Rustler,* April 9, 16, 30, 1909; Thermopolis *Record,* April 10, 17, 24, May 1, 8, 15, June 12, October 23, 30, November 6, 13, 1909; Lovell *Chronicle,* May 8, October 23, 1909; Denver *Republican,* October 30, 1909; *Wyoming Industrial Journal,* May, 1909; Mokler, *op. cit.,* 365–68; Charles Lindsay, "The Big Horn Basin," 233–34, Ph.D. dissertation, University of Nebraska; Tacetta B. Walker, *Stories of Early Days in Wyoming: Big Horn Basin,* 104–107.

[61] *Wyoming Industrial Journal,* October, 1909.

[62] Wentworth, "Sheep Wars of the Nineties in Northwest Colorado," *The Brand Book,* Vol. II, No. 7 (July, 1946), 20.

[63] Peake, *op. cit.,* 90n.

[64] Raine and Barnes, *op. cit.,* 262–63.

Blue Mountain and, in the following year, used grain treated with strychnine to kill about 300 west of Craig.[65]

With sheepmen electing officials in many counties and with their rewards an incentive to sheriffs, it was no longer safe to raid the sheep camps. Besides, many of the cattlemen discovered, somewhat reluctantly, that they could raise sheep profitably as well as cattle. The sheep, if grazed loosely, improved the sod with their hoofs instead of destroying it. Moreover, the sheep droppings, though they disintegrated less quickly, were more valuable as fertilizer than cow droppings. Put on the same range, the cattle ate the long fibers, too coarse for the sheep, while the woolies nibbled the short grass and tender shoots that the cows could not reach and some of the weeds they spurned.[66] In Wyoming a Meeteetse ranchman, David Dickie, found that he could increase his profits about one fifth by putting cattle in his valleys and lower slopes and sheep in his timbered areas and mountain heights.[67] Several leading cattle raisers in that state later came to be numbered among the most successful sheepmen.

Putting cattle and sheep, and sometimes Angora goats, on the same range became common practice in parts of Texas, which was soon the leading sheep state. In poor market years many a Texas cattleman began, apologetically, to run a few sheep as a hedge against low beef prices. His hands may have objected at first, but most of them adjusted themselves to the changed situation. Some of the Texas ranchmen referred to their woolies as "mortgage-raisers." "Whenever I see a cowman putting a flock of sheep on his ranch," remarked A. A. Hartgrove, "I guess he has a mortgage he's trying to raise."[68] In time, old scars were healed, even to the extent that some of the cattlemen learned to eat lamb chops.

[65] Wentworth, "Sheep Wars of the Nineties in Northwest Colorado," *The Brand Book*, Vol. II, No. 7 (July, 1946), 20–21.

[66] Winifred Kupper, *The Golden Hoof*, 116–17.

[67] Charles Wayland Towne and Edward Norris Wentworth, *Shepherd's Empire*, 202; Edward Norris Wentworth, *America's Sheep Trails*, 523.

[68] Mrs. Dale S. Campbell of Dallas, daughter of Hartgrove, to the author, 1945. Referring to cattlemen's sheep as "mortgage raisers" became common in western Texas.

The despised sheepman, who seldom rode a horse or carried a gun, had won the longest and bloodiest range war in the West. He could graze his flocks without fear of human molestation. In Texas he usually had his own spreading ranch, carefully fenced. Elsewhere he could obtain a grazing permit for public pasture land as readily as the cowman could. His struggle had cost the lives of many thousands of woolies and of dozens of herders. It had covered several decades—a period in which, in Texas and Wyoming, cattle raisers had engaged in equally bitter range wars among themselves. Yet no one could dispute the victory of the sheepman.

6. The Fence Cutters

They say that heaven is a free range land—
Good-bye, good-bye, O fare you well—
But it's barbed wire for the devil's hat band
And barbed-wire blankets down in hell
—EWIN FORD PIPER, *Barbed Wire and Wayfarers*

DROUGHT hit the Texas cow country a staggering blow in summer, 1883. The sky was empty except for the blazing sun that parched and cracked the earth. Dust hovered over the plains and settled on what was left of the brown, shrunken grass. From the coals of careless campers or the sparks of locomotives, fires raced over many of the pastures, leaving only charred, blackened turf. When even the stubble was gone, the cattle browsed on chaparral, munched prickly pear, and chewed the blooms of Spanish dagger.

Still worse than the lack of enough grass was the scarcity of water. Creeks that had served vast herds were so dry that a crawfish could not wet his whiskers. Settlers on the upper reaches of the Brazos and the Colorado said they never had seen those rivers so low.[1] In some streams the trickle which still flowed was so salty that cattle refused to drink it. Water holes which had lasted through other hot summers dried up. Some cattle that waded into the mud to suck up the ooze and green scum sank into the mire and suffocated.

Leathery longhorns, toughened to hardship and scant fare, were crazed by thirst. They rolled their tongues in agony and bawled for water. Day by day their moaning grew weaker. Their bodies thinned, and their eyes became more sunken. From some of the herds many head were lost, first the cows with

[1] Albany *Echo,* September 1, 1883.

young calves, then the calves and yearling steers. The smaller cattlemen suffered first and most severely. Those who could move their piteously lowing herds to better pasture and water did so but found their stock restless and hard to control.

For many ranchers this situation was disastrous. It was made worse by the fact that the ranges were overstocked for even a normal year, in that era when few cattlemen had means for hoarding water. Feverish activity and speculation had come from the rising prices of cattle and land. Ordinary Texas cattle that sold at seven dollars a head in 1880 brought eleven dollars the next year, sixteen in 1882, and often twenty-five in 1883.[2] Men who foresaw the end of the open range and its free grass wanted to grab all the land and cattle they could, even by borrowing big sums at 18 to 24 per cent interest. Outside capital was coming in from the East and from Britain.

Some cowmen whose herds were hit by the shortage of water and grass blamed the newfangled barbed-wire fences for their predicament. Barbed wire had been brought into Texas for eight years. Ridiculed and resisted at first, it soon proved its value in making fences that were pig tight, horse high, and bull strong. Enterprising young John W. Gates and other salesmen were kept busy handling orders. In the early eighties, barbed wire was shipped in by the carload, and even by the trainload, to make hundreds of miles of fences around the larger pastures. In the Panhandle the Frying Pan Ranch spent $39,000 in 1882 for wire and posts, at wholesale, to put a four-wire fence around a 250,000-acre pasture. Some stockmen still feared that the barbs would injure their horses and cattle, but no one any longer doubted the strength of the wire to hold. On plains almost devoid of timber and stone, it offered the only satisfactory means for enclosing livestock.[3]

Many stockmen who continued to graze their cattle on public or other unoccupied lands were enraged as more and more of what had been open range was fenced in. This was especially true in the drought year of 1883. All the good streams and water holes and most of the remaining grass seemed to be in-

[2] *National Live Stock Journal*, July, 1883.

[3] Walter Prescott Webb, *The Great Plains*, 280–318.

side the fences. Some of the less settled cowmen moved farther west, but the barbed-wire fences were quick to catch up with them. Stockmen in two counties petitioned the legislature to ban fences west of the one-hundredth meridian. Land west of that line, they said, was suitable only for grazing.

To advocates of a continued open range and to buyers who came too late to acquire choice sites along streams, application of the English common law of riparian rights seemed unfair. In the arid plains, the men who bought land on rivers or creeks had a big advantage. By fencing their land, they could keep away from the streams all stock except their own and thus make the land farther back almost worthless. Those who grazed their herds on the upland pastures argued that the water should belong to all the land, since the rain which filled the streams fell on the whole plains region.

Opponents of fencing included not only farmers and small stockmen but also some big cowmen who owned thousands of cattle but had no land. These men had been grazing their herds without either buying or leasing an acre, and were determined to keep on doing so. They considered free grass and access to water to be inherent rights which the legislature was legally bound to preserve. They were all the more enraged when big pastures were bought and enclosed by corporations and foreign capitalists. One leading ranchman, Charles Goodnight, said that antipathy to fencing "originated among the cattlemen themselves, a class of holders who did not want to lease or buy land and hence did not want anyone else to, their aim being to keep the range free and open."[4]

The conflict over fencing was by no means confined to Texas. It brought about clashes in nearly every part of the western range country. It was a renewal of the ancient struggle between the nomadic herdsman and the settled stockman. The rapid spread of barbed wire merely brought the conflict to a head. In Texas the clash was sharpened by the fact that the public land

[4] Charles Goodnight, letter to R. D. Holt, October 31, 1927, quoted by Holt in "The Introduction of Barbed Wire Into Texas and the Fence-Cutting War," *West Texas Historical Association Year Book*, Vol. VI (June, 1930), 65–79, a comprehensive discussion of the fence troubles and their causes.

was owned not by the federal government, as elsewhere in the West, but by the state. When drought pushed the landless cowman to the brink of financial ruin, violence was inevitable.

The Texas Greenback party encouraged resistance to fencing. It viewed barbed wire as the symbol of a monopoly that sought to convert farmers and small stockmen into serfs. The agrarians were inclined to lump this and other complaints into one loud wail. This tendency was shown in a note found posted on a street in Coleman:

> Down with monopolies! They can't exist in Texas and especially in Coleman County. Away with your foreign capitalists! The range and soil of Texas belong to the heroes of the South. No monopolies, and don't tax us to school the nigger. Give us homes as God intended and not gates to churches and towns and schools. Above all, give us water for our stock.[5]

Along with the frustrated farmer and the landless cowman, antagonists to the fence builders often included the cow hand who feared he might be thrown out of work and the rustler who saw his prey protected and his shady activities hampered. Some of the opponents had worthier motives. There was widespread resentment against fencers who blandly took in too much territory. Along with the ranchmen who strung their barbed wire around only their own ranch lands were others who neither owned nor leased the pastures they enclosed. Still others had title to part of the land they fenced but included farms and grazing lands belonging to neighbors. E. S. Graham, a pioneer real-estate man, was critical of the big enclosures. He asserted that the ranchmen brought their troubles on themselves "by fencing up large bodies of land that did not belong to them and by trampling on the rights of the public."[6]

These overambitious fencers, along with some of those who enclosed only their own extensive holdings, often had little or no regard for the convenience of travelers. They set up mile after mile of fence without making a gate. These obstructions

[5] Fort Worth *Gazette,* November 7, 1883.
[6] *Ibid.,* September 19, 1883.

cut off roads, thereby leaving some schools and churches inaccessible to people who had to travel on horseback. In Archer County even the county seat was blocked off so that farmers and stockmen could not reach the courthouse except by snipping someone's barbed wire.[7] Jones County residents fared little better. Their county seat was completely surrounded by a fence, fifteen miles distant, with only two gates. In Gonzales County, fences cut off post routes, leading a United States district attorney in San Antonio to promise prosecution of those persons who obstructed roads used in mail delivery.[8]

Even the ranchman who fenced only his own property was a target for bitter epithets when—allowing his fenced land to remain ungrazed—he kept his herds on the common range until its grass was gone, and then moved them to his enclosed pastures. This practice, while lawful, was a sure means of stirring up the anger of the landless cowman.[9]

Smoldering resentment against fencing was touched into flame by the 1883 drought. Persons who viewed barbed wire as an instrument of the devil began to gather in small groups, muttering and grumbling. When letters and telegrams to legislators and the governor brought no action, men who opposed the fences began to formulate their own plans. They banded in secret groups, with passwords, spies, and messengers. They began making excuses to their wives for being out at night.

Soon the work of these *saboteurs* was the talk of the state. Some ranchmen had their pastures burned. More found their fences cut in the night, often with an added warning against rebuilding. At first, most of the fences cut were those which obstructed roads or enclosed other people's land. A man sent to repair the government telegraph line from Fort Griffin to Coleman had no hesitancy in cutting a fence he found in his way on Jim Ned Creek near Camp Colorado. When an army captain and several soldiers from Fort Elliott found a fence across a road in Clay County, the captain had his men cut it despite the pro-

[7] Galveston *News,* June 1, 1883.
[8] *Ibid.,* September 17, 1883.
[9] Fort Worth *Gazette,* September 1, 1883.

tests and threats of the owner. Later he had the fence builder convicted and fined in a district court.[10]

Before long the cutting became widespread and less discriminate. Abel H. (Shanghai) Pierce, one of the cattle kings of the coastal plains, who had built a fence around approximately three leagues of land, had every strand of wire cut.[11] On Tehuacana Creek, nine miles southeast of Waco, the fencing of a seven-hundred-acre ranch brought pasture burnings as well as wire snipping. Referring to a tank that had been on private property since it was built, the fence cutters left a penciled note that read:

> You are ordered not to fence in the Jones tank, as it is a public tank and is the only water there is for stock on this range. Until people can have time to build tanks and catch water, this should not be fenced. No good man will undertake to watch this fence, for the Owls will catch him. There is no more grass on this range than the stock can eat this year.[12]

Secrecy was the rule, but there were exceptions. A letter from Devine station estimated that twenty miles of recently completed fence had been cut in a week on land of the Hickey Pasture Company. This letter reported:

> Never before has such bitter feeling existed against the pasture company. No man can cast reflections upon the members of the company individually, as they are real gentlemen; but the pasture encloses convenient water for such dry season as is now prevailing. This caused people of small means to unite in a regular organization to resist. Wire-cutting is not done secretly or underhandedly. Those engaged in it can be heard for miles, and it would not be safe for anyone not a member of the wire-cutting organization to approach them while they are at the work of destroying fences.[13]

[10] Goodnight, letter to R. D. Holt, October 31, 1927, quoted by Holt in "The Introduction of Barbed Wire Into Texas and the Fence-Cutting War," *West Texas Historical Association Year Book,* Vol. VI (June, 1930), 65–79.

[11] Galveston *News,* September 11, 1883.

[12] *Ibid.,* August 9, 1883.

[13] *Ibid.,* June 30, 1883.

Much of the work of cutting was well organized, with armed guards posted to protect the men as they worked. Possession of a pair of nippers was a badge of membership in the resistance movement. Conversely, seeing a pair in a neighbor's pocket was ground for suspicion on the part of anyone who had had his fence cut. As the snipping progressed, many of the cutters became less concerned over correcting inequities in fencing and more determined to destroy all range fences. Some recruits joined the nocturnal groups for devilment and others for pay.

With irresponsible persons gaining control and with many lawful fences wrecked, the cutters came to be viewed less as crusaders and more as outlaws. The leading newspapers of the state denounced them, while most of the politicians remained cautiously silent. Meanwhile, troubles mounted for the cattlemen whose fences were demolished. At the stone store in the crossroads village of Trickham, one harassed Coleman County ranchman, J. L. Vaughn, aired his woes, which were common to many. He said he wished the man who invented barbed wire "had it all wound around him in a ball and the ball rolled into hell."[14]

Ranchers in Tom Green County suffered from an epidemic of fence cutting late in 1883.[15] Night workers cut the fence of L. B. Harris for nineteen miles, using their nippers between each pair of posts. Then they piled a carload of wire on a stack of cedar posts and lighted a $6,000 fire.[16] John R. Nasworthy and John R. Frost suffered similar losses. C. D. Foote not only had his fence cut but lost ten head of shorthorn cattle, including a fine imported bull. The cutters who drove off these animals left on a post a crudely lettered sign that read, "If your bull you hunt for, call at the first ranch this side of hell, and brand him when you get him."[17]

Ranchmen whose fences were cut held indignation meetings and devised neighborhood strategy against the marauders.

[14] Harry Hubert in *Semi-Weekly Farm News*, Dallas, April 4, 1924.

[15] Fort Worth *Gazette*, December 11, 1883; R. D. Holt, "The Saga of Barbed Wire in the Tom Green Country," *West Texas Historical Association Year Book*, Vol. IV (June, 1928), 32–49.

[16] Fort Worth *Gazette*, December 11, 1883.

[17] Galveston *News*, December 19, 1883.

The Law and Order Association of Tom Green County, formed late in 1883, was one of several groups that tried to check fence cutting and to prevent the enclosing of land not owned or leased by the fencer.[18] But rewards offered for the conviction of fence cutters generally went unclaimed. One of the few convictions was that of an army lieutenant who, with a group of men on a hunting trip, removed posts and wire to get through a fence and failed to replace them.[19]

Occasionally, defensive gunfire was effective. One moonlight night a young preacher-farmer in central Texas, Ed Featherston, went out with a neighbor youth, Will Satterwhite, to guard fences. Ed fell asleep in a thicket but was awakened by the sound of wire clipping. He and Will skirted the live oaks until they could see the cutters; then Ed fired at one of them with an old shotgun. They took to their heels, however, when their shots were returned by the intruders. The fence wreckers also made a quick retreat, stopping two miles away to abandon to the wolves and wild hogs a horse that had died from a wound caused by Ed Featherston's shot. The riders, who had been snipping wire for pay, decided that they had had enough of fence cutting.[20]

Bands of fence cutters often gave themselves such names as Owls, Javelinas, or Blue Devils.[21] When their warnings against restringing the wire were disregarded, they usually took it down again and destroyed the posts. A Castroville farmer found on his fence a card with a bullet hole through it and this threat: "If you don't make gates, we will make them for you." In Hamilton County fifteen men, after snipping the barbed wire from a pasture, left a picture of a coffin. With it was a note saying they were determined to have free grass and free water, even at the risk of their lives.

In a similar circumstance, an Albany paper reported the

[18] *Texas Wool Journal*, January 1, 1884.

[19] Fort Worth *Gazette*, December 13, 1883; Austin, *Daily Statesman*, December 18, 1883.

[20] Galveston *News*, January 15, 1884; Edward Baxter Featherston, *A Pioneer Speaks*, 73–89.

[21] Fort Worth *Gazette*, August 11, December 20, 1883; Albany *Echo*, August 18, 1883.

nailing of a coffin to one of the posts of a cut fence.[22] Wire cutters in Live Oak County, after destroying a fence, took time to dig a grave, dangle a rope in it, and leave a sign that said: "This will be your end if you rebuild this fence." Some of the cutters tried to justify their course in unsigned letters or doggerel sent to local newspapers. At Brownwood nearly two score fence cutters brazenly took possession of the courthouse for one day.

Fence cutting was reported in more than half of the Texas counties. It was especially common in a wide belt extending north and south through the center of the state. This was the frontier where farmers and settled ranchmen were pushing landless cowmen farther west. Local officers did little to halt the cutting; at Victoria a pasture fence within three blocks of the courthouse was cut in fourteen places in one night. The Texas Rangers did better, but there were not enough of them to cover all the trouble spots. At Waelder, in Gonzales County, a few Rangers disarmed a large band of fence cutters and induced them to return home peaceably. In DeWitt County the owners of a large ranch persuaded three Rangers to leave the service and guard their pasture. In spite of the fact that gunfire marked many skirmishes between fence owners and cutters, only three men were reported killed.

In proportion, sheep ranchers who had fenced their land suffered from wire cutting as much as, and probably even more than, the cattlemen. In Tom Green County, C. B. Metcalfe had completed the first four miles of fence on his ten-thousand-acre Arden ranch on the Middle Concho River when every span of wire was cut by men from a neighboring cow outfit. After rebuilding the fence, Metcalfe went to town with a shotgun and sought out the responsible cowman. What he said must have been effective, for his fence was not again molested. In Coleman County a sheepman found his fence cut on both sides of each post for a distance of several miles. When he was having the fence repaired, a coffin was left on his porch one night, with a note that said: "This will be your end if you keep fencing." He used the coffin as a water trough—and kept on fencing.[23] Another Coleman County sheepman, Horace B. Starkweather, had

[22] Albany *Star*, December 12, 1883.

his wire fences cut and two thousand cedar posts burned, along with his sheepfolds and herders' homes. When he rebuilt the fence, it was cut again, and scabby sheep were turned into his flock, forcing him to dip eight thousand head.

Soon the fence cutters had a reputation outside Texas. When Starkweather went to Chicago to borrow money on his ranch, he was confronted with big headlines in the daily papers:

HELL BREAKS LOOSE IN TEXAS!

WIRE-CUTTERS DESTROY
500 MILES OF FENCE
IN COLEMAN COUNTY

Without getting his loan, he took the next train home, where he found so much trouble that he later had to sell his ranch.[24]

Serious as the wire-snipping mania was to victimized ranchmen, it was often a subject of levity among others and brought forth many fantastic proposals. An Albany paper reported that one Texas solon

> thinks seriously of presenting a bill in the Legislature to build a Chinese Wall around Coleman County, put all the fence-cutters inside it, furnish them with wire and nippers, and tell them to wade in. As the fence-cutters prefer to do their cutting at night, the plan proposes stretching a great awning over the county, painting it black to represent night, probably cutting holes in it to represent stars. They would then be able to cut all the time, and they would abstain from sleeping so long that they would die of sheer exhaustion. Our friend thought the free state of Brown or Hamilton would be the proper place but after careful study has decided that Coleman County is the best locality.[25]

In a few instances, conciliatory methods brought peace to local warring factions. At Gonzales, Doc Burnet found some of his neighbors' cattle standing at the gate of his pasture, looking longingly at the water within. He opened the gate and let the

[23] Roy Holt, "The Woes of a Pioneer Texas Sheepman," *Sheep and Goat Raiser,* Vol. XXI, No. 3 (December, 1940).

[24] Harry Hubert in *Semi-Weekly Farm News,* April 4, 1924.

[25] Albany *Echo,* December 15, 1883.

cattle in, afterward inviting his neighbors to bring their herds to his water and offering to roll up his fence until the drought ended. His property was not molested. At Henrietta five spokesmen named by the wire cutters met with Clay County ranchmen. The two groups reached an amicable agreement by which fences were removed from across public roads and from land not owned or leased by the fence builders, gates were provided for the farmers' use, and wire cutting was ended.[26]

In most localities, factional antagonisms were too strong to allow peaceful discussion. Destruction went on through the fall. No compilation of the total damage was made, but one estimate placed the loss from destroyed fences at twenty million dollars. The Fort Worth *Gazette* declared that tax valuations had declined by more than thirty million dollars as a result of the fence troubles.[27] Property losses in Brown County alone were said to exceed one million dollars.[28] Prospective settlers were scared away from Texas, and some of the small farmers who had recently come sold out and left. One legislator feared that some of the newly organized counties would lose so many residents that their county governments would be disbanded.[29]

Finally Governor John Ireland—"Ox-Cart John," the railroad men called him—could dodge the fence-cutting issue no longer. On October 15, he called a special session of the Texas Legislature to meet in Austin on January 8, 1884.[30] He asked the lawmakers "to consider and find a remedy for wanton destruction of fences, to provide a more efficient system of highways, and to amend the law providing for enclosing school lands." When the legislature met, it was deluged with petitions and bills and was the scene of heated debates. One man called the snippers "the rag-tag and bob-tail ruffians, these hell hounds of Texas."[31]

There was no doubt that the lawmakers would make fence

[26] Galveston *News,* September 4, 26, 1883; Fort Worth *Gazette,* September 9, 1883.

[27] February 8, 1884.

[28] Galveston *News,* January 11, 1884.

[29] *Ibid.,* June 1, 1883.

[30] H. P. N. Gammel, compiler, *The Laws of Texas,* IX, 538–39.

[31] Fort Worth *Gazette,* January 29, 1884.

cutting a felony. They passed laws providing a penalty of one to five years in prison for fence cutting and terms of two to five years for malicious pasture burners. The main controversy came over the regulation of fencing. After weeks of fiery argument, the solons made it a misdemeanor to fence public lands knowingly or to enclose lands belonging to another without the owner's consent. Persons who had built such fences were given six months to take them down. Ranchers who built fences across public roads were required to place a gate every three miles and to keep the gates in order.[32]

Enforcement of these laws gradually decreased the fence troubles, but some of the people thought the legislators punished the builders of illegal fences too lightly, in view of the much heavier penalties imposed on wire cutters and pasture burners. The fence cutters' war, in its earlier stage, had been a well-intentioned effort to seek justice through group violence. It was a reaction, spurred on by the drought, against the inequities imposed by many of the fencers. But, while these conflicts brought legislation to correct the injustices, they failed to halt the spread of fencing.

Sporadic outbreaks of fence cutting continued in Texas for a decade, especially in periods of drought; but the flurries were local and usually were of minor consequence. In Navarro County in the late summer of 1888, fence cutting became too prevalent for local officers to stamp out. In response to a call for help, two Texas Rangers were sent there. Sergeant Ira Aten and Jim King arrived in an old farm wagon drawn by a horse and a mule. They took jobs picking cotton and doing other farm work, and in the evening King often entertained a crowd with his fiddle. Soon they became acquainted with the fence cutters, whom Aten described as "a hard lot," including small cowmen, ranch hands, and thieves. Aten bought dynamite and began making bombs to string along the fences. Orders from Austin directed him to stop his work and return to the capital, but grapevine reports of the bombs were enough to halt the wire cutting.[33]

[32] H. P. N. Gammel, *op. cit.*, IX, 566–69.

[33] Sergeant Ira Aten, letters to Captain L. P. Sieker, quartermaster of the Frontier Battalion, 1888, in Adjutant General's papers, Austin.

In the same year, R. A. Davis of near-by Ellis County placed a four-strand barbed-wire fence around a thousand-acre tract, only to have it snipped in 3,500 places within two days. The cutters worked systematically, removing two out of every three panels around the whole pasture. Davis promptly had the wire spliced and replaced, despite threats that, if he did, his fence would be cut again, his grass would be burned, and his tanks would be emptied of water. None of these threats was carried out.[34]

At Boerne in 1889, W. G. Hughes offered a $100 reward for information that would lead to the imprisonment of those who had cut the Hamilton pasture on the Bandera road. In Uvalde County in 1893, a young county judge, John N. Garner, asked for "about three good Rangers" to come and catch marauders who were cutting fences. In Brown County in 1898, men who signed themselves "White Cappers" burned pastures, cut many fences, and threatened those who replaced the wire with death. Their letters warned the fence builders that stock would be poisoned and homes dynamited. On one occasion they rode up in daylight to a group repairing a fence. Pushing the muzzles of their guns against the men, the White Cappers threatened them with extinction if they continued.[35] As late as 1939, the 1884 law against fence cutting was invoked in Dallas County, in a complaint from near Mesquite.[36]

Fence cutting in other states was less extensive and less spectacular than in Texas; but instances were reported from many parts of the Great Plains and the Rocky Mountains, particularly from New Mexico, Colorado, and Wyoming. In the Dakota Badlands the Marquis de Mores, who had bought long strips on each side of the Little Missouri River in 1883, incurred the wrath of his neighbors when he began to fence his land because the fences kept all cattle except his own from the river. The other ranchers got out their nippers and wrecked the fences; and when he had the wire restrung, they cut it again. Soon after-

[34] Ross W. Davis of Waxahachie, Texas, grandson of R. A. Davis, letter, December 3, 1945.

[35] Walter Prescott Webb, *The Texas Rangers,* 426–28.

[36] Dallas *Morning News,* January 31, 1939.

ward, three hunters, fortified with drink, protested against the fencing by shooting up the town of Medora. For good measure, they fired a few bullets into the Marquis' twenty-eight-room chateau. This incident led to a gun fight in which one man was killed and another suffered a broken leg.[37]

Elsewhere, fencing by settled ranchmen and by farmers—nesters, or "fool hoe men" to the cowmen—pushed the cattle trails and the open range westward and finally closed most of the trails. At the time of the Texas fence cutters' war, many cattlemen were making unlawful enclosures of the public domain in Nebraska, Colorado, Wyoming, and Montana. Several Kansans strung their wire around whole counties.

Hundreds of complaints poured into Washington from western stockmen whose herds were cut off from grass and water by the illegal fencing of federal lands. These disgruntled stockmen reported that even some persons who had no herds fenced public lands and rented the enclosed pastures to cattlemen. In addition to those fencing public land, there were many men who obtained large tracts by fraudulent operation of the homestead laws. In 1883 the district court at Cheyenne enjoined one of the big cattle companies in Wyoming from fencing public lands and ordered it to remove fences by which it had enclosed eleven sections of federal land, thus keeping the cattle of other owners from grass and water.[38] In 1886 a territorial governor, George W. Baxter was removed from office for having unlawful fences.[39] In that year ten large cattle companies were listed as having had illegal enclosures in Laramie County. One of these companies was reported to have had 130 miles of unlawful fences.[40]

[37] Bruce Nelson, *Land of the Dacotahs,* 190–201.

[38] Injunction order of district court, First Judicial District, Laramie County, Wyoming, in case of *United States* v. *Alexander H. Swan et al.,* August 30, 1883, No. 45, J. 7, p. 172.

[39] New York *Tribune,* December 3, 1886; Cheyenne *Sun,* December 9, 1886; *Daily Boomerang,* Laramie, December 13, 1886; Harry B. Henderson, Sr., "Wyoming Territorial Governors," *Annals of Wyoming,* Vol. XI, No. 4 (October, 1939), 250.

[40] Annual Report of the Commissioner of the General Land Office, 1896.

"Some morning," the *Wyoming Sentinel* warned, "we shall wake up to find that a corporation has run a fence about the boundary lines of Wyoming, and all within the same have been notified to move."[41] In Nebraska in 1883 one company had fencing for eleven miles in one direction and twelve to fifteen miles in the other. In that year another Nebraska company sold four enclosed pastures, one of them containing 143,000 acres.

In Custer County, Nebraska, where the Brighton Ranch Company had enclosed a pasture about fifteen miles square, disrupting postal service, several settlers located homesteads inside this fence in the fall of 1884. These settlers asked the company to remove the illegal fence within thirty days. When their request was ignored, they destroyed part of the fence and used the posts as rafters in their sod houses. The ranch foreman had the homesteaders arrested for this action, and while they were in town for trial, the foreman and some of his cow hands tore down the sod houses to recover the posts. In the end, the grangers were freed, and the ranch foreman was fined for destroying the houses.[42]

In 1883 the Secretary of the Interior advised homesteaders to cut all fences from federal land on which they wanted to settle. This invitation led to much snipping, some of it on the fences of privately owned ranches.[43] Two years later Congress passed a law to expedite prosecution of persons who built fences on federal lands. Suits filed under this law brought the removal of many fences. Yet a survey by the Public Land Commission in 1904-1905 showed illegal fences remaining in many sections.

While in other states much communal grazing land remained, barbed wire quickly closed the open range in Texas. The fence cutters' war of 1883 was the last spurt of a dying social order. The farmer and the ranchman who owned their land won out over the landless cowman who expected the state to provide him with grass and water. Wire sales rocketed again, and within a year the chief salesman was being called "Betcha-a-Million Gates." Settlers continued to push westward, and soon

41 Louis Pelzer, *The Cattlemen's Frontier*, 175–76.

42 S. D. Butcher, *Pioneer History of Custer County*, 185–86.

43 Peake, *op. cit.*, 73.

they were followed by windmills, water tanks, and higher grades of livestock.

The barbed-wire fence, despite the inequities and temporary hardships it brought to some, was a badge of permanent settlement. It halted the almost nomadic grazing practices that had prevailed since Spaniards introduced the first cattle and sheep. It played a major role in the settling of the western plains, a task in which the fence cutters were only a momentary impediment. It opened the plains to homesteading, encouraged improvement of the land, and gave rise to thriving cities on what had been a few decades earlier the range of the buffalo.

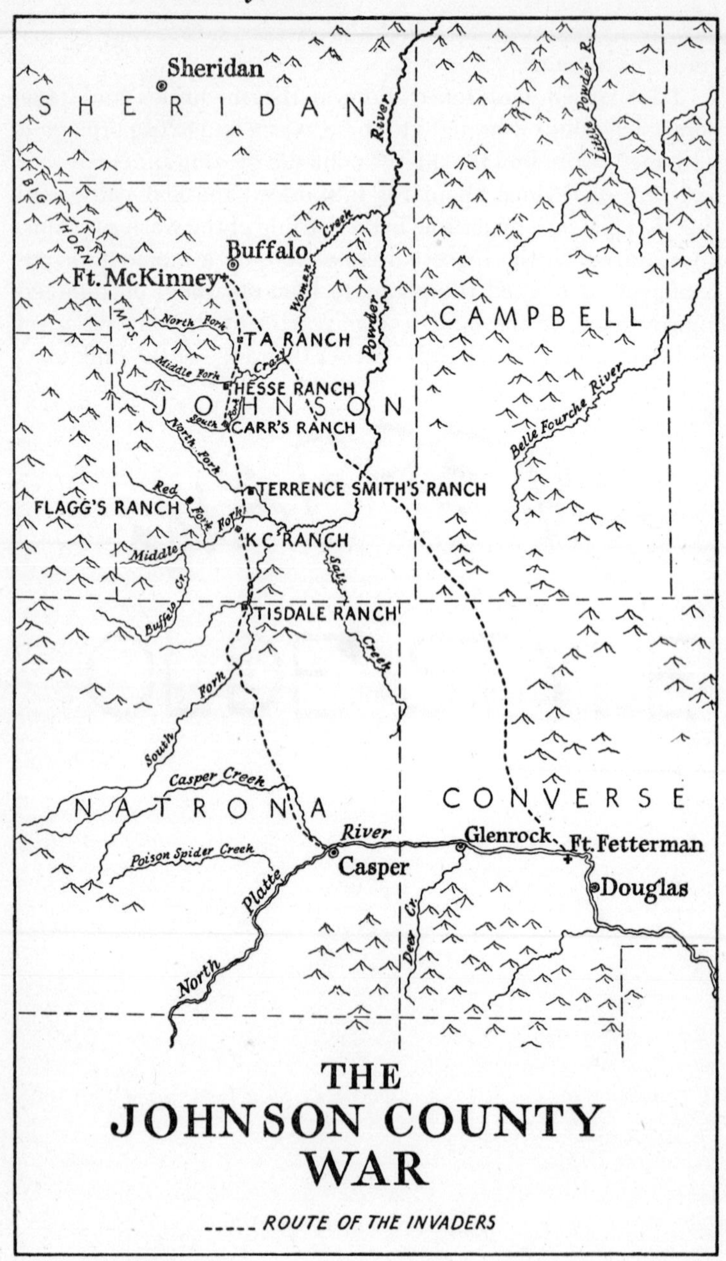

Sheridan
SHERIDAN
BIG HORN MTS.
Buffalo
Ft. McKinney
Women Creek
Powder River
Little Powder R.
CAMPBELL
North Fork
T A RANCH
Crazy
Middle Fork
HESSE RANCH
JOHNSON
South Fork
CARR'S RANCH
North Fork
Belle Fourche River
Red Fork
TERRENCE SMITH'S RANCH
FLAGG'S RANCH
Middle
K C RANCH
Salt Creek
Buffalo Cr.
TISDALE RANCH
South Fork
Casper Creek
NATRONA
CONVERSE
River
Glenrock
Ft. Fetterman
Poison Spider Creek
Casper
Douglas
North Platte
Deer Cr.
THE JOHNSON COUNTY WAR
----- ROUTE OF THE INVADERS

7. Wyoming Invasion

> The Johnson County cattle war marks the dividing line between the old West, under the rule of the big cattle kings, and the new West of the pioneer homesteader.
>
> —D. F. Baber, *The Longest Rope*

RUMOR and speculation spread through Cheyenne with the arrival of a mysterious train at five-twenty on the afternoon of April 5, 1892. This mixed special had come up from Denver over the Union Pacific. The shades of its single chair car were tightly drawn, but no attempt had been made to hide the camp equipment and the three Studebaker wagons on its flat car. In addition, there were three stock cars containing more than fifty saddle horses, a baggage car, and in the rear a caboose.[1]

This train had been chartered by a group of big ranchmen in an effort to stamp out cattle thieving. The final destination of the expedition was Buffalo, a frontier town of twelve hundred people, on Clear Creek, at the foot of the Big Horn Mountains. Buffalo was the seat of Johnson County, where many men had been indicted for cattle rustling, but only a few had been convicted.

At Cheyenne, the train pulled on past the station to the east end of the switching yards. It stopped at the stockyards near Crow Creek, on a track of the Cheyenne and Northern. There it acquired another engine and crew. In a few minutes it took on more passengers and horses and a large assortment of ammunition and supplies, including army rifles, dynamite, strychnine, tents, bedding, and thirty-five saddles and blankets. Curi-

[1] Cheyenne *Daily Leader*, April 8, 1892.

ous persons were kept away from the train. About six o'clock it pulled out for Casper, nearly two hundred miles to the northwest. It carried fifty-two heavily armed men and ammunition enough to wipe out the entire population of Wyoming.

The war was on! Big cattlemen of Wyoming had been preparing for months for this invasion. They were determined to settle a conflict that had been brewing for several years. Small cattlemen and farmers had been pouring into the state. The lure that brought most of them was free land, easily obtainable under the Homestead Act of 1862 and later land laws. With the homesteaders had come cattle rustlers who had been run out of Montana or Texas.

This influx of people was a blow to the monopolists who, in earlier days, had fraudulently grabbed much of the best land. Homesteaders forced some of the big outfits to take down unlawful fences and to give up high-handed control of streams. The cattle barons resented the small fry as intruders and nuisances, and complained bitterly of their loss of cattle. Many of the monopolists suspected that the small holder was either a rustler who ranched on the side or a rancher who rustled on the side. In some instances the foremen were stealing their own employers' cattle from isolated pastures.

The small stockmen and grangers, some of whom lived in crude dugouts, were equally resentful of the big operators. They accused the latter of obtaining control of streams and choice land by trickery and fraud, of allowing their herds to destroy crops, of poisoning water holes, and of branding as their own the calves that belonged to the smaller cowmen. The newcomers were aware that many of the wealthy cattlemen had gained their start by branding strays and by other questionable practices of which they now righteously complained.

In the seventies and early eighties, public ranges in Wyoming had proved a bonanza for pioneer cattlemen. Calves worth only five dollars each at birth were turned out on free grass to become, in four or five years, beeves that sold at forty-five to sixty dollars each. Longhorns from Texas and farm cattle from the Middle West were imported by the hundreds of thousands. Careless range practices provided an opportunity for many who had no capital—or scruples. Edgar Wilson (Bill) Nye wrote in his Laramie *Boomerang* in 1883 that "three years ago a guileless tenderfoot came to Wyoming leading a single Texas steer and carrying a branding iron. Now he is the opulent possessor of six hundred head of fine cattle—the ostensible progeny of that one steer."[2]

This speculative boom ended in a crash in 1886–87. With the ranges overstocked and drought stunting the grass, Chicago cattle prices dropped to a new bottom in the fall of 1886. Late in November a heavy snow covered the remaining grass, and the last days of January brought the worst blizzard the ranchmen had known. In the spring thousands of dead cattle were piled like driftwood in the coulees. The emaciated survivors had eaten the bark of willows as high as they could reach. Many of them had frozen ears, tails, and feet and were barely able to move. Cattlemen not ruined by this disaster learned not to depend on range grass alone but to grow hay for winter feeding. A depression that began in the late eighties brought another shrinkage, but stockmen and grangers kept coming.

By the spring of 1892, the rift between the big Wyoming cattlemen and the settlers had become deep and wide. Several acts of violence had helped to arouse public feeling to a fever pitch. One was that which involved James Averill and Ella Watson, also known as Cattle Kate. For some time, they had been homesteading on adjoining claims on the Sweetwater River. Averill, who had served as postmaster, was justice of the peace and ran a small store and saloon. He had no livestock; but he had incurred the enmity of the big cattlemen by contesting a land claim of one of them and by writing a letter to the Casper *Weekly Mail,* in which he condemned them as speculators and fraudulent landgrabbers.[3] Ella Watson entertained cow hands and, in exchange, acquired in time fifty to eighty head of young cattle, some of which may have been stolen.

On the night of July 20, 1889, ten cattlemen captured Ella Watson and Averill, accused them of being cattle thieves, and

[2] *Rocky Mountain Husbandman,* June 14, 1883, quoting Bill Nye in the Laramie *Boomerang.*

[3] Casper *Weekly Mail,* April 7, 1889.

ordered them to leave that part of the country. When they refused, the stockmen took them out and, without trial, hanged them to a stunted pine in Spring Canyon. A coroner's jury found that this crime had been committed by prominent landowners; but since one of the witnesses died soon afterward and the other departed without explanation, there was no prosecution.[4]

The wrath of the big cattlemen fell next on Tom Waggoner, a thrifty homesteader of German descent, who had a place northwest of Newcastle. He raised and broke horses, and had about a thousand head at the time. There was, however, no evidence that he did any stealing. On the morning of June 4, 1891, while he was at home with his wife and young children, he was called out by three strangers. One of the visitors pretended to be a deputy United States marshal and said he had a warrant for Waggoner's arrest. Believing a mistake had been made, the rancher told his wife he would be back soon and then went out to talk with the men. Eight days later his body was found hanging from a cottonwood several miles away. At least one of the lynchers was known, but there was no prosecution.[5]

Less than five months later, just before dawn on the morning of November 1, two armed cattlemen pushed into the ranch cabin of W. H. Hall, on the Powder River, while two others remained outside. Hall was not there, but two men who lived with him were asleep in their bunks. These occupants were Ross Gilbertson and Nathan D. Champion, the latter a top cow hand from Williamson County, Texas. As the gunmen advanced with drawn pistols toward the sleepers, one of them shouted, "Give up, boys! We've got you this time!" He fired at Champion but missed, causing only a powder burn.

Awaking suddenly, Champion reached over the side of his bunk for his gun and began firing so quickly and so accurately that the attackers fled, two of them wounded. Since they left their overcoats behind, there was no difficulty in identifying them; yet only one of them was arrested. He forfeited his $5,000 bond and left the state.[6]

[4] Laramie *Boomerang*, July 23, 25, 27, 30, 1889; Casper *Weekly Mail*, July 26, 1889.

[5] Wyoming *Derrick*, June 25, 1891.

The next efforts against the settlers were more carefully planned. On the evening of November 28, Orley E. (Ranger) Jones was driving home from Buffalo. A youth of twenty-three, he had been a broncobuster for the C Y. He had gone to town to buy lumber to complete his cabin and was expecting to be married as soon as his home was ready. As he crossed the high bridge over Big Muddy Creek, fourteen miles from Buffalo, driving two horses to a buckboard, he was shot three times by an assassin hiding under the bridge. The buckboard was taken off the road, with the body left in it; and the horses were turned loose.

Two evenings later, John A. Tisdale, who lived on a Powder River ranch about sixty miles south of Buffalo, started on a similar trip home. He drove a wagon and was taking home grain, groceries, and toys for his children. Uneasy because he had overheard a man in a saloon telling another that he would "take care of Tisdale," he had bought a double-barreled shotgun for protection. That night he stayed at the Cross H Ranch, six miles out of Buffalo. He told the hands there of his fear and carefully kept his window shades down.

The next morning Tisdale resumed his homeward trip. Two or three miles away, he crossed a small stream at Haygood's gulch. Just after he had rumbled over the bridge and started up the hill, he was ambushed and killed in the same manner as Jones. His wagon was taken out of sight of the road, and the horses were shot. His body was discovered soon afterward, and in the wagon blood was mingled with Christmas toys. Tisdale's fate led to a search for Jones, who was overdue home. When the two frozen bodies were brought into Buffalo, antagonism to the big cattlemen rose to a new high. Tisdale had ridden range for Theodore Roosevelt. He and Jones both had good reputations and had not been accused of cattle rustling. Frank Canton, a former sheriff, whose horse was found near the murder scene, was arrested in the Tisdale case; but he was released after a preliminary hearing.[7]

[6] Buffalo *Bulletin,* November 5, December 17, 1891.

[7] *Ibid.,* December 3, 10, 1891; *Natrona Tribune,* December 9, 1891; *Wyoming Derrick,* December 10, 1891; Coroner's report on the death of

While Johnson County seethed, big stockmen in Cheyenne were remarking that there were "too many people and not enough cattle" in Wyoming,[8] and were forming plans for an invasion aimed at wiping out the rustlers. To them, that seemed the only way to obtain justice and to make their herds safe. At least unofficially, the powerful Wyoming Stock Growers' Association, dominated by the cattle companies, took the initiative. The minutes of its meetings for this period were left conveniently blank,[9] but its leaders did not deny their responsibility.[10]

The first blow of the association was made in October, 1891, through the state Board of Live Stock Commissioners, that organization being under the influence of the association. Instructions to the commissioners were to take all cattle bearing the brands—presumably of the rustlers—which appeared on a list provided by the association. The commissioners were told to disregard all bills of sale for such cattle, to sell the animals, and to hold the money. This plan allowed the board to confiscate almost all cattle offered for sale by anyone except members of the association. Small ranchers, cow hands, and grangers were assumed to be guilty of stealing the few cattle they had raised unless they could prove their innocence.[11]

This practice aroused bitter condemnation and turned against the association several newspapers which previously had been among its defenders. The Cheyenne *Daily Leader* regretted "the revival of the old spirit of intolerance by the Wyoming Stock Growers' Association" and "an un-American spirit of dominance which would ride roughshod over the weaker ele-

---

John A. Tisdale; Asa Shinn Mercer, *The Banditti of the Plains,* 14–18. Mercer, a graduate of Franklin College, had served as the first president of the University of Washington, 1861–63, before coming to Wyoming. Cattlemen tried to suppress his biting, partisan account of the Johnson County war, the original edition of which became a collectors' item.

[8] Cheyenne *Daily Leader,* July 12, 1892.

[9] Minute books, Wyoming Stock Growers' Association, University of Wyoming library.

[10] Ernest Staples Osgood, *The Day of the Cattleman,* 249.

[11] Cheyenne *Daily Leader,* October 28, 1891.

ments and force them to immigrate or crawl, cowed and subdued, at the feet of a fierce and implacable oligarchy."[12]

Small cattlemen of northern Wyoming met at Buffalo in the early spring of 1892. They decided to disregard as unfair the Board of Live Stock Commissioners' division of the state into roundup districts. Forming the Northern Wyoming Farmers and Stock Growers Association, they began plans to hold a roundup of their own on May 1, weeks ahead of the one set by the commissioners. This action further outraged the big cattlemen, who viewed it as an effort to collect the mavericks before the large companies could get hold of them.

Talk of an armed invasion of Johnson County had begun in the summer of 1891. Preparations were systematic and thorough. Leaders of the association raised a big war fund and saw that dispatches were sent to newspapers in Denver, Chicago, and other cities, intimating that the rustlers had imposed a reign of terror on the ranges. To head the expedition they chose chubby Major Frank Wolcott of Glenrock, a cattleman and former army officer, originally from Kentucky. He had been advocating such a foray for a long time.

Wolcott sent recruiters to Montana, Idaho, and Colorado to enlist gunmen, without much success; but Tom Smith did better in Texas. A former Texan, Smith had been a deputy sheriff in Fort Bend County and a deputy marshal in the Indian Territory. From several Texas towns, including Paris, near the Red River, he picked up twenty-three young fellows who liked excitement, were good shots, and feared nothing. Some of them were experienced in law enforcement. Smith was said to have received $2,500 and to have offered the Texans $1,000 each and expenses.[13]

In Denver the cattlemen arranged for a special train and

[12] *Ibid.*, March 23, 1892.

[13] Robert B. David, *Malcolm Campbell, Sheriff*, 154. David's book gives the most detailed and—despite its partiality to the invaders—the most reliable account of the Johnson County war. The Buffalo *Bulletin* of April 14, 1892, said the Texas gunmen were hired at five dollars a day, plus a $3,000 accident policy and a bonus of fifty dollars to each man for every rustler killed.

bought supplies. They procured horses from a ranch north of Denver and picked them up on the way. To assure adequate and favorable publicity, they took along two war correspondents, Ed Towse of the Cheyenne *Sun* and Samuel T. Clover of the Chicago *Herald*.[14] The latter's detailed reports gave the impression that the expedition was entirely proper.

The cattlemen informed the acting governor, Dr. Amos W. Barber, of their plan. He co-operated by presenting the expedition with a case of new guns and by having the adjutant general issue a general order on March 23, 1892, instructing the Wyoming National Guard to obey no orders to assemble except those received from the state headquarters. This order clearly violated a state law of 1890 which empowered a sheriff or mayor or local judge to call out these forces in any emergency. It seemed to put Johnson County at the mercy of the cattlemen's private expedition. Barber must have known, too, that the invasion itself ran counter to Article XIX of the constitution of Wyoming, which banned the bringing into the state of any police force or other armed body of men to suppress domestic violence, except on order of the legislature or the governor.[15]

On April 4, the day before their invasion train arrived from Denver, the Wyoming Stock Growers' Association held its annual meeting in Cheyenne. The association did little, officially, except to pass a resolution commending the work of its puppet, the Board of Live Stock Commissioners, in protecting the herds of its members from outlaws.[16] But there was much anxiety among the cattlemen. People in the town knew that something big was afoot.

In Cheyenne the next afternoon a visitor from the Platte valley became suspicious of the strange train and began questioning railroad men. The answers he received were so evasive and unsatisfactory that he surmised the purpose of the expedition. When he realized what was happening, he tried to telegraph a warning to his friend, Sheriff W. G. (Red) Angus of Johnson County; but an agent of the cattlemen had already cut

[14] Samuel Travers Clover, *On Special Assignment.*
[15] Constitution of the state of Wyoming, Article XIX, Section 1.
[16] Cheyenne *Daily Leader,* April 5, 1892.

the wires. The stranger was told that no messages were going through, so he wrote Angus a letter and sent it by the regular train the next day.

As the invasion train left Cheyenne, Wolcott called out, "Put us at Casper and we will do the rest." There were on board more than a score of cattlemen, the hired Texans taken on in Denver, the two newspapermen, and a Philadelphia surgeon, Dr. Charles Bingham Penrose,[17] who had come to Wyoming for his health. The passenger car was thick with smoke and with talk of the adventure ahead. While some of the Texans played cards, Wolcott unfolded a map and explained the strategy he had planned. As the night wore on, lights were dimmed and most of the men tried to sleep. The train stopped at Douglas for water, and at Fort Fetterman it took on a cow hand and a horse from Senator Joseph M. Carey's ranch.

Before daybreak the invaders reached the outskirts of Casper, which nestled at the foot of snow-crested mountains. Quickly the men began unloading their horses and equipment, which included tents and blankets stamped as property of the United States Army. They were disappointed in failing to find confederates who had promised to meet them there. Some were disturbed by a rift that arose when Wolcott ordered Frank Canton from the baggage car. Seeing that the Texans took the part of Canton, who was from their state and was a friend of Tom Smith, Wolcott resigned his command. Canton was chosen in his place; but as he showed little initiative, the pudgy major gradually reassumed active leadership.[18]

At Casper the invaders saddled their horses and loaded the wagons. Then they set out across the sagebrush plains to the northwest. They were headed for the ranch headquarters of D.

[17] *Rocky Mountain News,* Denver, April 15, 1892; Charles Bingham Penrose, "The Rustler Business," manuscript, Penrose papers, University of Wyoming library. Dr. Penrose was a classmate and friend of Acting Governor Amos W. Barber and a brother of Senator Boise Penrose of Pennsylvania.

[18] William C. Irvine, letter dated Ross, Wyoming, December 6, 1913, to Dr. Charles B. Penrose, Philadelphia, in Penrose papers, University of Wyoming library. Irvine, one of the invaders, was a member of the Wyoming Board of Live Stock Commissioners.

R. Tisdale and State Senator John N. Tisdale, who were members of the party. This ranch was on the South Fork of the Powder River, nearly fifty miles from Casper. With no more excitement than a little trouble with wagons and horses and the turning back of a few curious strangers, they reached the ranch on the second evening, April 7. They now were at the southern edge of Johnson County.

The tired men lost little time in bedding down at the Tisdale place. While there they were met by a rider from the north. This was Mike Shonsey, foreman of the big ranch of the Western Union Beef Company. He had information that caused the leaders to change their plan a bit. Two of the men the invaders were looking for, Shonsey reported, were staying at the K C, or Nolan, Ranch, fourteen miles farther north, on the Middle Fork of the Powder. These men were Nathan D. Champion, who had narrowly escaped five months earlier, and Nick Rae, a former Missourian. Rae had leased the K C Ranch from John Nolan. Champion, who had staked a claim two miles farther north, was bunking with him. The big cattlemen had accused these two of being rustlers but had never produced any evidence against them. Friends protested that Champion and Rae were honest settlers.

After resting at the Tisdale ranch on the eighth of April while their supply wagons caught up with them, the invaders set out that night—all except Dr. Penrose, Ed Towse, and one Johnson County cattleman, who decided they had had enough. Through a biting wind and flurries of snow, they proceeded to the K C Ranch, which they reached a little after daybreak on Saturday, the ninth. The ranch headquarters consisted of a three-room log and frame cabin, a barn, and a pole corral. Because of the light, the attackers dared not approach the house openly but hid in a near-by brush ravine. Although the storm had delayed them and had cooled the combativeness of some of the men, they had the place almost surrounded before they saw any sign of life in the cabin.

Soon an elderly man left the house with a bucket and walked to the stream for water. Then a younger man came from the cabin and went to the barn. They proved to be trappers, Ben

Jones and William W. Walker, who had spent the night at the ranch. The attackers captured and held them. Champion and Rae, the trappers said, were the only persons left in the cabin.

A few minutes later, Rae, who was a lanky fellow, opened the door and stepped out. He was greeted with a fusillade from a dozen Winchesters and fell with a bullet in his head. On his hands and knees, he tried to drag himself back to the cabin but soon received a shot in his back and collapsed with a groan. At this, Champion sprang out of the house. Using one hand to drag Rae in by the collar, he fired at the attackers with his pistol and tried to dodge the bullets that fell about him. He got back inside with his friend and banged the door.

The attack continued, but cautiously. Inside the cabin, Champion realized that he had little chance to get out alive. To leave a record for his friends, he took his pocket notebook and began a diary, writing in pencil between shots. His jottings had the simplicity of the letter he had written to the Buffalo *Bulletin*, describing the earlier attempt on his life. His first entries were:

Me and Nick was getting breakfast when the attack took place. Two men here with us. Jones and another man. The old man went for water and didn't come back. His friend went out to see what was the matter, and he didn't come back. Nick started out, and I told him to look out. I thought there was someone at the stable and would not let them come back. Nick is shot but not dead yet. He is awful sick. I must go and wait on him. It is about two hours since the first shot.

Nick is still alive. They are still shooting and are all around the house. Boys, there is bullets coming in like hail. Them fellows is in such shape I can't get at them. They are shooting from the stable and river and back of the house.

Still afraid to leave their cover for a frontal attack, the invaders kept pouring lead into the cabin from their various hiding places. In his temporary haven, which was growing more precarious by the hour, Champion wrote:

Nick is dead. He died about nine o'clock. I see smoke down at the stable. I think they have fired it. I don't think they intend to let me get away this time.

At midday, as the grim siege continued, Champion made another notation:

> It is about noon now. There is someone at the stable yet. They are throwing a rope out at the door and dragging it back. I guess it is to draw me out. I wish that duck would get out farther so I could get a shot at him. Boys, I don't know what they have done with them two fellows that stayed here last night.

Such an attack could not be kept secret for long, even in thinly settled Wyoming. On their way up from Casper, the invaders had told persons they met that they were surveyors on their way to the Bald Mountains; but no one was fooled. Those travelers who were turned back and others who were captured temporarily and then released obeyed fearfully the injunction of silence. But early on the morning of the attack against the K C Ranch, Terrence Smith, a ranchman who lived four miles to the north, on the North Fork of Powder River, heard the firing and rode over to see what was up. What he saw sent him racing to Buffalo to warn the sheriff. On the way, he met six men at the Crazy Woman Ranch and sent them to keep an eye on the fight.

Early in the afternoon another neighbor approached the scene of battle. This was Oscar H. (Jack) Flagg, who had come from Texas with a cattle herd in the fall of 1882 and had settled on a ranch not far from the K C. That day Flagg was traveling toward Douglas with his seventeen-year-old stepson, Alonzo Taylor. The youth was driving a team of bay horses to a stripped wagon, and Flagg was riding a horse about fifty yards behind. They reached the K C Ranch about two thirty and were uncomfortably close when they realized that it was under attack. When some of the men jumped up and ordered the boy to halt, he urged his horses on and raced for the bridge, with Flagg galloping behind. Then seven men came out on horseback and ordered Flagg to stop. When he refused, one fired his Winchester and all of them started in pursuit.

Major Frank Wolcott
Leader of the invaders

Chapman Collection, University of Wyoming Library

As Flagg caught up with the wagon, his stepson handed him his rifle. With this he kept the pursuers at a distance while the youth unhitched one of the horses and mounted. The two soon outdistanced their attackers, who apparently had little relish for a fight in the open, and hastened to John R. Smith's ranch. There they found three men who were on their way to Cheyenne. These travelers changed their plans, quickly saddled their horses, and hastened to Buffalo to arouse the people.

From his cabin, Champion saw the Flagg incident and noted it in his diary:

Boys, I feel pretty lonesome just now. I wish there was someone here with me so we could watch all sides at once. They may fool around until I get a good shot before they leave. It is about three o'clock now. There was a man in a buckboard and one on horseback just passed. They fired on them as they went by. I don't know if they killed them or not. I seen lots of men come out on horses on the other side of the river and take after them.

I shot at the men in the stable just now; don't know if I got any or not. I must go and look out again. It don't look as if there is much show of my getting away. I see twelve or fifteen men. One looks like Frank Canton. I don't know whether it is or not. I hope they did not catch them fellows that run over the bridge toward Smith's. They are shooting at the house now. If I had a pair of glasses, I believe I would know some of those men. They are coming back. I've got to look now.

With Jack Flagg and his stepson gone, the attackers, who had been unaware of the earlier warning by Terrence Smith, knew they would have to complete their present job quickly. So they decided to try to set the cabin on fire and thus force Champion out. Taking the wagon Flagg had abandoned, they wheeled it to the barn about four o'clock and loaded it with hay and pitch pine. Then five men backed it against a window of the house, using it as a shield for themselves, and set it on fire. Under cover of smoke, they dashed back to the barn.

As they did this, the besieged man made two more entries in his diary:

Well, they have just got through shelling the house like hell. I heard them splitting wood. I guess they are going to fire the house tonight. I think I will make a break when night comes, if alive. It's not night yet.

The house is all fired. Good-bye, boys, if I never see you again.[19]

The cabin roof caught fire quickly from the blazing wagon. In a few minutes the north wall was a sheet of flame. Smoke began to pour out through the plastered cracks between the pine logs. Flames leaped fiercely through the rooms of the cabin; knots in the logs cracked and popped; smoke made a black cloud across the prairie to the south; and sparks set the grass afire.

The sharpshooters stationed to down Champion as he came out began to think they were not needed. "Reckon the cuss has shot himself?" one remarked. "No fellow could stay in that hole a minute and be alive."

He had hardly finished speaking when someone west of the cabin shouted, "There he goes!" With a Winchester in his hand and a pistol in his belt, Champion rushed out through the back door, in his stocking feet and bareheaded. He started across the burned open space toward the ravine. He had fired only one shot when a bullet struck his rifle arm. Before he could draw his pistol, he stumbled and fell, riddled with twenty-eight bullets, several of them in his heart.

Champion's body was far enough from the blazing cabin to avoid being burned. As the fire died down, the attackers examined their victim, took his guns, and searched his clothes—gray shirt, vest, overalls, and red sash. They found the diary in his pocket, read it, and slashed out the name of Frank Canton. To Champion's blood-stained vest they pinned a card that Clover had lettered at the request of one of the stockmen. It read, "Cattle thieves, beware!"[20]

The invaders had killed two of the men they regarded as rustlers but had a few casualties of their own. Two of the at-

[19] Cheyenne *Daily Leader,* April 13, 14, 20, 1892; Buffalo *Bulletin,* April 14, 21, 1892; Mercer, *op. cit.,* 41–42.

[20] Chicago *Herald,* April 15, 1892.

tackers were wounded so seriously that they were sent back to Casper. Another, with lesser wounds, decided to go on. As their wagons caught up with them in the evening, the tired gunmen enjoyed a warm meal. Still sixty miles from Buffalo, they decided to travel all night and set out soon after nine o'clock. After riding for several hours, they stopped at the headquarters of the big ranch of the Western Union Beef Company. This ranch was managed by George W. Baxter, whom President Grover Cleveland had removed from the territorial governorship in 1886 for unlawful fencing. There they changed to grain-fed horses which had been made ready for their use.

Meanwhile, in Buffalo and other places, the alarm was spreading. About seven thirty Saturday evening, Terrence Smith arrived in town and immediately told Sheriff Angus what he had seen at the K C Ranch. Angus, who had already received the letter of warning from Cheyenne, called on the local commander of the National Guard to help him repel the invasion. The commander refused, citing the order he had received from the adjutant general. The commander of Fort McKinney, three miles west of town, likewise declined to help without an order from the governor. The sheriff tried to telegraph the governor, but the wire was cut.

Finally, Angus sent a telegram to Sheriff Malcolm Campbell at Douglas: "Fight on Powder River between White Caps and rustlers. Arrest and hold all suspicious parties." Then he quickly swore in several deputies and headed for the K C Ranch, gathering reinforcements on the way. His departure may have saved his life, for he heard rumors later that Buffalo sympathizers of the invading cattlemen had been detailed to kill him that night.

Flagg and Taylor and the men they had picked up stopped Saturday evening at a ranch about thirty miles north of the K C. There they were joined by the men Terrence Smith had sent back. The enlarged party decided to head south to meet the invaders. Near Dick Carr's ranch on Crazy Woman Creek they found some bales of hay and used them to block the road. When the cattlemen and their reinforcements failed to arrive, the Flagg party went on down the road to look for them. But the accidental discharge of a gun warned the invaders, who cut one of the Carr fences and detoured around their opponents. Flagg and his men then camped for the night.

The invaders, after passing the Carr ranch, hastened northward. About two o'clock Sunday morning they stopped at the 28 Ranch of one of their party, Fred Hesse. There they had hot coffee and rested for two hours. Soon after they had resumed their ride toward Buffalo, twenty-two miles to the north, they saw someone coming frantically toward them on a foaming horse. It was Phil Duffran, a cattlemen's detective. Duffran told them that Angus had not been killed. He added that the citizens were warned and were preparing to defend the town. "Turn back," he yelled. "Take to cover if you value your lives."

At this news, Major Wolcott held a war council and decided to stop at the T A, or Harris, Ranch, a few miles ahead. As the invaders reached the headquarters of this ranch, they received more bad news. A little earlier, Charley Ford, who lived in the neighborhood, had been given permission to ride ahead and see his wife. One of the Texans, six-foot James Dudley, who had a troublesome horse, went with him in search of a gentler mount. At the T A the party learned that Dudley's horse had started bucking and had thrown its rider. The fall loosened and accidentally discharged Dudley's Winchester, seriously wounding him in the left leg. Wolcott decided to send him, in Ford's spring wagon, to the army hospital at Fort McKinney. He told Dudley to say he had shot himself by accident.

Meanwhile, Flagg and his companions went on into Buffalo Sunday morning. On their way, they saw the invaders fortifying their position on the T A Ranch, fourteen miles south of town. The Flagg party found Buffalo popping with excitement. Horsemen had been sent in all directions to spread the warning and to call for volunteers. Robert Foote,[21] who owned the biggest store in Buffalo, invited the defenders to come in and take what guns and other equipment they needed, without charge.

[21] Foote, then fifty eight years old, was of Scottish birth and had been an Indian fighter, a post trader, and a freighter. Soon after the Johnson County invasion, he was elected to the Wyoming Legislature. Mrs. Charles Ellis, "Robert Foote," *Annals of Wyoming*, Vol. XV, No. 1 (January, 1943), 50–62.

As these men outfitted themselves, Foote mounted his black stallion and paced the streets, calling for recruits. "Wyoming has been invaded," he boomed. "This murderous gang is now marching on our village to murder our citizens and destroy our homes. Now is the time to show your colors. I call on you to shoulder arms and go to the front to fight the approaching foe." One of the local preachers recruited forty of his parishioners to help defend the town.

Buffalo's defenders were all the more aroused when they heard of the plot to kill Sheriff Angus. With armed settlers pouring into the town, it would have been unsafe to even whisper anything favorable to the invaders. By eight thirty Sunday evening, forty-nine men were ready for battle. Led by Arapahoe S. Brown, a former squaw man who had settled down to homesteading and to running a small flour and feed mill in Buffalo, they departed for the T A Ranch. They arrived there about midnight, and, finding pickets posted, they decided to wait for daylight.

The T A Ranch, in a bend of Crazy Woman Creek, was admirably suited for defense. It had a large log house, set among trees. Near by were an ice house, a hen house, a dugout for storing potatoes, and a stable with corrals and a haystack. The buildings were surrounded by a tightly built log fence, with barbed wire on the outside. Gullies and a ravine made the headquarters hard to approach. The site commanded a view of low hills in all directions, with the snow-clad Big Horns off to the west.

Near the corrals Wolcott found a pile of heavy timbers that had been brought for putting up additional buildings. He decided to use these to improvise a fort on rising ground just west of the ranch buildings. Although the men were tired, they went at this work quickly. Before long they had made a barricade about twelve by fourteen feet and added earthworks and trenches.

While these defense preparations were going on at the T A, Sheriff Angus and his men reached the scene of the Saturday battle at the K C. There they found embers still smoking. They came upon Champion's body where the gunmen had left it and removed that of Rae, horribly burned, from the ruins of the cabin. Leaving the bodies to be brought in by wagon, they sped back to Buffalo, where they arrived about one o'clock Monday afternoon, April 11.

By that time Buffalo was an armed camp. The wagon bearing the wounded Dudley had passed through the town, stirring excitement and suspicion. The townspeople refused to believe Dudley's story and assumed that he had been wounded by Champion two days earlier. But they allowed the sufferer to be taken on to the hospital at Fort McKinney, where, after two days of fever and delirium, he died.

Before sundown Monday, Angus hurried off to the T A Ranch with forty men, leaving arrangements for others to follow. That evening one of his posses captured the three supply wagons belonging to the invaders. These contained food, bedding, ammunition, handcuffs, kerosene, strychnine, and two cases of dynamite. With the drivers were three other men, including the Chicago reporter. One of the teamsters gave the names of the men in the invading party. In Frank Canton's valise was a list of seventy men believed marked for death.[22]

As recruits poured in, the settlers greatly outnumbered the besieged cattlemen. They were increasing their strength almost hourly. Behind the barricades, the invaders were becoming worried. They held another war council Monday evening and decided to try to send out an appeal for help. Major Wolcott wrote a telegram to the Governor. George Dowling, a cow hand who had been captured by the party on its way north from the K C Ranch, volunteered to try to slip out. While the moon was blacked out by clouds, he stole down Crazy Woman Creek and escaped through the picket lines. After finding a mount, he rode into Buffalo, where he learned that the telegraph wires had been cut. Only by going southward to Hathaway's Crossing was he able to get his message forwarded to Cheyenne.

The besiegers spent much of Monday night digging rifle pits

[22] Cheyenne *Daily Leader,* April 20, 1892, quoting an April 14 letter of Mary S. Watkins of Buffalo in the Laramie *Boomerang;* Penrose, "The Rustler Business," 1914. Penrose Papers, University of Wyoming library, 40; David, *op. cit.,* 237.

and throwing up breastworks. In the night a cold drizzle set in, changing to snow by morning. Each side fired random shots but was unable to penetrate the other's defenses. By Tuesday afternoon Sheriff Angus had in his command more than 250 men, some of them farmers from Prairie Dog and as far north as the Tongue River. His lieutenants were Arapahoe Brown, the Reverend M. A. Rader, a fiery Methodist preacher, and E. U. Snider. After serving under General George Crook, Snider had been a post trader at Fort McKinney and had held office as sheriff, probate judge, county treasurer, and territorial legislator.

On Tuesday, while Angus tried unsuccessfully to obtain artillery from Fort McKinney, Brown and Snider conferred on attack strategy. They worked out a plan like the one used by the invaders to rout Champion from his cabin on the preceding Saturday. They had the gear of two of the captured wagons placed side by side, several feet apart, and fastened them together with heavy timbers. In this way they made a movable breastwork of logs and baled hay. Their plan was to load the captured dynamite on this "go-devil," push it backward into the cattlemen's stronghold, and explode it. Then their sharpshooters would pick off the cattlemen and the Texans as they tried to escape.

Meanwhile Governor Barber and others in Cheyenne were becoming alarmed. Reports indicated that the cattlemen's invasion party, which had intended to drive out or kill off the Johnson County rustlers and to subdue the homesteaders, was surrounded and in danger of being captured. On Tuesday, Barber sent frantic telegrams to President Benjamin Harrison, to both of Wyoming's senators, and to Brigadier General John R. Brooke of Omaha. In these messages he asserted incorrectly that a state of insurrection existed in Johnson County and asked that United States troops stationed at Fort McKinney be sent to quell it.

That night the Wyoming senators went to the White House and routed the President from his bed. At their insistence, the Commander-in-Chief ordered the War Department to give the requested aid. From General Brooke, commander of the Department of the Platte, Colonel James J. Van Horn at Fort Mc-

Kinney received his order at twelve thirty on the morning of Wednesday, April 13. He replied that he would have three troops of cavalry moving in two hours. Colonel Van Horn had been in close touch with the situation and was not fooled by the Governor's misrepresentation. He stated in his telegram to General Brooke: "The entire country is aroused by the killings at the K C ranch, and some of the best citizens are in the sheriff's posse."[23]

By the time the troops arrived at the T A Ranch, about six forty-five Wednesday morning, the besieged men were haggard from strain and lack of sleep. The sheriff's men, by pushing bales of hay ahead of them and by digging rifle pits at night, had edged dangerously close to the fort. They were about ready to put their go-devil to use. Colonel Van Horn, bearing a flag of truce and accompanied by his aid-de-camp, Captain C. H. Parmelee, and Sheriff Angus and Arapahoe Brown, approached the besieged fort. As the firing ceased, he demanded the surrender of the defenders.

"I will surrender to you," Major Wolcott replied. "But to that man"—pointing to Sheriff Angus—"never."

Quickly the soldiers took charge of the cattlemen and their hired Texas gunmen. The captives, forty-six in all, were glad to be relieved of their unforeseen predicament. They gave up forty-three rifles, forty-one pistols, forty-six horses, and about five hundred rounds of ammunition. Within two hours they were on their way to Fort McKinney. The 320 homesteaders and townsmen left for home or for Buffalo, well satisfied with their success in thwarting the invasion in its main objective.[24]

But Sheriff Angus was not content. On the next day he wired the Governor, asking him to have the prisoners at Fort McKinney turned over to his custody for civilian trial. The Governor refused, on the ground that they might become objects of violence in Johnson County.

[23] *Rocky Mountain News,* April 14, 1892.

[24] Cheyenne *Daily Leader,* April 14, 15, 1892; Mercer, *op. cit.,* 45–48. In 1947 Clarence Gannon, owner of the T A Ranch, still could point out to visitors such scars of the 1892 battle as portholes and bullet marks in the barn.

Sheriff W. G. (Red) Angus
Defender of Johnson County

Wyoming State Library

On Friday, six days after their deaths, Nate Champion and Nick Rae were given a big funeral in a vacant store building in Buffalo. There was a profusion of flowers. Women filled most of the seats, while the men stood outside in the spring sunshine. The Reverend W. J. McCullom, a Baptist, prayed "that the law may be strengthened—that if we cannot get justice here, then in the other world." The Methodist preacher who had been with Angus' posse at the T A, the Reverend M. A. Rader, eulogized the two dead men as having been law-abiding citizens. The procession to the cemetery included five hundred persons. Jack Flagg led the horses of Champion and Rae, with empty saddles.

On the following day, Saturday, April 16, a coroner's jury at Buffalo found that Champion and Rae were murdered and named thirty-nine men as alleged killers. Early in the next week, as murder charges were being prepared against them,[25] the prisoners were taken from Fort McKinney, in accord with the Governor's wishes. Three troops of cavalry escorted them—through rain, sleet, and snow—over the Bozeman Trail to Fort Fetterman. They arrived in mud-caked clothes, with stubbly beards and peeling noses.

At Fort Fetterman the prisoners were met by a detachment from Fort Russell, near Cheyenne, and were taken to the latter fort by special train. Nominally the men were confined for sixty days; but Wolcott, Senator Tisdale, and others were paroled. The remaining stockmen and the Texans spent much of their time in Cheyenne.

Meanwhile Ben Jones and Bill Walker, the trappers who had stayed overnight with Champion and Rae at the K C Ranch, had begun talking. Although they had witnessed the battle there, the cattlemen had regarded them as harmless fellows who might be encumbrances if carried along as prisoners. So they released the pair and told them to head south and to keep quiet about what they had seen. A few days later, Jones and Walker turned up in Casper. There they learned what had hap-

[25] Amended information, *State of Wyoming* v. *Frank M. Canton et al.*, district court, Second Judicial District, Johnson County, filed May 9, 1892, Doc. 3, No. 365. The original information was filed April 20.

pened at the T A Ranch. On finding public sentiment almost wholly with the Johnson County settlers and against the invading cattlemen, the trappers began telling their eyewitness stories. Soon these were published in several newspapers.[26]

Sheriff Angus was fearful of what might happen to these star witnesses. Since Casper had no jail, he arranged to have them taken to Douglas for safekeeping. This was done, and the trappers were given bunks in the sheriff's office in the front part of the jail. There, while Sheriff Campbell was away in Washington and his deputy was out of town, the trappers were approached by a Douglas lawyer and a local livery stable keeper. Both had been hired by the cattlemen to get Jones and Walker out of the state. These agents offered large bribes for a disappearing act and threatened dire punishment if the pair remained.

Fearful for their lives, the trappers finally agreed to leave. They were escorted out of town on horseback late one night, headed eastward. Before they had gone far, they were transferred to a train, on which they were guarded by armed ruffians. In the next few days they went through several comic-opera adventures. The Douglas lawyer represented the complaining Jones as being an insane uncle whom he was taking to an asylum.[27] The two trappers were kidnaped several times. In Omaha they were arraigned in a federal court on trumped-up charges of having sold liquor to the Indians.[28]

From Omaha the trappers disappeared from public view. Much later their Wyoming friends learned that they had been taken, by way of Kansas City and St. Louis, to Rhode Island. There they were kept for eleven months, with their bills paid, then released to discover that the checks they had been given for their silence were worthless.[29]

Indignation over the kidnaping and disappearance of the two trappers added fuel to the fires of protest that already were sweeping through the interior Wyoming counties. Citizens of

[26] Cheyenne *Daily Leader*, April 19, 1892; *Rocky Mountain News*, April 19, 1892.

[27] *Rocky Mountain News*, May 7, 9, 10, 1892.

[28] *Ibid.*, May 11, 1892.

[29] William W. Walker's story, as he told it years later to Mrs. D. F. Baber, is given in her book, *The Longest Rope*.

Johnson County had held a mass meeting at the courthouse in Buffalo on April 27. They had adopted resolutions condemning the cattle barons and their association, labeling the invasion as a great outrage perpetrated by unprincipled scoundrels, branding the Governor as a traitor to his people, and calling for a boycott of two Cheyenne newspapers, the *Sun* and the *Tribune*. The resolutions did, however, denounce cattle stealing and pledge vigorous prosecution of rustlers.[30]

On May 3, more than sixty Converse County homesteaders and businessmen met at Glenrock, the home town of Major Wolcott, and approved similar resolutions. They made the same charge against the Governor, referred to the invaders as a murderous gang of cutthroats, pledged action against cattle thieves, and offered protection to the cattle companies "as long as they are willing to abide by the laws of the land."[31]

Casper, on the evening of June 11, was host to what was described as the largest and most enthusiastic mass meeting ever held in central Wyoming. Joel L. Hurd, the region's biggest sheep raiser and heaviest taxpayer, presided. Resolutions, passed at this meeting of Natrona County people, made the usual denunciations and noted that agents of the invaders had spirited out of the state the only witnesses of their murder and arson. They condemned the effort to have martial law imposed in the range country and called on the President and Congress to inquire into the Wyoming troubles.[32]

In the early summer of 1892, while some of the prisoners were enjoying their farcical imprisonment at Fort Russell, a score of the big cattlemen petitioned the Governor to declare martial law in Johnson County. They said such a measure was necessary to protect their stock against stealing and misbranding. This was not done; but in June additional cavalry forces were sent into Wyoming, and on June 30, President Harrison issued a strange proclamation ordering all unlawful assemblages to disperse by August 3.[33]

[30] Buffalo *Bulletin,* April 28, 1892.

[31] *Rocky Mountain News,* May 9, 1892.

[32] *Ibid.,* June 13, 1892; *Wyoming Derrick,* June 16, 1892.

[33] James D. Richardson, *Messages and Papers of the President,* IX, 290.

On July 5 the invaders were taken to Laramie for a preliminary hearing. One of the cattlemen's lawyers, Willis Van Devanter, argued against holding the trial in Johnson County. He contended that a fair trial was not possible there.[34] After two weeks of deliberation, the court ruled in favor of a trial in Cheyenne, and the prisoners were returned to that town.

On Saturday, August 6, the defendants appeared in the district court in Cheyenne. There they pleaded "not guilty." After three days in which jurymen were chosen, Sheriff A. D. Kelley asked the court for an order to protect him against personal responsibility for the cost of housing, feeding, and guarding the prisoners. He said this cost amounted to one hundred dollars a day and reported that Johnson County, whose treasury was empty, had sent no money for this purpose. The next morning, August 10, Judge Richard H. Scott announced that, since Johnson County had not provided for maintenance of the prisoners, he would release them on their own recognizances. Each then signed his own bail bond and was released with an order to appear in the next term of court, in the following January.[35] The Texans were paid off promptly and equipped with new guns. Nearly all of them left for Fort Worth that afternoon.

On January 21, 1893, most of the cattlemen appeared again in court, but the Texans were absent. "On the bench," reported John Clay, one of the onlookers, "was Judge Scott, slow, solemn, impartial, a little embarrassed, knowing full well that the trial was a mere puppet show."[36] As no witnesses appeared against the defendants, the case was dropped.[37]

At the annual meeting of the Wyoming Stock Growers' Association in Cheyenne on April 4, 1893, spokesmen for the cattlemen admitted the illegality of the invasion of a year earlier, which had cost them $105,000. Yet most of them seemed proud

[34] David, *op. cit.*, 337–39. Van Devanter served as associate justice of the Supreme Court of the United States, 1911–37.

[35] Cheyenne *Daily Leader*, August 11, 1892.

[36] Denver *Republican,* January 22, 1893; John Clay, *My Life on the Range,* 284.

[37] Dismissal order in case of *State of Wyoming* v. *Frank M. Canton et al.,* district court, First Judicial District, Laramie County, January 23, 1893, Crim. Doc. 3, No. 363, J. 13, p. 441.

of their achievement. Years later one of the invaders, Frank M. Canton, sought to justify their action. "It never has been any trouble since to convict a cattle thief in Johnson County," he wrote. "We made it safe for an honest man to live in that county and enjoy the fruits of his labor."[38]

The homesteaders, however, had a stronger claim to victory. The invasion aroused such bitter opposition that some of the participants found it advisable to leave the state, at least temporarily. The Republican party, which had become identified with the big cattlemen, lost the state and Congressional elections of 1892.[39] Although the invasion probably drove some cattle rustlers from Johnson County and reformed others overnight, it boomeranged against its perpetrators. Its main effect was to strengthen the claims of the small homesteaders, whether farmers or stockmen, and to further weaken the influence of the big cattle companies that had dominated the ranges. Up and down the Powder River the grangers regarded the victims of the K C fight as martyrs. For years cow hands quieted their herds with songs of the Johnson County war, one of them a crude ballad based on the diary of Nate Champion.[40]

Except for troubles between sheepmen and cattlemen, which persisted in several states, the Johnson County invasion was the last of the serious range wars. Big and little stockmen learned to get along as neighbors. Cattle rustling became less common and no longer called for mass violence. Those Westerners who continued to take justice into their own hands were mainly citizens banded as vigilantes. Their activities, which had begun much earlier, were directed against individual offenders whose guilt was clear but who seemed beyond the reach of statutory law.

[38] Frank M. Canton, *Frontier Trails,* 106.

[39] Osgood, *op. cit.,* 254.

[40] Struthers Burt, *Powder River: Let 'er Buck,* 279–99; Levette J. Davidson, "A Ballad of the Wyoming Rustler War," *Western Folklore,* Vol. VI, No. 2 (April, 1947).

VIGILANTES

8. California Ropes

The early vigilantes were the outgrowth of a demand for justice against organized crime when and where law enforcement did not exist.
—CHARLES SHIRLEY WALGAMOTT, *Six Decades Back*

IN Dry Diggings, a California mining camp nine miles from the Coloma sawmill where gold had been discovered a year earlier, five bandits slipped into the bedroom of a gambler named López one night in January, 1849. While one of the intruders held a pistol at the head of López, the others took his valuables. But before they could escape, the gambler gave an alarm. The miners gathered quickly and seized all of the robbers.

As there was no jail in which to place the culprits, the miners decided to hold an immediate trial and chose twelve of their number as jurors. These men found the defendants guilty and ordered them each to receive thirty-nine lashes. After the miners had inflicted this punishment, they tried three of the bandits for robbery and attempted murder on the Stanislaus River in the preceding autumn. All three were declared guilty.

"What shall we do with them?" the impromptu judge asked the two hundred assembled gold seekers.

"Hang them!" shouted one miner.

Another objected but was overruled by the crowd. The miners placed ropes about the necks of the prisoners and hanged them from the branches of a tree near the center of the camp. Thereafter the camp was known as Hangtown until a later change made it Placerville.[1]

[1] E. Gould Buffum, *Six Months in the Gold Mines,* 83–85; Hubert Howe Bancroft, *Popular Tribunals,* I, 144–45.

Such informal hangings soon became common in the California gold rush. The miners showed a determination to administer swift and decisive justice in communities that were without jails and formal courts. Improvised courts sprang up in nearly all the early California diggings, not so much from choice as from necessity. The loose alcalde system, a vestige of Mexican rule, was alien to the miners' traditions and was insufficient to meet their needs.

The earliest miners' courts were formed more to handle civil problems than to try criminal cases. They fixed the size of the claims, which varied greatly from one camp to another. They also determined the boundaries of districts and made simple rules governing the working and abandoning of claims and trespassing on the claims of others. These courts were called into activity only when occasion arose and were administered by miners chosen by popular acclaim. Seldom was anyone with legal training available to give the proceedings a smattering of legal phraseology.

As the first rush of gold seekers scrambled for nuggets and dust in 1848, there was little crime in the primitive camps. Men could pile gold-bearing gravel on their claims or leave thousands of dollars' worth of gold dust in their tents without worry. But in 1849 and later, as hardened criminals from the Eastern states and unscrupulous fortune hunters from Mexico, Panama, and Chile joined the honest gold seekers, protection against crime became a serious problem in the camps. Ways had to be found quickly to punish those who jumped claims, robbed sluice boxes, stole horses, or used their pistols too freely.

In the smaller camps, guilt and punishment were often determined by the whole assembly of miners. In the larger mining communities, this responsibility usually was delegated to a jury; and sometimes the plaintiff and defendant had counsel assigned them. Because there were no jails, penalties were usually limited to banishment, whipping, or hanging. In Grass Valley in 1850, a man who stole a mule was given thirty lashes. In Nevada City in the following year, one who took a sack of flour in the wake of a fire received twelve lashes. In one camp a storekeeper was flogged for swindling the miners of gold dust with false balances.

In Calaveras County a thief caught with gold dust that belonged to someone else was given twenty lashes and sent out of the camp.

Sometimes the miners hanged men for serious or repeated robbery, as well as for murder, since there seemed no other way to stamp out this form of crime. Whether justice was administered by an alcalde, the more common miners' court, or a committee of vigilance, technicalities were dispensed with, and penalties were carried out without delay or appeal. To make sure that a condemned man did not get away and to have the unpleasant business done with, men were often hanged within an hour or two of their conviction.[2]

Summary justice of this sort saved the mining camps from anarchy and met the approval of most visitors from the East. Bayard Taylor, who spent six months in the mining region in the fall of 1849, reported in his letters to the New York *Tribune* that camp regulations were obeyed faithfully and that crime was checked by just and deliberate punishments.[3] Typical of California newspaper comment was that of the Sacramento *Transcript*. "This is the only sure means of administering justice," said this paper. It cited "the present unsafe sort of prisons and the lenity shown offenders" as justification for the improvised courts.[4]

The miners' courts varied greatly. Although some in the larger camps approached the formality of statutory courts, those in the small camps met infrequently and generally did not keep records. In camps where there was neither an alcalde nor a miners' court, maintenance of order often depended on a voluntary committee of vigilance. This group usually was even less formal than the miners' court. In some instances the committee was one of long tenure. In others, it disbanded as soon as its immediate task was completed, and a new one was formed when the next emergency arose. These committees had no more hesitation than the miners' courts in inflicting death penalties.

[2] Charles Howard Shinn, *Mining Camps: A Study in American Frontier Government,* 109–81.

[3] Bayard Taylor, *Eldorado, or Adventures in the Path of Empire.*

[4] February 12, 1851.

Committees of vigilance and people's courts marked a decided advance over the feuds and range wars which brought violence to many frontier settlements. They represented not factions seeking vengeance or selfish gain but an informally organized society taking protective action against lawbreakers. Their verdicts were not partisan but were the embodiment of community judgment.

California's vigilance committees had their highest development not in the mining camps but in the boom metropolis of San Francisco. This was the chief port of entry for the gold seekers and was the scene of appalling crime waves in the gold-rush period. An outgrowth of the trading town of Yerba Buena, San Francisco had few more than eight hundred inhabitants when Jim Marshall found gold in the tailrace of John Sutter's lumber mill. Most of the men rushed to the mountains in search of nuggets; sailors deserted their ships; and soldiers absented themselves without leave.

Soon San Francisco was a bustling center of miners' outfitters, saloons, and gambling halls. The streets were so deep with mud and ooze that sometimes mules and riders were drowned in them. At night pickpockets, thugs, and painted women were out to prey on the adventurers who came off the ships or miners back from the diggings with bags of gold dust. Before long, criminals from many countries made up an underworld with which the local alcalde was unable to cope.

Especially active and insolent was a group of desperadoes known as the Hounds. This band, which terrorized San Francisco in the early summer of 1849, had as its nucleus New York rowdies who had enlisted for the Mexican War and, after their discharge, had gone to the California mines. Disappointed at the diggings or driven out of the camps because of their misbehavior, they had drifted back to San Francisco to join hands in many kinds of villainy. From headquarters in a large tent dubbed Tammany Hall, they paraded the streets on Sundays, with flying colors and a fife and drum corps. By night they went out with bludgeons and pistols to engage in barbarous outrages. In particular, they took advantage of the city's antiforeign prejudices to make brutal attacks on minority groups, especially

Mexicans, Peruvians, and Chileans. To placate critics, they changed the name of their band to the Society of Regulators; but their activities remained as lawless as before.

On the night of Sunday, July 15, following a rowdy afternoon parade, the Hounds made a night-long raid on the foreign quarter, yelling, killing, and looting. This was too much for the more orderly people of San Francisco. The next day Samuel Brannan, who had started the first newspaper in the city two years earlier, mounted a barrel on a street corner and began to address those who gathered about him. Soon the crowd was so large that it adjourned to the Plaza. There Brannan and Frank Ward spoke from the roof of the alcalde's home, denouncing the Hounds and calling for the extermination of the gang.

When some of the Hounds mingled in the crowd, brandished pistols, and threatened to burn his home, Brannan became all the more biting in his invectives. The citizens formed four companies of a hundred men each to clean out the Hounds and raised a fund for the relief of their victims. Nineteen of the gangsters were rounded up, including the leader, who was taken from a ship on which he had sought to escape the city. The citizens quickly formed a court to try these Hounds. This informal tribunal observed the legal forms. It allowed the defendants counsel and called in witnesses. After several days, it convicted nine men. Since no jail or prison was available, banishment was the only punishment imposed.[5]

Its work done, the people's court disbanded. San Francisco then resumed its slow progress toward maintaining order through formal means. Citizens at a mass meeting put licenses on gambling halls and taxes on property to provide funds for policemen and street lights. That year the hulk of the brig *Euphemia* was bought and converted into a floating jail. In April, 1850, the city was incorporated; and on May 1, local officers were chosen. Colonel John C. Hays, who had distinguished him-

[5] Charles V. Gillespie, "The Vigilance Committees," 5–6, manuscript statement, Bancroft Library, University of California, Berkeley; Frank Meriweather Smith, editor, *San Francisco Vigilance Committee of '56*, 7–8; Brancroft, *Popular Tribunals*, I, 76–102; Mary Floyd Williams, *History of the San Francisco Committee of Vigilance of 1851*, 100, 105–109; James A. B. Scherer, *The First Forty-Niner*, 69–82.

self in the Texas Ranger service and in the Mexican War, was elected sheriff.

Yet these and other measures were insufficient to keep down crime in the growing city. Newcomers in droves kept swelling the population. By the end of 1850, San Francisco had nearly fifty thousand inhabitants. Along with honest adventurers, a great horde of criminals had come to California without any intention of ever working in the mines. Among them were many released criminals and other hard characters from Australia. These ruffians came to be known as the Sydney Ducks or the Sydney Coves. The Coves lived in tents and hovels in Sydney Town, at Clark's Point, on the outskirts of the city. They were among the most active in waylaying and robbing miners in the dark streets and stabbing patrons of the crowded bars and gambling dens. Many persons accused them of starting the fires that devastated large sections of the city.

Soon the underworld denizens became so bold that many citizens were afraid to leave their homes at night. More than a hundred persons were murdered within a few months; yet not one of the killers was punished. Local officers and courts seemed helpless. The few thugs arrested promptly hired shyster lawyers, who usually kept them out of jail. It was almost impossible to find witnesses to a crime who dared to testify against the culprits. If prosecution witnesses were in prospect, defense lawyers sometimes had the trial delayed until they could be killed.

Early in 1851 some of the merchants organized a night patrol as a special agency to protect their property. A few of them talked of organizing a vigilance committee but did not want to take such a step if it could be avoided. Meanwhile, killings, robberies, and other outrages increased. Often a score of major crimes took place in a single night. In the spring, two merchants consulted Sam Brannan on the need for direct action. They found him strongly interested, and together with Brannan they conferred with other leading citizens. Early in June those persons wishing to participate in such action formed a committee of vigilance and adopted a constitution and bylaws. These documents were signed by about two hundred men, including some of the most prominent in the city.[6]

Disdaining secrecy, the vigilantes had their constitution and bylaws published in the local newspapers. The signers called attention to the insecurity of life and property. They gave notice that, while seeking only to sustain the laws, they were prepared to take direct action to prevent criminals from escaping punishment through the laxity or corruption of officials, the insecurity of jails, or the quibbling of lawyers. The committee was to be called out by two strokes upon a bell, this summons to be repeated at intervals of one minute.[7]

The underworld of San Francisco quickly learned that the vigilantes meant business. On the night the constitution was adopted and signed, after most of the committee had gone home, the first culprit was brought to the assembly room. He was John Jenkins, an Australian with a criminal record in his home country and a bad reputation in San Francisco. He had just been caught stealing a small safe from an office. Two vigilantes who assisted in his capture chose to bring him to their headquarters instead of to the police station.

Confronted with Jenkins, the leaders of the committee decided upon an immediate trial. One of them took a stick of wood and began striking the assembly signal on the bell of the California Engine Company. In a few moments the bell of the Monumental Engine Company was echoing the call. San Francisco men began tumbling out of their beds. Citizens who were not members of the committee did not know what the signal meant but realized that something serious was afoot. Several thousand of them gathered in the streets about the vigilante headquarters to learn what was taking place.

Inside, Jenkins was tried quickly and was convicted on indisputable evidence. As the statutory penalty for grand larceny was death, the verdict was to hang him immediately. A cleryman was summoned to talk with him, but the prisoner remained

[6] William T. Coleman, manuscript statement, 17–18, Brancroft Library; James Neall, Jr., manuscript statement, 1–3, Brancroft Library; Brancroft, *Popular Tribunals,* I, 201–13; Williams, *op. cit.,* 163–207.

[7] *Alta California,* San Francisco, June 13, 1851; San Francisco *Herald,* June 13, 1851.

defiant and insulting. Brannan went out and reported the action of the committee to the crowd. Most of the men outside shouted enthusiastic approval of the verdict. Soon afterward the pinioned prisoner was brought out under armed guard and marched down a roped-off passage through the crowd to the adobe Custom House in the Plaza. The chief of police made a perfunctory pass to rescue the prisoner, and some of his fellow Sydney Coves made an ineffectual effort to free him. Finally a noose was placed about his neck and the other end thrown over a beam.

"Every lover of liberty and good order lay hold of this rope!" shouted Brannan. As many as could reach it grabbed the rope and pulled, hoisting Jenkins to a quick death.[8]

A coroner's jury blamed members of the committee for the hanging, but San Francisco newspapers were unanimous in approving the summary riddance. "No man need be afraid," said the *California Courier*, "to let his children know he took part in that transaction."[9]

There was some opposition to the committee of vigilance; nevertheless, it was swamped with applications for membership following the hanging of Jenkins. Local officials made no effort to dissolve the growing organization. The committee published its membership list and delegated much of its work to an executive committee of twenty which had been formed on the night of the Jenkins execution. For the first month, Sam Brannan was the head of both groups. The whole general committee was organized systematically. Each member was assigned specific duties, and painstaking records were kept.

During the remainder of June, the committee investigated some of the more undesirable members of the San Francisco underworld. Four men who had especially bad records—two of them innkeepers whose places had been resorts for thieves and incendiaries—were sent back to Australia. Many criminals

[8] J. D. Farwell, "Vigilance Committees in San Francisco," 6, manuscript statement, Bancroft Library; George Everett Schenck, manuscript statement, 35–38, Bancroft Library; Bancroft, *Popular Tribunals,* I, 226–39; Williams, *op. cit.,* 208–26.

[9] *California Courier,* San Francisco, June 14, 1851.

Brig Euphemia
San Francisco's first jail

Soule's Chronicles of San Francisco

left voluntarily, without waiting for investigation or formal notice.[10]

The committee not only banished undesirable residents but kept a check on all persons coming in from Australia. They were determined to enforce an 1850 statute which banned the immigration of criminals, even though the Supreme Court of the United States had declared similar legislation in Massachusetts and New York unconstitutional. Vigilantes boarded each arriving vessel to examine the passengers and their records. They turned back convicts, paying their fares from committee funds. In this activity, the committee had the co-operation of local United States officers dealing with immigrants. Soon the inspection of incoming passengers by the committee became a routine part of the San Francisco marine news.[11]

A month after the execution of Jenkins, The San Francisco vigilantes had a second candidate for their hanging rope. James Stuart, who at sixteen had been banished from England to Australia for forgery, came to California in 1850, where he gained notoriety as a horse thief, robber, and burglar, and finally murdered a mining-camp merchant. A man mistaken for Stuart had been convicted in a regular court. He was released only after the vigilantes captured the real villain and, with persistent effort, extracted from him an admission of his identity and a confession of his many crimes.

As it became known about the city that the vigilantes had Stuart in custody, a lawyer who formerly had defended this villain obtained a writ of habeas corpus to have the prisoner brought into court. But Sheriff Hays made only perfunctory and fruitless efforts to get hold of Stuart. On the morning of July 11 the vigilante assembly signal was struck on the Monumental bell. While nearly four hundred of the nine hundred members of the committee completed deliberations begun several days earlier, a throng of people filled the adjoining streets. That afternoon when the crowd, still waiting impatiently, was in-

[10] San Francisco *Herald,* June 12, 18, 21, 1851; Williams, *op. cit.,* 227–33.

[11] *California Courier,* June 16, 1851; Isaac Bluxome, Jr., manuscript statement, 15, Bancroft Library.

formed of the verdict of hanging, it shouted its almost unanimous approval. Then the members of the committee emerged from their headquarters and marched in platoons, ten abreast, to the water front. At the Market Street wharf, the loose end of the vigilante rope was thrown over a derrick and seized by a score of hands. While the men in the crowd bared their heads and those on ships in the harbor raised their flags and fired their cannons, eager executioners jerked the prisoner into the air. After he had swung for half an hour before the crowd, his body was lowered and turned over to the coroner.

The hanging of Stuart, a more deliberate circumvention of statutory authority than that of Jenkins, aroused some opposition. But Governor John McDougal, who personally approved of the work of the committee, satisfied himself by issuing a nominal proclamation asking citizens to abstain from unlawful acts. Mayor Charles J. Brenham, who was closer to the scene, published an open letter calling attention to the dangers and illegality of the committee's actions. He asked members to withdraw from its ranks, and, with that note of warning, he let the matter drop. Judge Alexander Campbell of the Court of Sessions denounced the hanging as an inexcusable outrage and impaneled a grand jury to indict those persons responsible. This jury, which included two of the vigilantes and others who sympathized with the work of the committee, refused to take such action.[12]

San Francisco newspapers condemned Judge Campbell's attitude as futile and supported the vigilantes. The editors said that these men had inflicted no penalties except those which elected officials should have carried out much earlier, had the latter not been remiss in their duty. The *California Courier* blamed public officials for the prevalence of crime. The *Herald* asked, "Whenever the law becomes an empty name, has not the citizen the right to supply its deficiency?"[13]

By that time, outrages by Joaquín Murrieta and other bandits had aroused direct action elsewhere in the state. Committees of vigilance were busy in Marysville, Sacramento, Santa

[12] Bancroft, *Popular Tribunals*, I, 267–334; Williams, *op. cit.*, 252–74.

[13] *California Courier*, July 14, 1851; San Francisco *Herald*, July 14, 23, 1851.

Clara, Sonora, and Stockton. In Monterey, determined citizens convicted and hanged a horse thief. The San Francisco vigilantes continued their fight against crime, driving out desperadoes and searching for associates of the late James Stuart. Some of these villains had fled the city after being implicated by Stuart's confession. Two of the Australian thugs were apprehended soon. Sam Whittaker, after eluding vigilantes who were on his trail, was arrested in Santa Barbara. Sheriff V. W. Hearne took him to San Francisco by steamer to deliver him to Sheriff Hays; but, arriving there, he allowed the vigilantes to take Whittaker from the ship and accepted their reimbursement of expenses. The other gangster, Robert McKenzie, had been arrested at San Francisco and brought back.

Although the vigilantes had begun turning some lesser offenders over to local officials, when assured of prompt and vigorous prosecution, they decided to handle these two robbers and gunmen themselves. Whittaker, who said his real name was Gibson, was a Briton who had been sentenced to a penal colony in Van Diemen's Land. From there he had escaped and had come to California. He was one of the worst criminals in San Francisco. McKenzie was equally brutal. Examined separately, both men confessed.

It had been known for some time that the vigilantes had Whittaker and McKenzie in custody, and the proceedings of the committee had been published in the newspapers. These facts made it difficult for local and state officials to avoid taking notice of the situation. This was especially true after opponents of the vigilantes pressed for action. On August 19, Governor McDougal heard that the committee planned to hang both men on the next day. Hastening to San Francisco, he conferred with Mayor Brenham late that night; and the two found a judge willing to issue a writ demanding immediate surrender of the two prisoners. At three o'clock the next morning, McDougal and Brenham roused Sheriff Hays from his bed and handed him the writ.

The sheriff had no relish for such a chore but had little choice. Calling his deputy, John Caperton, he reluctantly accompanied the state and city officials to the committee headquarters, with which he and Caperton were familiar. They entered without opposition. Caperton readily obtained and brought out the prisoners, to whom almost any prospect was better than the one they had been facing. The two thugs were quickly locked in the new jail which had replaced the brig in the harbor. By daybreak, people were milling in the streets, wondering what the vigilantes would do.

The outraged committee concerned itself first with placing the blame on its own guards for the loss of the prisoners. Two days later, Sunday, August 22, on the assumption that Whittaker and McKenzie would be acquitted if tried in the courts, the executive committee ordered Captain J. W. Cartwright to detail a guard, arrest the two prisoners, and bring them before the general committee. On the preceding day, scouts from the vigilantes had visited the jail. One of them had seen the prisoners. Another had invited Sheriff Hays to see a Sunday bullfight at the Mission Dolores.

On Sunday morning twenty-nine picked vigilantes appeared outside the jail and separated into three squads. At a signal indicating that the weekly religious service in the main hall had just ended, one group of vigilantes entered the front door of the jail. At the same moment, another crushed the back door with a sledge hammer and entered by that passage. The third squad stood guard at the front door. While some of the officers scuffled with the vigilantes, the prisoners scurried for the protection of their cells. The two men whom the committee wanted were captured after a brief struggle. They were bound quickly, taken to a carriage waiting outside, and driven to the committee headquarters.

There they saw nooses dangling from projecting beams above the doorways on Battery Street. In a few moments, as an alarm was struck on the Monumental bell and crowds gathered in the streets, Whittaker and McKenzie were swinging. From an open doorway, Sam Brannan and another member of the executive committee addressed the crowd. They reminded their hearers that the executed pair were confessed criminals and asserted that any other course on the part of the vigilantes would have put a premium on crime.[14]

This double hanging threw such fear into the remaining Sydney Coves and other criminals that many of them soon left the city. As a result, city and county officials were able to keep order more easily, and there was less emergency work left for the vigilantes. In September the committee was reorganized on a less strenuous basis. Some of the vigilantes won public posts in the next city election. With the organization less active, membership and financial support gradually declined, and rifts arose within the ranks. Although the committee never formally disbanded, its activities diminished until, early in 1853, it went out of existence.[15]

In other California communities the committees of vigilance —most of them patterned after the one in San Francisco—also became less busy as the need for emergency action passed. As in the booming seaport, many of the members continued to work for order and law enforcement in the capacity of jurymen or public officials. Where strong jails were available and courts were able to preserve order and to punish wrongdoers, vigilante action began to be frowned upon.

The San Francisco reformation of 1851, however, did not prove permanent. By the spring of 1855 the city administration had become so corrupt and crime so prevalent again that the *Herald* called for a return of the "good and vigorous days of the vigilance committee."[16] Several months later, on the evening of November 17, trouble started in the Cosmopolitan Saloon. Charles Cora, of Italian birth, a gambler and a machine politician adept at stuffing ballot boxes, quarreled with General William H. Richardson, United States marshal. Later that evening they left the saloon, still arguing. Outside, Cora drew his pistol and shot Richardson, who was unarmed. Cora was hurried off to jail. That night a summons rang out from the bells of the fire stations. At the Oriental the fiery Sam Brannan addressed a

[14] San Francisco *Herald,* August 25, 1851; Bancroft, *Popular Tribunals,* I, 335–66; San Francisco *Chronicle,* October 3, 1915; Williams, *op. cit.,* 275–304.

[15] San Francisco *Herald,* May 7, October 28, November 17, 1852; Bancroft, *Popular Tribunals,* I, 393–406; Williams, *op. cit.,* 323–55.

[16] San Francisco *Herald,* April 22, 1855.

crowd and called for immediate execution of the killer. Those persons present, however, decided to give the courts an opportunity to punish him.[17]

Cora appeared unworried over his predicament. The jailer was one of his cronies; and his mistress, well supplied with money and influence, retained several of the ablest lawyers in San Francisco. The *Bulletin*, established a short time earlier by a former vigilante, James King of William, published a report that forty thousand dollars was being spent to get the murderer acquitted. Both this paper and the *Alta California* suggested that the committee of vigilance might be revived if justice miscarried in the court.[18]

Cora, when brought to trial on January 3, 1856, was jauntily defiant. He had reason to be so. The jury was fixed, the witnesses were rehearsed in perjury, and the proceedings were a farce. On the seventeenth the jury reported disagreement, as planned by Cora, and was discharged. Commenting on the depravity brought to light in this trial, the *Alta California* predicted that crime would become so frequent that it no longer could be endured and that vigilante action would be revived.[19] The *Bulletin* issued an extra edition which asserted that "the money of the gambler and the prostitute has succeeded." This paper referred to technicalities of the law that "call into action the heated blood of an outraged community."

King continued to explode his indignation in the *Bulletin*. But soon after the *Bulletin* was on the streets, Casey called at court, and several San Francisco newspapers had mentioned it. On May 14, he mentioned that James P. Casey, a city supervisor, ballot-box stuffer, and editor of the *Sunday Times*, had been an inmate of Sing Sing prison. Casey had admitted this fact in

[17] *Alta California*, November 18, 20, 1855; Smith, *op. cit.*, 15–18; Bancroft, *Popular Tribunals*, II, 1–35.

[18] San Francisco *Bulletin*, November 20, December 12, 1855; *Alta California*, December 8, 1855. While living in Washington, D. C., before he migrated to California, James King had added his father's given name as a trailer to his own name. He did this to distinguish himself from several other James Kings residing in the capital.

[19] *Alta California*, January 17, 1856.

King's office and objected to having his past raked up again. King ordered him out and told him never to come back. The visitor stalked out, still full of wrath. That evening, as King walked home through a fog, Casey stepped from behind an express wagon and shot him.

As Casey was rushed off to jail, the call of the Monumental Engine Company bell brought ten thousand men into the streets. Three hundred guarded the Pacific Express office, where the dying editor lay. Others milled about the jail, crowded the corridors, and even climbed upon the roof. Some shouted for hanging the killer immediately. Many passed on rumors that the committee of vigilance was being revived. When the mayor stepped out in front of the jail and tried to disperse the crowd, voices shouted:

"Look at poor Richardson! How is it in his case? Where is Cora now? Down with such justice! Let's hang him!"[20]

There was little sleep in San Francisco that night. The crowds in front of the jail and the express office refused to disperse. Several men who had been members of the 1851 committee of vigilance asked one of their number, William T. Coleman, to head a new committee. Coleman, thirty-two years of age, was a former Kentuckian and a graduate of St. Louis University. After coming to California as a forty-niner, he had become one of the principal merchants of San Francisco and an outstanding civic leader. When urged to head the vigilantes of 1856, he declined the honor at first but was drafted for the post.

That night Coleman and his associates issued a call for the former vigilantes to gather in a vacant hall the next evening. They prepared a notice hastily and inserted it in the newspapers the following morning. Determined men filled the hall and approved the formation of a new committee with Coleman at the head. In the next two days, 5,500 members were enrolled. Many other persons expressed sympathy with the aims of the committee and sent contributions for its expenses.

[20] *Ibid.*, May 15, 1856; William Taylor, *Seven Years' Street Preaching in San Francisco, California,* 243–56; Smith, *op. cit.*, 33–39; Bancroft, *Popular Tribunals,* II, 35–64; Gertrude Atherton, *California, an Intimate History,* 174–89; Stanton A. Coblentz, *Villains and Vigilantes,* 114–60.

Governor John Neely Johnson attended a meeting of the committee to protest against its projected activities. While there, he was so swept away by Coleman's eloquence that he slapped the vigilante leader on the back and shouted: "Go to it, old boy! But get through as quickly as you can. Don't prolong it, because there is a terrible opposition and a terrible pressure." Before long the Governor himself succumbed to this pressure, but his defection did not deter the committee from its course.

The temper of the citizens was shown when the *Herald* made an about-face and became the only local newspaper to condemn the committee. It was immediately boycotted by many advertisers and subscribers. Overnight it dropped from the top to the lowest place among the city's daily papers and, consequently, had to cut its size in half.

By Sunday, May 18, scores of the militiamen guarding the jail had deserted their companies to join the vigilantes. On that day Charles Doane, chief marshal of the committee of vigilance, rode a white horse at the head of five hundred marching men with rifles and bayonets. At the jail they were met by Coleman and another vigilante leader, who arrived in a carriage. Coleman threatened to destroy the jail with a cannon if Sheriff David Scannell did not open the door in five minutes. Scannell could see the gunner waving his fuse. The door was opened. Coleman and another went in and brought out the killers they wanted—Cora and Casey. The marchers escorted their prisoners to the committee headquarters as the mayor and Governor Johnson viewed the proceeding helplessly from the roof of the International Hotel.

Two days later Cora came to trial before a vigilante court that was much more dignified and much more fair-minded than the statutory one in which he had appeared four months earlier. But early that afternoon the proceeding was interrupted with the news that James King of William had died. As the word of his death spread through the city, almost every place of business was closed. Most of the buildings, except the saloons and gambling houses, were draped in black. Ships in the harbor had their flags lowered to half-mast. Bells tolled from the churches

SAN FRANCISCANS IN ACTION
End of Hetherington and Brace, July 29, 1856

From a contemporary newspaper

and the fire stations. Crowds surged through the streets in one of the greatest tributes ever given by a city to a private citizen.

King's funeral, on the twenty-second, was viewed by many thousands from the streets and the housetops. The procession of carriages to the cemetery was a mile long. It seemed as if nearly all the inhabitants of the city who were not in the carriages were accompanying them on foot. But before the procession reached the cemetery, a rumor spread among those afoot. It caused ten to twelve thousand of them to turn about and hasten back. Many broke into a run after they were beyond the view of the procession and the sound of its solemn music.

There was ground for the rumor. The trials of Cora and Casey had resulted in verdicts of guilty. The condemned men had been sentenced to be hanged Friday noon, the day after King's funeral. But to avoid possible counter-action, the executive committee of the vigilantes had decided to hang the pair a day earlier, while most of the free people of the city were on their way to the cemetery. The condemned men were notified, and hinged wooden platforms were extended from the second-story windows of the committee headquarters on Sacramento Street. No attempt being made to rescue them, the two killers were executed early that afternoon. After the bodies had swung in public view for nearly an hour, they were cut down and turned over to the coroner.[21]

This double hanging did not end the work of the 1856 committee of vigilance. The group remained in action for three months, swelling its membership to more than eight thousand. During this period, San Francisco had only two murders, compared with more than a hundred in the six months before the committee was formed. Nine days after the hanging of Cora and Casey, a prisoner at the vigilante headquarters, having confessed to political frauds, killed himself with a knife. In June and July the committee presented many of the city thugs with

[21] San Francisco *Herald*, May 15, 1856; Miers L. Truett, "Vigilante Committees in San Francisco," 1–2, manuscript statement, Bancroft Library; Smith, *op. cit.*, 39–56; Josiah Royce, *California From the Conquest in 1846 to the Second Vigilance Committee in San Francisco*, 437–53; Bancroft, *Popular Tribunals*, II, 64–243; Atherton, *op. cit.*, 190–200; Coblentz, *op. cit.*, 158–92.

one-way tickets for outbound ships and saw that they did not miss getting aboard.[22]

Summary action of the opposition came through a Law and Order party. But members of this group were embarrassed at finding themselves in partnership with the underworld and by having their hidden arms captured by the vigilantes. One of the Law and Order leaders was Judge David S. Terry of the California Supreme Court. Terry stabbed a vigilante policeman, Sterling A. Hopkins, in the neck as he was trying to make an arrest.[23] Such incidents, however, did not dampen the ardor of the vigilantes. On July 29, they hanged two more murderers, the English-born Joseph Hetherington and a desperado from upper New York, Philander Brace.

In August the committee concluded that its work was about done. It began preparations to wind up its affairs and to turn its self-assumed responsibilities back to city and county officials. On the fourteenth, it took down its barricade; on the sixteenth, it opened its headquarters to the public; and on the eighteenth, it held a triumphal parade and review. In this final fling, more than six thousand members marched in military order. The equipment of the organization was not sold at auction until October, and its executive committee continued to hold meetings in smaller quarters until late in 1859. Yet the parade of August, 1856, virtually marked the end of the San Francisco vigilante activities. At that time there were no prisoners in the jail awaiting trial, and the more notorious criminals had departed, either by choice or by request.[24]

In shelving their bayonets and their hanging ropes, the San Francisco vigilante leaders disclaimed any desire to seek or to accept public office. "It is seldom," observed the London *Times*, "that self-constituted authorities retire with grace and dignity, but it is due to the vigilance committee to say that they have done so." Yet the determination that spurred San Francisco

[22] John L. Durkee, "Vigilance Committees in San Francisco," 23, manuscript statement, Bancroft Library.

[23] Gillespie, *op. cit.*, 10; Truett, *op. cit.*, 3–6; Durkee, *op. cit.*, 3–5.

[24] *Alta California*, June 22, 1856; San Francisco *Bulletin*, June 23, 1856; Smith, *op. cit.*, 56–83; Bancroft, *Popular Tribunals*, II, 244–547; Atherton, *op. cit.*, 210–17.

citizens to direct action against crime did not quickly die. In 1859, three years after its activities ended, a stranger asked a San Franciscan what had become of the city's vigilance committee. The reply was, "Toll the bell, sir, and you'll see."[25]

Elsewhere in California, as in other Western states, there still was occasional need for people's tribunals. Vigilance committees found work to do in Monterey in 1864 and in Tulare and adjoining counties in 1872–74. In Truckee, banditry and murder became so common in the fall of 1874 that citizens formed a Committee of 601, which cleaned out the desperadoes. By that time, statutory courts were effective in nearly every section of the state, with the effect that such informal action soon ceased.

Over a period of twenty-five years, the California vigilantes had cleaned up many intolerable situations. In addition, they had provided a pattern that, with many variations, was followed in the mining towns of Colorado, Montana, and elsewhere on the western frontier. In these isolated outposts, committees of vigilance often attained order and security in the absence or impotence of formal law.

[25] Bancroft, *Popular Tribunals*, II, 695.

9. Montana Roundup

> Vigilantes served a great need on the frontier in stamping out lawlessness with swift justice and so held down desperate situations until the coming of proper legal procedure.
>
> —Robert B. David, *Malcolm Campbell, Sheriff*

IN the mushroom mining town of Bannack, wind-bitten gold seekers turned out in their Sunday best on the spring afternoon of May 24, 1863, to elect officials for their district. This frontier Montana community had become the chief center for gold placer mining on the eastern slope of the Rockies. In addition, it had acquired a bigger crew of outlaws than almost any other town of its size.

Bannack, which boasted a thousand inhabitants, was less than a year old. It had emerged from the Grasshopper Diggings that a small party of prospectors had established in July of the preceding year on Grasshopper Creek, a tributary to the Beaverhead River. Adventurers from Idaho and Colorado had swarmed in throughout the late fall and the winter. Houses were so scarce that many families had had to spend the cold months in emigrant wagons. With the prospectors had come gamblers, bandits, and dance-hall girls to relieve the miners of their gold dust and nuggets. As Montana did not yet have even a territorial government, there was almost no curb on lawless activities.

For two months Bannack had had a sheriff of a sort in Hank Crawford. Hank was a butcher who had been chosen temporarily for this post in January at the trial of a pair of killers before a group of citizens. In the spring he had become involved in a shooting scrape with a desperado leader, Henry Plummer. Crawford wounded Plummer but was so impressed with the latter's threats of retaliation that a week later, on March 13, he left for his former home in Wisconsin.

At their May election, with more than five hundred present, Bannack citizens chose a presiding officer and a secretary. The presiding officer then appointed judges and tellers to hold the election, by ballot, of a judge, a sheriff, and a coroner for the district, which included all the camps east of the Bitter Roots. The temporary officers and the men chosen as judge and coroner were all respected members of the community. But for some reason never entirely clear, the choice for sheriff was the notorious Henry Plummer. Some evidence indicates that this meeting was not dominated by the rough element of the town, as sometimes happened; and, certainly, the Bannack voters were not yet aware of the full extent of Plummer's villainy. Too, many may have believed it more important to fill this post with a daring pistoleer than with an honest man.[1]

Plummer, in his late twenties when elected sheriff, was a man of good appearance. He could make a favorable impression on strangers when he wished to do so. From an eastern state he had emigrated to California in 1852. In the following year he and a partner opened a bakery in Nevada City, California, where three or four years later he was elected marshal. Before his term expired, he killed a man with whose wife he was having an affair. For this crime he was convicted and sent to prison, but after a few months his friends persuaded Governor John B. Weller to pardon him.[2]

On his return to Nevada City, Plummer went into the bakery business again—but not for long. After seriously injuring a man

[1] Minutes of the Bannack election of May 24, 1863, D. H. Dillingham, secretary, manuscript in the library of the Historical Society of Montana, Helena.

[2] Thomas J. Dimsdale, *The Vigilantes of Montana*, 218–21. Dimsdale, of English birth and education, came from Canada to Montana in the gold rush. In the fall of 1863, he opened a private school in Virginia City. Soon after the Territory of Montana was created, in the spring of 1864, Governor Sidney Edgerton appointed him superintendent of public instruction. Late in that year he also became editor of the *Montana Post*, which had been established in August. A popular feature of this frontier newspaper was a series of articles by Dimsdale on the Montana vigilantes, which he later prepared for publication in book form. He died in 1866.

in a bagnio brawl, he joined a band of stagecoach robbers at Washoe. Later he went back to Nevada City, where he became embroiled in another fight and killed a man. Breaking out of jail with the aid of two pistols that had been smuggled in to him, he moved on, but stopped in turn at Walla Walla, Lewiston, Idaho, and the diggings at Orofino.

Arriving at Lewiston in the spring of 1861, Plummer operated as a gambler and soon made himself the head of a band of highwaymen, horse thieves, and cutthroats who worked over a wide area. He remained in town and generally avoided suspicion while he directed in detail the operations of his brigands and shielded them from harm. When a respectable Lewiston saloonkeeper was killed without provocation, the citizens held a meeting to organize for their protection; but Plummer spoke so eloquently against rash action that nothing was done. Later another saloonkeeper, Patrick Ford, who denounced this inaction as cowardice, was killed by Plummer and two of his men in Orofino. Plummer then moved his headquarters to Florence.

In the late summer of 1862, Plummer built two roadhouses, called "shebangs." One of these was between Alpwai and Pataha creeks, about twenty-five miles out from Lewiston on the Walla Walla trail. The other was at the foot of Craig's Mountain, between Lewiston and Orofino.[3] The shebangs were manned by ruffians ever ready to relieve travelers of their gold dust or anything else of value. Plummer's agents in Lewiston watched miners as they outfitted there. The agents made notes of the mounts and saddles, then sent faked bills of sale for these horses by fast courier to the shebangs. Bandits intercepted the miners, presented the bogus bills of sale, and dispossessed the travelers.

An action that took place in Florence in the fall of 1862 may have influenced Plummer to move on to Bannack. On the road from Florence to Walla Walla, a pack train was held up in October by masked men who took fourteen pounds of gold. But

[3] Nathaniel Pitt Langford, *Vigilante Days and Ways*, I, 83–84. Langford, a prominent resident of Bannack in its turbulent days, was a fearless opponent of outlawry. He was well acquainted with Plummer and some of the other desperadoes. His two-volume work, along with the earlier one by Dimsdale, is a mine of reliable information on the Montana vigilance activities.

the bandits were recognized, and three of them were caught separately by vigilance groups and taken to Florence for trial. There the citizens, fearing a rescue, entered the jail at night and hanged all three of the desperadoes.[4]

When Plummer arrived at Bannack, late in 1862, he was accompanied by another malefactor—Jack Cleveland, with whom he recently had quarreled over a woman. Cleveland, less subtle than Plummer, soon became known in Bannack for the bandit he was. Plummer feared that his former associate would talk too much of his past, and in February, 1863, he killed Cleveland in a saloon fight and made his action look like self-defense. Plummer soon attempted to kill Sheriff Hank Crawford, because he feared that his own past might have been revealed to the officer by the dying Cleveland.

By the time he became sheriff at Bannack, Plummer had an intricate network of bandits, agents, and hideouts in southwestern Montana. His main base of operations was Rattlesnake Ranch. He often visited this headquarters and sometimes joined his gunmen in tests of marksmanship, using as a target a signpost in front of the cabin. Other resorts were Robert Dempsey's Cottonwood Ranch, whose owner dared not report the brigands, and Peter Daley's "Robbers' Roost," a roadhouse at Ramshorn Gulch. These and several other places served as hideouts for the bandits and provided cover for their loot.[5]

His election as sheriff in May added to Plummer's standing in the community. Now it was easier for him to carry on banditry without being caught. Soon he had a hundred highwaymen, or "road agents" as they generally were called, terrorizing travelers on the mountain trails about Bannack. He had spies in every store and saloon. These men put secret marks on stagecoaches to identify them for the bandits. In some instances, Plummer's agents wore a certain sailor's knot in their ties to enable their fellows to recognize them. His men called themselves "the Innocents."

Soon after his election, Plummer went down the Beaverhead and across a mountain trail to a fort on the Sun River, where a

[4] *Ibid.*, I, 134–41.
[5] Dimsdale, *op. cit.*, 22.

farm girl, Electa Bryan, was awaiting him. He arrived on the second of June, and on the twentieth the couple were married by a priest at St. Peter's Mission. The bride wore a brown calico dress, while Plummer was in a blue suit foxed with buckskin. Soon afterward the pair drove back to Bannack in a borrowed army ambulance. Their wedded life lasted only a few weeks. On September 2, the disillusioned bride departed, by way of Salt Lake City, for her parental home in Cedar Rapids, Iowa.

In naming his deputies before leaving to be married, Plummer showed where his main interest lay; for three of the men named were among his toughest bandits. While serving as officers, they continued to steal horses, hold up stagecoaches, and engage in other crimes. The fourth deputy, perhaps picked to satisfy the honest citizens of Bannack, was D. H. Dillingham, who had served as secretary of the meeting at which Plummer was elected. While Plummer was gone, Dillingham, who was under no delusions about his fellow deputies, informed Jim Dodge that one of the deputies and two other bandits were planning to hold him up on the road to the new diggings in Alder Gulch.

On learning that news of their plot had leaked out, the bandits were enraged at Dillingham and set out to kill him. They found him on June 29 in the new town of Virginia City, which was sprouting from the Alder Gulch diggings. There a district court was trying civil cases in a brush wickiup. While the court was in recess, the brigands called Dillingham out and shot him without giving him a chance to defend himself. Another of Plummer's deputies, who was in on the plot, quickly reloaded the gun used, to make identification more difficult.

On that day and the next, the three assassins were tried by a hastily formed people's court. One was acquitted. The other two were condemned to die, and men were appointed to build a gallows and dig two graves. But by the time this was done, women in the crowd began weeping and imploring, "Save the poor young boys' lives!" Someone read aloud a faked letter which one of the defendants was said to have written to his mother. These defense stratagems induced those in charge to take two more votes. In the confusion and in the multiple voting of the bandits' friends as they passed through the line to be counted, the assassins seized an Indian's horse and galloped out of the gulch. Glancing at the unused gallows, one of the guards remarked, "There is a monument to disappointed Justice."[6]

In the next few months, Plummer was at the height of his power. He obtained recruits for his bands of road agents by finding miners who were not doing well and promising them big rewards. There was an abundance of potential loot, for many miners were coming into town with their gold or taking it back East. Any miner who turned down Plummer's proposal knew that his life would be worthless if he said anything against the two-faced sheriff.

Plummer himself took part in a number of the robberies. Pretending to be an expert judge of ores, he would have one of his agents, dressed as a prospector, come into town with some specimens and ask him to go out into the hills with him to examine a silver lode. On other occasions, he would have a fake warrant brought in to him and would ride off to the hills on the pretense of having to make an arrest.[7] Robberies increased, and occasionally they were accompanied by murder. In October, Plummer tried unsuccessfully to kill N. P. Langford because the latter refused to recommend him for appointment as a deputy United States marshal. Langford apparently was one of the first men in Bannack to recognize Plummer's double role.[8]

Other persons soon had occasion to become suspicious. On the evening of November 14, young Henry Tilden was robbed by several armed horsemen as he rode toward Bannack from Horse Prairie, ten miles south. He recognized the leader of the bandits as Sheriff Plummer and so reported when he reached town. He was told to keep quiet for his own safety, but his news spread by grapevine.

That afternoon, before Tilden had come back to town with his alarming report, Colonel Wilbur F. Sanders, his uncle, had

[6] *Ibid.*, 63–71.
[7] Langford, *op. cit.*, I, 388–89.
[8] *Ibid.*, 386–88.

noticed that Plummer and some of his men were preparing to leave town. Plummer said they were going to rescue some horses from Indian thieves. Sanders thought the party really was going to the new silver mines to stake out and record claims. He asked to be taken along to obtain a claim for himself, but Plummer found excuses for not taking him. He said that if any claims were filed, he would enter one for Sanders even though he was not present.

After the sheriff's party had left, ostensibly for Rattlesnake Ranch, fifteen miles away, Sanders headed in that direction on a mule. Arriving late that night, he discovered that Plummer had not been there. He stayed for the night but was awakened several times by the arrival of some of Plummer's brigands. He learned enough to suspect that Plummer was the head of the organized road agents, and his suspicion was confirmed when he returned home and heard what had happened to his nephew.

Despite the whispering against him, Plummer was still powerful. On Thanksgiving he gave a big dinner, serving a turkey for which he had sent to Salt Lake City and paid forty dollars in gold. Among the guests were Colonel and Mrs. Sanders and several other leading citizens.[9] It was a festive occasion, but most of the guests were already becoming aware of their host's real character.

Aside from the three deputies, Plummer's chief lieutenant was George Ives, a handsome young desperado who had worked as a hostler for a livery stable in Virginia City. When a traveler left his horse or called for it, Ives would make casual inquiries concerning his destination. If the traveler were worth robbing, Ives would pass the essential information on to the brigands stationed on his route. A few who discovered his role would tell him they were going in some other direction than the one intended.

Ives, who had come from a good family in Wisconsin, occasionally took part in the holdups and murders. When short of funds, he would exact a "loan" of an ounce or two of gold dust, at the point of a gun, from some merchant or saloonkeeper. At near-by Nevada City he killed a man who had threatened to

[9] Hoffman Birney, *Vigilantes,* 174–75.

expose him and the other bandits. At Ramshorn Creek, about the last of November, Ives robbed Anton M. Holter of his money and cattle and tried to kill him. In the Stinkingwater Valley a few days later, he robbed a ranch hand, Nicholas Thibalt, of two hundred dollars and a fine pair of mules. Then he killed Thibalt and dragged his body into the bushes.

Nine or ten days later, William Palmer, while hunting grouse, found Thibalt's frozen body and had it hauled into Nevada City, where it was on display for half a day, causing great excitement. This cold-blooded murder proved to be a turning point in Montana history. At ten o'clock that evening, about twenty-five citizens of Nevada City rode out of town. They picked up another man at a ranch on their way and, at three-thirty the next morning, crossed Wisconsin Creek, seven miles below Dempsey's Cottonwood Ranch.

The party surrounded the ranch house and at daybreak closed in and captured Ives and several others. On the way back to Nevada City, Ives escaped his captors. On a fleet horse, he headed across the plain for the mountains about Biven's Gulch; but he was soon retaken. He asked to be tried in Virginia City, knowing that there Plummer might have a better opportunity to get him free. His request was denied.

Crowds lined the muddy streets of Nevada City when the party arrived. Since the weather was mild for that season—it was December 19—the vigilantes decided to begin the trial before the assembled townsmen that afternoon. The remainder of that day and all of the next were used in taking testimony and in argument. There were two attorneys for the prosecution and two for the defense. One of Ives' associates testified that the defendant had boasted of shooting Thibalt while he was kneeling in prayer.

On the twenty-first of December the jury brought in a verdict of guilty. The crowd voted to accept this decision and to punish Ives by hanging. When Ives asked for a delay in the execution, someone in the crowd yelled, "Ask him how long a time he gave the Dutchman." He was given only enough time to dictate his will and a few letters. While he was doing this, two men prepared a scaffold by projecting the butt of a small pine from a near-by building. Ives was placed on a large dry-goods box and the noose fastened about his neck. Then the guards shot the box from under him and let him swing in the evening breeze.[10]

Those who sent George Ives swinging knew they had put in a good lick for order and law. In the early West, vigilance committees and people's courts were spontaneous expressions of the American spirit of democracy. They showed that men in isolated communities could cope with a difficult social problem without awaiting formal action from the outside. Their activities contrasted sharply with the lynching bees of the South. The latter usually represented a deliberate flouting of statutory laws and of elected officials who—except in some instances in the Reconstruction period—were able and ready to handle the situation. The informal actions in the West, on the other hand, were not a mockery of law, because there was no effective law. They were the only alternative to anarchy in places where statutory law did not prevail. They were the forerunners of the established courts.

In the instance of Ives, the hanging had immediate and widespread effects, even though his confederates were freed. It threw fear into the Montana road agents and spurred the formation of vigilante bands to clear the mining country of outlaws. While the trial of Ives was still in progress in Nevada City, five men met in a store in Virginia City and took the first steps in organizing a vigilance committee there. In Nevada City, on the evening of December 23, two days after the hanging, two dozen men held a meeting behind closed doors. They bound themselves together to arrest thieves and murderers and to recover stolen property.

The oath which the Nevada City vigilantes signed that

[10] *The Banditti of the Rocky Mountains and Vigilance Committee in Idaho,* 90–93, an extremely rare item of which Fred A. Rosenstock of Denver has a photostatic copy; Dimsdale, *op. cit.,* 71–102, 223; Langford, *op. cit.,* II, 46–76.

[11] Oath and signatures of the Nevada City vigilantes, December 23, 1863, manuscript in the library of the Historical Society of Montana, Helena.

night[11] pledged them to secrecy, to law observance, and to loyalty to each other and to their standard of justice. Soon there were similar groups in Bannack and other mining towns, and these forces maintained close co-operation. The miners began to lose their fear of Plummer and his brigands and to seek safety on the side of law and order. The vigilance movement was speeded by news of the murder of a popular Lewiston merchant, Lloyd Magruder, and two of his men, who had left Virginia City in October with $14,000, to return to Lewiston.

While the slayers of Magruder were being caught in distant places, the Montana vigilantes found game near at hand. On December 23, a party of twenty-four, mounted on horses and mules, rode out of Virginia City in search of Alex Carter, an associate of Ives. Despite cold weather and deep snow, they scouted along the Stinkingwater, on the Big Hole, and past Divide. They camped at John Smith's ranch on Deer Lodge Creek, seventeen miles above Cottonwood.

On the trail, some of the men encountered Erastus (Red) Yager. He told them that Carter and his companions were drunk at Cottonwood. When they reached Cottonwood, the vigilantes found that the men they wanted had fled after being warned by a letter from George Brown in Virginia City. This letter had been brought by Red Yager, whom they had allowed to pass through their lines. Disappointed, the horsemen from Virginia City started to return home by way of Beaver Head Rock.

On the way back, they continued their scouting. After two days, on the twenty-seventh, they heard that Red Yager was at Rattlesnake Ranch, a cold ride of two days through snow and wind. There a contingent of the vigilantes captured Yager and started back with him toward Virginia City. At Dempsey's Cottonwood Ranch the captors met others of their party. They also found George Brown, the writer of the warning, and took him in tow. Brown had been a scout for General William R. Marshall in the Minnesota campaign of 1862 but had become one of Plummer's agents.

Resuming their journey back to Virginia City, the vigilantes stopped at Laurin's ranch on the Stinkingwater River near the mouth of California Creek. This place served as a trading post and a stage station. Some of the party remained there with the prisoners while the others rode on to Virginia City.

About ten o'clock on the night of January 4, 1864, the men who had gone on into Virginia City returned to Laurin's ranch. They waked the two culprits, who had gone to sleep on the floor of the barroom, and told them their hour had come. At this, Red Yager, the messenger, made a detailed confession that cleared up several crimes and explained how the Plummer outfit worked. He implicated Plummer and his deputies and many who had been serving as agents of the bandits in various mining towns. He explained the meaning of the sailor's knot in the neckties and related that the password was "Innocent."

Following this confession, the two prisoners were taken out across the snow to a pair of large cottonwoods. Yager remained cool and collected, but Brown cried for mercy. The Virginia City men clipped a few branches from a strong limb of each tree and tied the ropes. Then they pinioned the prisoners and stood them on stools with the nooses about their necks. As the stools were jerked out, the bodies of the freebooters swung in the winter wind. There they remained for several days, frozen stiff. Yager's back bore a label that spelled out, "Red! Road Agent and Messenger." The other was tagged, "Brown! Corresponding Secretary."[12]

Henry Plummer was in more danger than he realized. The vigilantes had been strengthening their organization during the holiday season. In Virginia City, between Christmas and New Year's Day, they had adopted regulations and bylaws similar to those which had prevailed in California in the days of the forty-niners. These provided for the election of officers, the keeping of records, and the trial of those accused of crime. In this case, the regulations stipulated only one punishment—death.[13]

On the afternoon of Sunday, January 10, some members of the Bannack group noticed the horses of Plummer and two of his deputies being brought into town. The presence of the mounts suggested that the trio might be preparing to escape.

[12] Dimsdale, *op. cit.*, 108–17.
[13] Birney, *op. cit.*, 218–22.

The Bannack committee, which had been considering Plummer's arrest, decided to act immediately. That evening, with an icy blast howling outside, a delegation called at the house of Mr. and Mrs. A. J. Vail, where the sheriff roomed. The visitors found Plummer in his bedroom and captured him without gunplay.

Bringing him out into the street, they soon were joined by other details which had taken into custody Ned Ray and Buck Stinson, the two deputies whose horses had been brought in with Plummer's. Ray and Stinson filled the winter air with curses. Plummer begged for his life and tried to convince his captors that he was innocent. But the men had deaf ears to such pleas. "It's useless," one of them told him. "You're to be hanged."

As the party arrived at the improvised gallows, someone threw a rope over the crossbeam and called out, "Bring up Ned Ray." Only the tightening of the noose choked off Ray's cursing. Loosely pinioned, he managed to get his fingers under the rope; but this only prolonged his agony.

"There goes poor Ned," whined Stinson, who a few moments later was dangling by his side.

Then came the call, "Bring up Plummer." The sheriff asked for time to pray but was told that he could make his prayers from the crossbeam of the gallows frame. At that he took off his necktie and threw it to a young man who had boarded with him. Plummer asked his captors, as a last favor, to give him a good drop. Then, as several strong men lifted him as high as they could and let him fall, Montana's most notorious bad man died without a struggle.[14] Ray's body was taken by his mistress. The others were placed in an unfinished building to await burial.

With Henry Plummer and five of his men hanged, some of the other road agents began to make quiet but quick exits; however, a few of them either did not act promptly enough or stayed on the assumption that the vigilante activities would die down with the death of Plummer. In this hope they were mistaken. The success of the citizens in doing away with Plummer spurred them to ferret out others of the desperado band who called themselves the Innocents. On the morning after the hanging of Plummer and two of his deputies, the Bannack committee

[14] Dimsdale, *op. cit.,* 126–29; Langford, *op. cit.,* II, 162–72.

decided to punish a Mexican, Joe Pizanthia. This villain had been guilty of several knifings and was suspected of being one of Plummer's henchmen. But when a delegation went to take Pizanthia from his cabin, he shot the two men who first appeared at his door. One of them was only slightly wounded; but the other, George Copley, died a few minutes later.

The death of Copley so angered the vigilantes that the larger group took Pizanthia in tow, after a gun battle. They strung him from a pole without the usual show of dignity. As he swayed on his clothesline rope, the crowd fired shots into his body and tore down and burned his cabin. A little later the body was cut down and thrown into the fire.

That evening Bannack had more excitement. It centered about Dutch John Wagner, one of Plummer's men who had several robberies and killings on his record. Wagner had been captured several days earlier, following his participation in the robbing of a pack train. He had made a confession and was being held in a cabin on Yankee Flat. When the committee notified him that he had only an hour to live, he asked permission to write a letter in German to his mother in New York. He did this with difficulty, as his fingers were frostbitten. Soon he was being marched to the place of execution. On the way, he passed the building where the bodies of Plummer and Stinson were laid out—one on the floor and the other on a work bench—but he seemed unmoved at the sight. A few minutes later the Montanans pulled a barrel from beneath him and let him swing.

The next to act were the determined men in Virginia City. Some of the Alder Gulch highwaymen, instead of fleeing to save their necks, had been threatening vengeance on the vigilantes. The latter moved swiftly. On the evening of January 13, the Virginia City committee made out a list of six desperadoes who were wanted. One of the six, suspecting danger, slipped out of town. The other five were brought before the committee the next morning.

The first to appear was Frank Parish, who confessed to more robberies than were charged against him. Next came George Lane, better known as "Clubfoot George." He pleaded innocence

We the undersigned uniting oursel
in a party for the laudible purpos
of arresting thievs & murderers & recove
stollen propperty do pledge ourselves up
our sacred honor each to all others
solemnly swear that we will reveal n
secrets, violate no laws of right & n
desert eachother or our standerd of
justice so help us God as witn
our hand & seal this 23 of Decembe
A D 1863

James Williams
Joseph Hinkley
G. S. Daddow
E. F. Reeves
Chs Brown
E. Moss
A. A. Balch
Wm. E. Maxwell
Nelson Kellock
S. J. Ross
Ch Beehrer
Thos Baume

Wm H. Brown
John Brown
Enoch Hodson
Hans J. Holt
H. Holt
Wm Gillon Jr
Wm Clark
Richd Tuff
C. S. Smith
W. Palmer
L. Seebold
M. S. Warden

Oath of the Vigilantes
Nevada City, December 23, 1863

but failed to convince his captors. Following him was Boone Helm, a former Missourian who admitted that he had killed two men. Jack Gallagher, Plummer's only surviving deputy, was found asleep in a gambling room of the Arbor Restaurant. He wore a swanky cavalry officer's overcoat, trimmed with Montana beaver. Informed of his fate, he issued a continual volley of oaths. The last highwayman brought in was Hayes Lyons, captured while eating griddle cakes in a cabin outside the town. After a brief examination, he confessed to the murder of Dillingham. His friends had advised him several days earlier to leave town, but he had been unwilling to part from his mistress.

The condemned men were disposed of on the day of their capture, January 14. The vigilantes marched them to an uncompleted log building at Wallace and Van Buren streets. This structure had its walls up but was not yet roofed. Five hanging ropes were thrown over a crossbeam and the ends tied to other parts of the building. Then five dry-goods boxes were placed under the nooses, each with a rope to be used in jerking it from under the desperado who stood upon it. By the time preparations were completed for the quintuple hanging, several thousand people had gathered to watch the event.

Before the prisoners were marched to the place of execution, the president of the vigilantes, Paris S. Pfouts, gave them an opportunity to make final requests and communications. All five declined. As their arms were being tied, Jack Gallagher tried to get at his knife to slit his throat and thus avoid a public hanging; but he did not succeed. On the way, Hayes Lyons asked for his mistress. His request was denied. The vigilantes recalled how women's cries for mercy had allowed the killers of Dillingham to escape punishment. "Bringing women to the place of execution," said one, "played out in '63."

Given another chance for last messages or requests, Jack Gallagher asked for a drink of whiskey, which was given him. Clubfoot George was the first to go. Seeing a friend in the crowd, he called out, "Goodbye, old fellow, I'm gone," and jumped off the box without waiting for it to be jerked from under him.

Jack Gallagher died cursing and invoking forked lightning on his executioners. Boone Helm looked calmly at the swaying body of Gallagher. "Kick away, old fellow," he said. "I'll be with you in a minute."

Frank Parish asked to have a handkerchief tied over his face. At this, someone took the bandit's own broad black tie from his neck, where it had been tied in a sailor's knot, and fastened it over his face. Hayes Lyons, the last to go, continued to beg for mercy. He asked that his body be turned over to his mistress and that her watch, which he carried, be restored to her.

The bodies were left hanging for about two hours, then were taken down and buried in Cemetery Hill. John X. Beidler, who had adjusted the nooses, was asked by one of his fellow townsmen, "When you put the rope around that poor fellow's neck, didn't you feel for him?"

"Yes," answered Beidler, one of whose friends had been killed by the road agents. "I felt for his left ear."[15]

That night's darkness covered a wholesale exodus of villains from the gulch. Most of them headed for Idaho. Yet enough were left to give the vigilantes grist for several more weeks. On the morning of January 15, twenty-one horsemen rode out of Nevada City to round up any road agents still within reach. That night they camped at Big Hole. They sent a detachment to Clark's ranch to look for Stephen Marshland, a bandit reported to be hiding there. The callers found Marshland laid up with frozen feet and a chest wound received while attacking a pack train in December. They captured him easily, and he admitted his crime. The next morning they hanged him from a pole that was stuck in the ground and leaned across a corral fence.

The vigilantes continued their scouting for several days. After camping at Smith's ranch on Deer Lodge Creek, about seventeen miles from Cottonwood, they went into that town after dark. There they captured William Bunton, who had been one of Plummer's most active men. Although he admitted nothing, they hanged him on the nineteenth from the crossbeam of the gate to Louis Demorest's corral. As he stood on a plank supported by two boxes, Bunton asked permission to jump off. This

[15] *Montana Post,* Virginia City, December 30, 1865; Dimsdale, *op. cit.,* 136–46, 221–23; Langford, *op. cit.,* II, 184–206.

granted, he called, "Here goes it," and leaped into the air, to have his neck broken by his vigilante collar.

The executions went on with grim regularity. On January 24, George Shears, a Plummer satellite, was hanged from a barn in the Bitter Root Valley. Before dawn of the following day, two more road agents, Cyrus Skinner and Alexander Carter, were strung by torchlight from poles fastened to a corral in Hell Gate. Later that day, a wounded leg failed to save John Cooper; he was brought to the corral by sleigh. Cooper and Robert Zachary met a similar doom from the same improvised gallows.

Two more bandits were rounded up in the next few days. On the twenty-sixth, William Graves, known as "Whiskey Bill," was captured at Fort Owen, in the Bitter Root Valley. The vigilantes put him on horseback, linked his neck with the limb of a convenient tree, then caused his horse to leap forward and leave him dangling. On February 3, William Hunter, the man who had escaped the Virginia City dragnet three weeks earlier, was hanged from a tree beside the trail, twenty miles above the mouth of the Gallatin.

In six weeks the Montana vigilantes had hanged twenty-two of their worst lawbreakers. In addition, they had banished several and had frightened many others into leaving. Their work made it easier to set up effective courts and enforcement agencies when the territorial government was formed a few months later. But their task was not yet fully accomplished. They had to deal next with Joseph A. Slade, a former Illinoisan who had settled in Virginia City with his wife a year earlier.

Slade had been head of one of the divisions of the Overland Stage Company. In Colorado, after a long quarrel, he had killed a man. With a bowie knife he slashed off his victim's ears, which he later carried as watch charms.[16] Because of his quarrelsome nature, Slade lost his stage job. He came to Montana in 1863 as the head of a freighting outfit. He was successful in this business and bought a small ranch near Virginia City. His main source of trouble was inability to hold his liquor.

[16] Lewis F. Crawford, *Rekindling Camp Fires,* 47–49. Doubt has been cast on the incident of the ear slashing, but several men who knew Slade asserted that they had seen the dried ears on his watch chain.

When drunk, which was increasingly often, Slade wanted to shoot up the town. His terroristic activities made him so obnoxious that he was given repeated warnings. Even after the vigilantes gathered on March 10 to hang him, they allowed him another chance. "Get your horse and go home," they told him. Instead, he stopped at a convenient saloon for more firewater. This was too much for the patience of the citizens. They hanged him from the crossbeam of a corral gate near the Pfouts and Russell store.

Throughout the summer the vigilantes kept their ropes handy. On June 15, they dealt summary justice to James Brady, a Nevada City saloonkeeper who had shot a man without provocation. After Brady was caught in Virginia City, he was returned to the scene of his crime and tried and convicted in Adelphi Hall. Then he was taken half a mile east of town and hanged from a butcher's hoist. In July a remnant of the Plummer band robbed a stagecoach en route from Virginia City to Salt Lake City and took $27,000 in gold dust from the four passengers. Vigilantes from Virginia City rode out in search of the bandits. They caught one of them, James Kelly, who was wanted also for horse theft. On September 5, they dangled him from a tree in the Port Neuf Canyon in Idaho. Another of this band, John Dolan, was hanged from a butcher's hoist about half a mile northeast of Nevada City on September 17.

Vigilance activities subsided in Montana for a time, although there were a few hangings in Bannack and Helena. But soon recurrence of stagecoach robberies brought the organized citizens into action again. In 1865, a year after the hanging of Dolan, a revived Virginia City committee published the following notice:

> To all whom it may concern: Whereas divers foul crimes and outrages against persons and property of the citizens of Montana have lately been committed and whereas the power of the civil authorities, though exerted to its full extent, is frequently insufficient to prevent their commission and to punish the perpetrators thereof, now this is to warn and notify all whom it may concern that the vigilance committee, composed of the citizens of the ter-

ritory, have determined to take these matters into their own hands and to inflict summary punishment upon any and all malefactors in every case where the civil authorities are unable to enforce the proper penalty of the law. The practice of drawing deadly weapons, except as a last resort for the defense of life, being dangerous to society and in numerous instances leading to affrays and bloodshed, notice is hereby given that the same is prohibited and offenders against this regulation will be summarily dealt with. In all cases the committee will respect and sustain the action of the civil authorities. This notice will not be repeated and will remain in full force and effect from this day.[17]

Helena citizens took a similar view. In that town, in the same week, the stiffening body of a thief, Tommy Cooke, was found swaying in the morning breeze. A few days later the corpses of two Idaho members of Rattlesnake Dick's band were seen hanging from a hay frame over the corral of a slaughter house up the gulch from Virginia City. The back of one of them bore the penciled note: "Road Agents Beware." Within another week, two other men were found hanging from the Prickly Pear tollgate about fifty miles from Confederate Gulch. Another dangled from a tree at Helena.

When a Nevada newspaper, the Carson *Appeal,* took the *Montana Post* to task for referring flippantly to these "little matters of necessity," the latter paper replied:

Upon general principle the majority of a community can be justified in taking the law into their own hands. It has been necessary here. Circumstances alter cases. Our vigilance committee is not a mob. Until justice can be reached through the ordinary channels, our citizens will be fully protected against these evil desperadoes, even if the sun of every morning should rise upon the morbid picture of a malefactor dangling in the air. Protection anyway is the prevailing sentiment of the honest people of Montana, of all creeds and factions.[18]

[17] *Montana Post,* September 23, 1865.

[18] *Ibid.,* November 4, 1865.

Civil authorities gradually took over the responsibility for keeping order in Montana, but informal bands still took occasional action. When the Missouri River steamer *Luella* was being unloaded at Fort Benton in 1866, a deck hand stole a case of patent medicine valued for its alcoholic content. Vigilantes caught the thief and, after convincing themselves of his guilt, whipped him until he was nearly dead. Captain Grant Marsh had no more trouble with pilfering from the *Luella*.[19]

In Argenta a score of the leading citizens formed a vigilance committee in December, 1866. Vigilantes were busy in the Lannon mining camp in May, 1868. In that month a committee in Dale City hanged three desperadoes and shot one. In the spring of 1870, a crowd, reported to have been more than a thousand persons, gathered in the courthouse square at Helena. Acting in the capacity of a people's court, the citizens tried two thugs who had robbed and killed an old man. A district judge protested against this irregular procedure and asked that the law be allowed to take its course, but the outraged citizens overruled him. They chose a committee of twelve to hear the evidence and to bring in a verdict. This jury found the prisoners guilty, and the crowd voted to hang them. Soon the pair decorated a big cottonwood.[20]

Montana continued to experience informal hangings for another fifteen years. Most of these were isolated cases of horse thieves who were caught and punished on the spot by small groups of stockmen. The ranchmen had no patience with horse thieves. They thought little more of dangling one of these villains from a tree than of shooting a wolf and throwing its skin over a fence. Often cow hands going out in the early morning would come upon the work of night riders. On a tree near the Smith Fork of the Judith River, in the fall of 1880, they found the swaying body of an unknown man. To his coat was pinned a paper with the words, "Horse Thief."[21]

That region had several such hangings in the summer of 1884. Early in June, ranchmen captured and killed one member

[19] Joseph Mills Hanson, *The Conquest of the Missouri*, 76–77.
[20] Helena *Daily Gazette*, April 30, 1870.
[21] *Yellowstone Journal*, Miles City, October 9, 1880.

of a band that had been stealing in the Judith Basin. On the twenty-sixth of that month, a horseherder encountered two desperadoes who were chasing off seven of the mounts in his charge. He shot and fatally wounded one of the thieves and captured the other. The latter was placed under guard in a stable. At two o'clock the next morning, vigilantes took him out and hanged him from a tall cottonwood near Judith Landing.[22]

A few days later, on July 3, ranchmen caught up with Sam McKenzie, a Scotch half-blood. Sam had been stealing Montana horses and selling them in Canada and then driving off Canadian horses and selling them in Montana. Ranch hands caught him in a canyon a few miles above Fort Maginnis, with two stolen horses. That night firm arms tied him to a cottonwood not far from the fort.[23] The next day two horse thieves, who had been celebrating with firewater, started to shoot up Lewistown but were killed in a gun battle with citizens.[24] On the evening of the same day, near the mouth of the Musselshell, other vigilantes hanged two men who had in their possession stolen horses and the hides of stolen cattle.[25] Later that month the bodies of seven men were found dangling in the same neighborhood.[26] The hanging of several other horse thieves was reported in September.[27]

Reflective opinion stood back of the tree trimming. Of the earlier organized committees in the mining towns, N. P. Langford of Bannack wrote later that "the people had perfect confidence in the code of the vigilantes, and many of them scouted the idea of there being any better law for their protection." These bands, he added, "made laws for a country without law and executed them with a vigor suited to every exigency."[28] The

22 *Mineral Argus,* July 3, 1884; Granville Stuart, *Forty Years on the Frontier,* II, 198.

23 *Mineral Argus,* July 10, 1884; Stuart, *op. cit.,* II, 198–201; John R. Barrows, *Ubet,* 202–204.

24 *Mineral Argus,* July 10, 1884; Stuart, *op. cit.,* II, 201–205.

25 Stuart, *op. cit.,* II, 205–206.

26 *Mineral Argus,* July 24, 1884.

27 *Ibid.,* September 11, 30, 1884. The Historical Society of Montana has a list of sixty men hanged by vigilantes in that state from 1862 to 1870, inclusive.

28 Langford, *op. cit.,* II, 447–49.

biographer of Captain Marsh, Joseph Mills Hanson, took a similar view: "The law of the vigilance committee was stern and uncompromising, but it seldom was unjust, for even the extremity of its punishments found excuse in the chaotic conditions of frontier society."[29]

Compared with the hastily formed groups on the ranges, the vigilance committees in the mining towns represented a more formal administration of justice. Their procedure more closely followed that of indictment and trial in statutory courts. Vigilante justice in the Montana mining camps was based in part on examples in the preceding decade in California, from which state many of the Montana miners had come.

If the Montana vigilante courts were less formal than the more celebrated ones of San Francisco, they at least were reasonably careful in gathering evidence. They had good leadership and seldom acted except in extreme cases. Usually they gave the defendant an opportunity to clear himself if he could. Most of the executions were by daylight and without use of masks. The vigilance committees were called into existence by frontier necessity. When the need for them passed, they quietly and quickly faded away.

[29] Hanson, *op. cit.*, 76.

10. Prairie Necktie Parties

> The vigilantes unquestionably served the frontier well in ridding it of desperado control. They bridged the gap between the lawless frontier and the orderly communities which came later.
> —Carl Coke Rister, "Outlaws and Vigilantes of the Southern Plains"

At Rapid City, in the Black Hills, the silence of a summer night was broken on June 20, 1877, when masked men surrounded a cabin of the stagecoach line. From the darkness, the visitors demanded that the guards deliver three prisoners who were inside. The guards complied readily. The wanted men had been captured outside the town that afternoon with six stolen horses in their possession. Four of these horses had been taken from the barn of the stage company at Crook City. The others belonged to a freighter there.

Two of the men had confessed the stealing but had insisted that the third had taken no part in it. He had been ordered out of Deadwood and Crook City because of other objectionable activities. He had started off afoot when the horse thieves overtook him on the trail and invited him to ride one of their spare mounts.

The midnight visitors marched their prisoners to a hill west of town where a sturdy pine had been defying the winds for many years. Quickly they made two small piles of rocks and placed nooses about the necks of the two thieves. Then they had them stand on the rocks, tied the other ends of the ropes to a branch of the tree, and kicked the stones from beneath their feet.

But what should they do with the third and younger man? "Up with him!" shouted one of the vigilantes. He reminded the group that dead men tell no tales and that the remaining prisoner was a disreputable rounder anyway. So up he went. The next morning the three bodies, with blackened faces and protruding tongues, still swung from the tree. Bob Burleigh, justice of the peace, went out and held an inquest. Then bystanders cut the ropes and buried the three in a level spot on the west side of the hill.[1]

On the western plains and in the mountains, frontiersmen viewed the horse thief as worse than a murderer. The cattleman had to use horses in his daily work. Without them he was almost helpless. Unhorsed far from home, he was exposed to every danger of the wilds. He might die of thirst or hunger. He might freeze in a blizzard or become prey to savage beasts or scalping Indians. Stockmen wanted to be sure that the mounts they turned out to graze at night would be within reach the next morning. Anyone caught with a stolen horse could expect no mercy. In the range country, horse thieves were the most frequent objects of committees formed to stamp out lawlessness. Any good calf rope could be used in decorating a tree.

In many instances, the man who filled the noose and those who tied it had gone to the West with similar motives. All wanted freedom from the restraints they felt in states farther east. The pioneers wanted independence. They wanted to escape financial panics, oppressive taxes, or crowding neighbors. The outlaw wanted to put himself beyond the reach of some sheriff or the frown of relatives. Once on the frontier, he may have tried his hand at farming or mining and failed. When he turned to crime, he found himself fighting against restraints that often proved more effective than those he had escaped.

The hanging outside Rapid City was not the first necktie party in the Black Hills in the era of the gold rush. Late in the afternoon of February 26, 1876, mounted vigilantes, without resort to masks or darkness, did away with a thief. He had been caught in the act of stealing a horse and had shot at the horse's owner, Peter S. Lambert. The captors stopped at a travelers' camp on the trail, on a snow-covered knoll about forty miles from Custer. They gave their prisoner, an Ohioan, time to write

[1] Jesse Brown and A. M. Willard, *The Black Hills Trails,* 292–96.

three letters. Then they had him mount a horse, tied his arms down, put a noose about his neck, and tied the other end of the rope to a branch of a scarred old cottonwood in Red Canyon. This done, one of the men gave the horse a blow that sent him rushing ahead and left the thief dangling and kicking. The vigilantes rode off, satisfied with their job. Later the travelers cut down the thief, rolled him in a saddle blanket, and buried him in the frozen red soil.

Another informal hanging took place in the summer of 1877. Two men operating a flourishing butcher shop in Deadwood were found to be selling beef stolen from neighboring ranges. The victimized cattlemen quickly joined to end this enterprise and located the rustlers and their loot at a spring about two miles east of Spearfish, at the foot of Lookout Mountain. Rousing the men from their sleep, they promptly swung them from pine limbs. The next day the bodies were cut down and buried.

Early in October, 1878, vigilantes captured two of a band of desperadoes about thirty miles from Fort Pierre. They left the pair hanging as a warning to others. In the same fall a notorious horse thief known as "Lame Johnny" organized a band of highwaymen and held up a stagecoach on a creek in Custer County. Soon afterward he was captured at Pine Ridge and taken to the Red Cloud stage station. Since he was wanted for mail robbery, he was shackled and handcuffed and put in a guarded stagecoach bound for Rapid City. Fresh horses were obtained at Buffalo Gap, and nothing unusual happened until the coach reached the site of the holdup. There Jesse Brown, one of the guards, who was riding a saddle horse behind the coach, heard a voice shout "Go back! Don't come any farther!" When he reached the coach a little later, the highwayman was swinging from the limb of an elm.[2]

Dakota Territory saw many similar instances of vigilante justice. In February of 1881, a newcomer in Custer City started to shoot up the town and killed a man who had befriended him. Before he could be taken to the jail, citizens grabbed him from the sheriff. They escorted him to the south side of the creek and strung him to a convenient tree. At Pierre, in the same winter,

[2] *Ibid.*, 298–301; Jack T. Sutley, *The Last Frontier*, 247–54.

vigilantes riddled with bullets a bullwhacker from across the river who, despite warnings, popped his gun in all directions and terrorized the people.[3] At Spearfish, six men took a wounded suspect from a hospital on an icy night, dragged him, clad in only his shirt, through a blinding snowstorm to the edge of town, and hanged him from a branch. There his frozen, blackened body was found the next morning.

As in other sections of the frontier, summary hanging was popularly accepted as the only just punishment for a horse thief or a cattle rustler. Of one suspect, the Huron *Tribune* remarked on August 11, 1883, "He will undoubtedly stretch hemp in the course of a few months, and we shall be glad to publish his obituary."

Nebraska vigilantes were no less expeditious. In 1875, where one of the cattle trails crossed the Platte River in the western part of the state, a bullwhacker shot to death a cattleman who had remonstrated with him for taking his beeves. The gunman was captured and was being taken to Sidney under guard when vigilantes intercepted the party north of that town. "One-Eyed Ed" died in a coulee with a lariat about his neck.

In the decade that followed, vigilantes dealt similar punishment to many of the Nebraska cattle rustlers, horse thieves, and other outlaws. On February 6, 1884, Kid Wade, leader of a band of outlaws and horse thieves, was taken from the sheriff of Holt County by a citizens' group which had been cleaning out the upper Elkhorn country. The next morning Wade's body was found hanging to a whistle-post ten miles east of Long Pine. At least ten others were said to have been put out of the way by this organization.[4]

In the same month, vigilantes accused the sheriff of Cherry County of being in collusion with horse thieves. They ordered him to leave the county immediately. The sheriff, who denied the charge, refused to leave. For his protection, he swore in thirty deputies and armed them heavily.[5]

[3] William Rhoads, *Recollections of Dakota Territory*, 29.

[4] Fort Worth *Gazette*, February 8, 1884; St. Paul *Phonograph*, February 15, 1884.

[5] St. Paul *Phonograph*, February 29, 1884.

The vast expanse of the unfenced plains made it hard to deal with outlaws except by applying strong-arm punishment to those caught. Farming areas, more thickly peopled than the grasslands, had less frequent need for vigilante action. But in some sections pioneers who used the ax and the plow to make the western prairies productive had to use the six-shooter and the hanging rope to make them safe.

Early Iowa settlers countered the activities of horse thieves and other outlaws by forming vigilance groups. In 1837, before the territory was organized, the Mississippi River town of Bellevue became the headquarters of a band of counterfeiters and horse thieves. Their leader was W. W. Brown, who built a frame hotel there. Brown's respectable appearance and engaging manners fooled his neighbors. They elected him to public office but soon thereafter discovered his real character. In January, 1840, while many Bellevue citizens were attending a ball, several of Brown's men robbed a residence and mistreated a young woman they found there. Luckily she recognized one of them and gave an alarm. In a consequent street encounter that night, one of the bandits was shot dead by the man whose house they had robbed.

Swearing vengeance, the outlaws retreated to a saloon and prepared to blow up the house they had burglarized. First, they broke into a store and took a tin can containing fifteen pounds of gunpowder. Next, they placed this in the cellar of the marked house and tried to set it off, but the gunpowder failed to explode. Discovering this plot, the aroused citizens obtained warrants for the arrest of Brown and a score of his confederates. Then they formed a posse of forty men and marched against Brown's barricaded hotel. In the ensuing fifteen-minute battle, Brown and two of his men were killed, thirteen were captured, and six escaped. The attackers lost four men killed and seven wounded.

Shouts arose for hanging the captured bandits, but the leading citizens demurred. After debating the issue in the home of one of their number, they decided to let the assembled townsmen choose between hanging and whipping. The vote was made by dropping white or colored beans into a box. The majority favored whipping. At that outcome, the wretches were given thorough lashings, placed in skiffs with three days' rations, and sent down the river with a warning that, if they returned, they would be hanged.[6]

Outbreaks of horse stealing and of killing in eastern Iowa in the middle fifties led to the formation of vigilance groups in several counties. In March, 1857, Jackson County citizens took from the Andrew jail a man who had murdered another for $150 hire. Quickly they heard his confession and hanged him. Two months later they took from another jail a man who had killed his former wife three years earlier and who had used technicalities to escape punishment. After bringing him back to Andrew, they strung him from the same tree they had used earlier.

At Montezuma, where the killer of a young emigrant couple had used legal loopholes to avoid conviction, two thousand enraged citizens gathered at the courthouse. The crowd dragged out the murderer and dangled his writhing body from the nearest tree. Elsewhere in this period, Iowans who called themselves "Regulators" hanged a number of suspected horse thieves, including one or two who may have been innocent.[7] Such summary actions soon became infrequent because the need for them passed. Yet as late as December 14, 1874, about 150 men, with blackened faces, entered the jail in Des Moines, knocked down and tied the jailer, took his keys, and removed a man accused of murder. They dragged him through the courthouse and hanged him from a lamppost.

Kansas, born in violence, had vigilance groups almost from its start. These stern plainsmen rid many communities of horse thieves and desperadoes. As elsewhere, the secret bodies sometimes degenerated into mob rule or were used for private vengeance. But usually they were made up of law-abiding, responsible citizens who wanted only to maintain order and to protect lives and property. Although at times they acted without warning, they often gave notice for offenders to leave. Those who failed to go were caught and put out of the way, usually by

6 Benjamin F. Gue, *History of Iowa,* I, 331–35.
7 *Ibid.,* I, 336–50.

hanging. Some of the vigilance committees were permanent organizations with elected officers and regular meetings. Most of them, however, were formed only as occasion arose and were disbanded as soon as their task was done.

Some of the early Kansas groups were more interested in promoting or opposing slavery than in checking outlawry. In June, 1854, a pro-slavery group formed the Squatters Claim Association in Salt Creek Valley, three miles from Fort Leavenworth, and appointed a vigilance committee of thirteen to protect its rights. Similar organizations were active in Linn County in 1857 and in Council City in the following year.[8]

As lawlessness remained rampant after the Civil War, vigilance committees sprang up in many communities. Topeka citizens put one outlaw to death. A Manhattan group scattered a band of desperadoes and killed several of its leaders. At Rising Sun, where a man had been killed while trying to save his cattle from thieves, a committee hanged four men from the same limb and tied two others there a few days later.[9] In the late summer of 1866, while a captured desperado was being taken from Mound City to Lawrence, more than a score of vigilantes seized him from the sheriff. They hanged their prisoner in the timbered bottoms of Big Sugar Creek.[10]

Horse thieves were a frequent menace in southern Kansas in the seventies. At the beginning of that decade, a large band of thieves was operating along the Arkansas River, between Wichita and Winfield. In the spring of 1870, this outfit drove 250 stolen mules to Texas. After this outrage, Winfield citizens quietly formed a vigilance committee and began systematic detective work. By fall they knew who the thieves and their agents were and began to act. At a crossing of the Walnut River near Douglass, in Butler County, they surrounded a house at which four agents of the thieves had stopped. The vigilantes ordered the men inside to surrender. Three who refused were

[8] Carl Coke Rister, "Outlaws and Vigilantes of the Southern Plains, 1865–1885," *Mississippi Valley Historical Review*, Vol. XIX (March, 1933), 551.

[9] Everett Dick, *The Sod-House Frontier, 1854–1890*, 136.

[10] J. T. Botkin, "Justice Was Swift and Sure in Early Kansas," *Kansas Historical Collections*, Vol. XVI (1923–25), 488–93.

shot, and the one who gave up was hanged from a near-by tree. The Kansans laid one body on the bank of a creek with a placard that said, "Sold for stealing horses."[11]

A few weeks later a band of about seventy-five citizens captured four Douglass men accused as stock thieves. They marched the quartet at night to the woods near Olmstead's mill, a mile and a half south of town, and hanged them. Then the vigilantes published the names of the remaining leaders and members of the horse-thief gang. As a result, several left the county in haste and horses were safe for some time.[12]

Men in southeastern Kansas were no less alert. Near Columbus, in Cherokee County, a mounted assailant shot and killed a cattleman who was on his way to Texas to buy stock. While the bandit was rifling his victim's pockets, men who had watched him from an adjoining field seized him. They hanged him from the nearest tree.[13]

At Caldwell, near the border of the Indian Territory, vigilantes captured a killer on Deer Creek in the spring of 1872 and brought him back to town where they shot him with his own pistol.[14] In May of that year a gun duel took place in the streets of Wellington, in the same county. An innocent bystander was killed, but the gunman who fired the fatal shot escaped, after putting the blame on his opponent. The latter was taken that night to the timber on Slate Creek and hanged. Since he was a tough character, the discovery that the wrong gunman had been strung up did not bring any obvious pangs of conscience.[15]

Caldwell and Wellington had more excitement in the latter part of July, 1874. Thieves stole nearly all the local horses and mules of a stage company and took a race horse and a pony belonging to Bob Drummond. Law officers and vigilantes, after scouring the countryside for ten days, recovered part of the stock

[11] Wichita *Vidette,* November 10, 1870; "Reminiscences of Arthur Walden," *Kansas Reminiscences,* III, 114, Kansas State Historical Society; Dick, *op. cit.,* 138–39.

[12] Winfield *Censor,* December 3, 1870; Wichita *Vidette,* December 8, 1870; G. D. Freeman, *Midnight and Noonday,* (2nd. ed.), 97.

[13] Floyd Benjamin Streeter, *Prairie Towns and Cow Trails,* 76.

[14] Freeman, *op. cit.,* 95–111.

[15] T. A. McNeal, *When Kansas Was Young,* 18–20.

VIGILANCE COURT IN SESSION
Harper's Weekly, April 11, 1874

Denver Library Western Collection

and learned the identity of the thieves. Three of them were captured soon thereafter and were taken on July 29 to the county jail at Wellington. On the evening of the following day, armed horsemen began gathering at the jail. At midnight they broke open the building, marched the prisoners about a mile out the road toward Caldwell, and hanged them on Slate Creek.[16]

Sumner County had another midnight party in the following month. After an argument over the price of a pair of boots, a temporary resident of Caldwell shot and killed a local shoemaker as he worked in his shop, unarmed, on August 20. That night the killer's body dangled from the limb of a tree on the small creek that ran past the eastern edge of the town.[17]

Dodge City, terminus of one of the cattle trails from Texas, formed a vigilance committee in 1875.[18] Similar organizations were at work in other parts of Kansas. At Ellsworth, citizens chased a desperado who, with two companions, took refuge in his cabin on the prairie. The pursuers set fire to the dry grass and soon had the cabin in flames. The three men came out shooting but were quickly mowed down.[19] In the summer of 1877, an Atchison County committee captured and hanged a ruffian who had killed two men.

Caldwell, although still a wild cattle town, was turning to formal methods. In 1883 and early 1884, it had as its marshal a fearless gunman, John Henry Brown. Before coming to Kansas, Brown had ridden with Billy the Kid and later had been the first constable of Tascosa, a frontier cow town in the Texas Panhandle. In Caldwell he kept order so well that grateful citizens presented him with a gold-mounted Winchester.

Late in April, 1884, Brown rode out of town with his assistant and two other men. He said they were going to look for horse thieves. On the morning of May 1, the four turned up in Medicine Lodge, sixty miles to the west. They rode to the Medicine Valley Bank just after it had opened, and Brown had one of his men watch the horses outside while he and his two other com-

16 Freeman, *op. cit.*, 238–59.

17 *Ibid.*, 260–64.

18 Topeka *Commonwealth*, July 14, 1875.

19 J. H. Beadle, *Western Wilds*, 213–14.

panions entered. Inside, the three ordered the president and cashier to throw up their hands. The cashier did so; but the president, E. Wylie Payne, reached for his gun. Thereupon the bandits shot both bankers, killing the cashier and mortally wounding Payne.

On hearing shots outside, the trio gave up their robbery plan and rushed out to their horses. Together with the fourth man, who was barely holding his own against the Medicine Lodge marshal, they mounted and rode off in a drizzling rain, with their pursuers close behind. Heading southwest for the Gypsum Hills, the bandits took refuge in the recess of a canyon where they were driven into waist-deep water and had to surrender.

The prisoners were brought into town in the afternoon and placed in the frame calaboose, under guard. About midnight a crowd of men surrounded the flimsy jail, overpowered the sheriff, and took out the bandits, who had removed their handcuffs. Brown slipped out of their hands and started to run. Before he had gone far, he was shot dead. The other three were taken to the river bottom and hanged from the limb of a big elm. Later Caldwell councilmen adopted a resolution heartily approving of this action.[20]

Every western state and territory had at least a taste of informal law enforcement. In southern Missouri the Bald Knobbers kept order in the Ozark fastnesses of Christian and Taney counties in the eighties, but overreached themselves and were disbanded. The Indian Territory had many impromptu executions, although lack of accurate reports made it difficult in some instances to distinguish these from killings by feudists and outlaws. Early in 1873, two bands of Choctaw Indians captured sixteen horse thieves of their own tribe. After obtaining confessions, they shot six of the leaders.[21] In southern Louisiana in 1872, Abbeville citizens rounded up a band of cattle thieves and hanged twelve at Vermillionville.[22]

Texas offered frequent occasion for vigilante action. This

[20] Freeman, *op. cit.,* 312–24; McNeal, *op. cit.,* 153–59.

[21] *Western Independent,* Fort Smith, Arkansas, February 6, 1873.

[22] Houston *Telegraph,* October 3, 1872, quoting the *Sugar Bowl* of September 1.

region had attracted, along with sturdy pioneers, many desperate characters. After a journey through Texas, Frederick Law Olmsted of New York wrote in 1856, with some exaggeration:

In the rapid settlement of the country, many an adventurer crossed the border, spurred by love of life or liberty, forfeited at home, rather than drawn by the love of adventure or of rich soil. Probably a more reckless and vicious crew was seldom gathered than that which peopled some parts of eastern Texas at the time of its first resistance to the Mexican Government.

"G.T.T.," (Gone to Texas) was the slang appendage, within the reader's recollection, to every man's name who had disappeared before the discovery of some rascality. Did a man emigrate thither, every one was on the watch for the discreditable reason to turn up. . . . If your life, an old settler told us, would be of the slightest use to any one, you might be sure he would take it, and it was safe only as you were in constant readiness to defend it. Horses and wives were of as little account as umbrellas in more advanced states. Everybody appropriated everything that suited him, running his own risk of a penalty. Justice descended into the body of Judge Lynch, sleeping when he slept, and when he woke hewing down right and left for exercise and pastime.[23]

In this early period, when Texas settlements were far apart and newspapers were few, vigilante activities seldom had notice in print. An exception was the case of Thomas D. Yocum, who lived near the Neches River and associated with a band of villains engaged in swindling, robbery, and murder. He was accused of stealing many cattle, horses, and Negroes, and of selling his loot in Louisiana. A number of killings were attributed to him, but he was never convicted. Finally, in 1841, he was caught in an attempt to swindle a man who lived on Cedar Bayou and was suspected of planning to kill this man. Indignant citizens called on Yokum and notified him to leave. At first he promised to do so, but later he gathered several of his friends together and defied the vigilantes. The latter then burned Yocum's house and captured him at the home of a relative on Cypress Bayou.

[23] Frederick Law Olmsted, *A Journey Through Texas,* 124–26.

They started with him toward the Trinity River, but a day or two later his body, pierced with five rifle balls, was found on the prairie near the San Jacinto.[24]

Farmers and stockmen in other sections of Texas were equally intolerant of outlaws. In the spring of 1857 the San Antonio *Ledger* reported that, within a few weeks, seven horse thieves had been hanged at different places along the San Antonio River. These actions appeared to be the work of the same committee, since in each case the thief's weapons and outer clothes were carefully placed beside the tree.[25] In August, 1864, three men accused as horse thieves were hanged by vigilantes in Smith County, in northeastern Texas.[26]

Following the Civil War, outlawry became still worse. For two decades the Gulf Southwest was infested with bands of desperadoes. These men stole cattle and horses, robbed stagecoaches, trains, and banks, and committed murder on slight provocation. One ranchman, John Hittson, estimated in 1873 that in the preceding twenty years thieves had driven 100,000 cattle from Texas.[27] Favorite scenes of operation, since they afforded easy access to refuge, were areas bordering on the Indian Territory and on the Río Grande.

Some of the bandits were former soldiers who turned to outlawry to prolong the sectional conflict or to offset unpopular Reconstruction measures. A larger group of bandits were local bushwhackers or guerrillas who had used the war as an excuse for terrorism and dared not return to civil life in their old homes. John Wesley Hardin and other notorious killers began criminal careers by disarming Negroes, sniping at soldiers, and shooting their way out of tight places. Other vandals robbed to recoup gambling losses or were tempted by the ease of cattle rustling on the unfenced plains. Jesse James, whose Missouri raiders were bringing terror to midwestern towns, had many a lesser counterpart in the Southwest.

[24] Houston *Morning Star,* October 7, 1841. On January 31, 1842, President Sam Houston issued a proclamation denouncing this killing.

[25] Trinity *Advocate,* May 20, 1857, quoting the San Antonio *Ledger.*

[26] *State Gazette,* Austin, November 25, 1865.

[27] San Antonio *Express,* February 27, 1873.

At Richmond, on the Texas coastal plain, townsmen took care of one horse thief on the night of April 26, 1869. This man, who lived in the woods, had been making nightly forays for several months and was blamed for the loss of fifteen to twenty horses and mules. In one instance he had sold a fine mare he had stolen; then he had again stolen and sold the same one. When arrested, he admitted some of the thefts and was placed in the county jail. The next day the sheriff and other county officers were disqualified by a Reconstruction order. That night the thief was taken from the jail and hanged from the west span of the iron bridge being built across the Brazos River.[28] Farther north, the Denton *Monitor* reported a month later that the business of horse stealing in Denton County had played out. "Horse thieves have been swung to limbs whenever caught, and cow thieves have not been slighted."[29]

Texas vigilantes were especially active in the seventies. Since they usually operated at night and were not inclined to talk, their work of trimming trees with outlaws lacked detailed publicity. Yet newspapers and other chronicles showed that they were busy in many communities. The annual report of Adjutant General F. L. Britton for 1873 quoted a warning to four alleged thieves in Hill County. This warning told them to leave the county within thirty days if they wished to avoid the fate of others of their kind. "The ropes and six-shooter balls are prepared for you."

At Denison, where thugs gathered after the Missouri, Kansas and Texas Railroad reached the Red River, citizens captured a horse thief on the night of January 12, 1874. They strung him from a tree a quarter of a mile west of the slaughter house. The next morning relatives found and cut down the body.[30] Preston, a few miles up the river, reported the killing of one horse thief and the wounding of another in a gun battle on the evening of March 6 of the same year.[31]

To the south, the murder of a sheepman and his wife near

[28] Galveston *News*, April 28, May 5, 1869.

[29] *Ibid.*, June 10, 1869, citing the Denton *Monitor*.

[30] Denison *Daily News*, January 4, 1874.

[31] *Ibid.*, March 22, 1874.

the Refugio Mission in June, 1874, aroused vigilante action that cost the lives of five Mexicans accused of this crime.[32] In the spring of 1877, cattlemen from northeastern Texas caught three rustlers in Grayson County. They swung them from a limb about two miles southwest of Goose Pond and placarded the bodies, "Cattle Thieves' Doom."[33] In the following August, stockmen from Arkansas pursued three horse thieves into Texas. They caught them in Red River County and hanged all three from the same tree.[34] Early in 1878 about 750 horse thieves were under indictment in Texas. Newspapers estimated that not one thief in ten was caught and that 100,000 horses had been stolen in Texas in the preceding three years.[35]

The inadequacy of the courts in dealing with horse thieves left much room for informal action. The Houston *Telegram* stated the prevailing view when it said:

> By common practice in the rural districts every man caught is either shot on the spot or hanged to the nearest tree. No instance is yet recorded where the law paid the slightest attention to lynchers of this kind. It is conceded that the man who steals a horse in Texas forfeits his life to the owner. It is a game of life and death. Men will pursue horse thieves for five hundred miles, go any length, spend any amount of money to capture them, and fight them to death when overtaken. That they will be totally exterminated admits of no doubt. The poor scoundrels cannot last long when the feeling of all civilization is so much aroused against them as it now is in Texas.[36]

The best-known and probably the most active vigilance committee in Texas was that of Fort Griffin. This group found much work in hilly country where mesquite and other growths provided cover for outlaws. It warned many lawbreakers and suspicious characters to depart. Some of those who ignored such

[32] J. Frank Dobie, *A Vaquero of the Brush Country*, 72–75.
[33] Galveston *News*, May 1, 1877.
[34] Dallas *Daily Herald*, August 19, 1877.
[35] Galveston *News*, February 25, 1878.
[36] *Frontier Echo*, Jacksboro, March 8, 1878, quoting the Houston *Telegram*.

notices were left swinging from trees along the Clear Fork of the Brazos. Often the bodies bore placards advertising them for what they were.

The Fort Griffin night riders went into action early in 1876. On the night of April 9, they caught a man in the act of stealing a horse and promptly dangled him from a pecan tree. Below his swaying body they left a pick and shovel for the convenience of anyone who might wish to dig a grave and put out of sight the gruesome spectacle. "So far, so good," wrote a local newspaper correspondent. "As long as the committee strings up the right parties, it has the well wishes of every lover of tranquillity."[37]

That was a busy spring for the Fort Griffin vigilantes. They engaged in a gun battle with four members of a band of horse thieves who had been operating between Fort Griffin and Fort Dodge. After shooting two, they captured the others and hanged them immediately. On the night of April 20, they took from the jail a fifth member of this band, who had been arrested by the town marshal. They hanged him from a tree on the Clear Fork and pinned to his clothing a card that read:

> Horse Thief No. 5 that killed and scalped that boy for Indian sign. Shall horse thieves rules the country? He will have company soon.[38]

He did have company, on the night of May 5, when the night horsemen saved near-by Eastland County the expense of a trial. They strung up, three miles from Fort Griffin, a man whom Eastland officials wanted for horse theft.[39] Then, on the night of June 2, they took two horse thieves from the Albany jail and hanged them along near-by Hubbard Creek, about a quarter of a mile from the courthouse.[40]

Two years later the Fort Griffin vigilantes dealt with a man who had served their county as sheriff. He was John M. Larn,

37 Dallas *Daily Herald,* April 23, 1876.

38 *Frontier Echo,* April 28, 1876.

39 *Ibid.,* May 12, 1876.

40 Denison *Daily News,* June 4, 1876; *Frontier Echo,* June 9, 1876.

an Alabaman who had come as a fugitive from Colorado about 1870 and had obtained work as a cow hand. He had married his boss' daughter and had started a cattle brand of his own. Elected sheriff of Shackelford County, he took office on April 18, 1876.[41] As sheriff he served acceptably at first but soon began to arouse suspicion. After he took a contract to provide the military garrison at Fort Griffin three beeves a day, cowmen noticed that, while Larn's herd remained the same size, losses from neighboring herds were regularly three a day.

Larn resigned as sheriff in March, 1877, and was succeeded by William Cruger.[42] Cattle continued to disappear, and two of Larn's cow hands vanished without explanation. Finally a neighboring nester reported that the hides of stolen cattle had been dumped into a deep water hole in the Clear Fork near Larn's slaughter pen. Some of these were fished out with grappling hooks. Soon afterward Larn and his partner shot and wounded the inquisitive farmer.[43]

Handed a warrant for Larn's arrest, Sheriff Cruger summoned a posse and rode off at night to his predecessor's ranch near Camp Cooper in adjoining Throckmorton County. He captured Larn at his cowpen and soon had him in the primitive jail in Albany. To prevent a rumored rescue by Larn's friends, he had his deputy, Henry Herron, take the prisoner to Charley Rainboldt's blacksmith shop and have shackles riveted to his legs.[44] He also posted a guard at the jail.

But the Fort Griffin vigilantes, too, had heard of the plans of Larn's associates to get him free. Hurriedly they saddled their horses, put on slickers and bandannas, picked up their Winchesters, and rode for Albany. Arriving before midnight on June 24, they overpowered the jail guards and found their man.

[41] Minutes of Shackelford County Commissioners Court, I, 99.

[42] *Ibid.*, I, 112.

[43] V. E. Van Riper, letter dated Headquarters Co. B, Frontier Battalion, Camp Sibley, June 15, 1878, to Major John B. Jones; G. W. Campbell, letter dater Fort Griffin, June 16, 1878, to Major John B. Jones, Adjutant General's papers, Austin.

[44] J. R. Webb, "Henry Herron, Pioneer and Peace Officer During Fort Griffin Days," *West Texas Historical Association Year Book*, Vol. XX (October, 1944), 32, quoting a statement made to him by Herron.

A volley of rifle shots quickly ended Larn's career. On their way home, the horsemen may have attended to another chore; for the next morning the body of an unknown man was found swinging from a tree on the outskirts of Fort Griffin.[45] In a little more than two years, the Fort Griffin committee had done away with nearly a score of stock thieves.

Vigilante justice cropped up almost everywhere in the western plains and in the mountains. At Fort Union, New Mexico, in 1872, a group of stern civilians induced officers at the post to turn over two outlaws who had killed a cavalry sergeant. They promptly put these culprits out of the way. At Albuquerque, late in 1883, citizens unable to find a convenient tree or lamppost took their prisoner to a railway flatcar and used a pile of ties to build a scaffold.[46]

In Arizona, Yuma had a vigilance committee as early as 1866. On July 3, 1873, Phoenix citizens seized Mariano Tisnado, who had stolen a cow from a widow; and soon he was dangling from the nearest tree. In the same town six years later, a committee of thirty men took from the jail one morning two killers—one who had knifed a saloonkeeper and one who had shot a ranchman. They strung both from cottonwood trees in front of the town hall. At Tucson, on August 8, 1873, a committee of public safety hanged four murderers from a scaffold built near the door of the jail. In 1879, vigilantes at St. Johns executed two men accused of murder. In the following year, Globe citizens took from their jail two men who had robbed an express messenger of $10,000 in gold in the Pinal Mountains and had killed the messenger and a Globe doctor who had pursued them. While a church bell tolled the death knell, the vigilantes took these outlaws to a near-by sycamore and let them stretch hemp.

Arizona necktie parties continued into the eighties. On the evening of December 8, 1883, an outlaw band led by John Heath robbed a Bisbee store and shot up the town, killing three persons. Posses caught the bandits, who were tried in Tombstone.

[45] Galveston *News*, June 26, 1878; *Frontier Echo*, July 5, 1878; Don H. Biggers, *Shackelford County Sketches;* Edgar Rye, *The Quirt and the Spur*, 99–115; Sophie A. Poe, *Buckboard Days*, 86–96.

[46] Fort Worth *Gazette*, December 11, 1883.

Five were sentenced to hang, but Heath was let off with a verdict of second-degree murder and a sentence of life imprisonment. Dissatisfied with this outcome, men from Bisbee and Tombstone stormed the jail on February 22, 1884, took Heath from his cell, and hanged him from a telegraph pole. Holbrook had a similar bit of excitement in 1885 when citizens captured two men wanted for killing and had them test a pair of ropes.[47]

Colorado vigilance committees engaged in many house cleanings. Near Sheridan, on the Kansas Pacific Railroad, one group hanged four men from a trestle bridge. To the north, on the Denver and Cheyenne road, another had seven culprits do strangulation jigs in a single night.

In April, 1859, pioneer Denver citizens crossed Cherry Creek to Auraria to join in a people's court. They helped hang, from a big cottonwood, John Stoefel, who had confessed to shooting a fellow prospector for his gold dust. In March, 1860, another people's assembly tried, condemned, and hanged from a scaffold Moses Young, who had killed a man on the west bank of Cherry Creek. Next to die by a vote of Denver citizens was Marcus Gridler, who, in June, 1860, had killed a fellow emigrant. Later in that month a freighter was sentenced to hang for killing one of his companions but escaped by bribing a guard.[48]

The most celebrated hanging of Denver's early days was that of James Gordon, who in 1860 had brutally slain a man who had declined to drink with him in a saloon. After escaping pursuers several times, Gordon was captured in southern Kansas and was taken to Leavenworth. There he barely escaped being hanged. He was returned to Denver on September 28 and was tried promptly and fairly by a people's court. The jury's verdict of death was applauded by hundreds who had assembled for the occasion. On October 6, Gordon was hanged before a crowd of several thousand, kept in strict order by mounted Jefferson Rangers.[49]

[47] William M. Breakenridge, *Helldorado,* 85–86, 195–97; Ward R. Adams, *History of Arizona,* 102–331; Frank C. Lockwood, *Pioneer Days in Arizona,* 267–71, 273–75, 333.

[48] *Rocky Mountain News,* Denver, January 6, 1878.

[49] *Ibid.,* September 25, 28, 29, 30, October 1, 2, 5, 6, 8, 1860; Alice Polk Hill, *Tales of the Colorado Pioneers,* 57–61.

On December 21, 1860, the Denver people's court conducted the last of its five hangings. This time the noose held Patrick Watters, an Irish farm hand who had shot his employer for his money.[50] In later years vigilance committees executed several other culprits, dangling some of them from the Blake Street bridge over Cherry Creek.[51]

In the eighteen sixties most of the camps in the Colorado mountains had miners' courts like those formed a decade earlier in California. Many of the valley towns had similar people's courts. An early historian observed that these courts "were about the only ones which were thoroughly respected and thoroughly obeyed." He added that their proceedings were open and orderly and that "they approached the dignity of a regularly constituted tribunal. They were always presided over by a magistrate, either a probate judge or a justice of the peace. The prisoner had counsel and could call witnesses if the latter were within reach."[52]

Committees of vigilance remained active in many communities, however. The committee at Pueblo was especially effective in the middle sixties and hanged several desperadoes. A dozen years later a similar group cleaned Leadville of its worst outlaws. In 1879, Leadville, at the height of its silver boom, was a lawless mining center of about 35,000 population. Fnding one to three or four dead men in the alleys back of the saloons and dance halls in the morning was nothing unusual. Thugs took over mining claims by intimidation. Others set up toll stations on Ten Mile Road to levy tribute from travelers. So many highwaymen operated along the stage roads that the express companies refused to haul bullion or coin.

Finally, in November, local officers jailed a bandit leader, Edward Frodsham. With several other brigands, Frodsham had engaged in a gun battle to get possession of a lot on which a house was being built. The outlaws had driven off the workmen,

[50] *Rocky Mountain News,* December 6, 19, 20, 21, 1860.

[51] William Littlebury Kuykendall, *Frontier Days,* 125–26.

[52] W. B. Vickers, editor, *History of the Arkansas Valley, Colorado,* 32; Thomas Maitland Marshall, editor, *Early Records of Gilpin County, Colorado, 1859–1861.*

wounding two, and had pulled down the timbers already in place. On the next Saturday night, the fifteenth, a Leadville barber, Carl Bockhouse, was returning to his home on State Street when he was held up by two armed footpads. As he raised his arms, he fired at these bandits. He killed one and wounded the other, young Patrick Stewart, who was captured quickly and jailed.

These outrages were too much for some of the leading citizens of Leadville. Quietly they began preparations to take the law into their own hands. Late Wednesday night the vigilantes posted guards about the jail. A little after one o'clock the next morning they captured the deputy sheriff. They forced him to let them into the jail, where they quickly found Frodsham and Stewart. Taking these gunmen from their cells, they hanged them from the rafters of a kitchen being attached to the jail. After daybreak the curious found on Frodsham's body a note of warning to footpads, lot jumpers, and other criminals. Some of them were listed by name. That day about four hundred of the lawless men of Leadville left town.[53]

Similar action marked the early history of other Colorado towns. At Del Norte one night, vigilantes took two cattle rustlers from the jail; but the pair managed to escape. Dismayed, the visitors shot up the town, accidentally killing one of their own men and wounding several. On the main street of Durango, citizens once engaged in an hour's gun battle with cattle rustlers and claim jumpers. At Ouray, in January, 1884, a committee hanged a man and his wife who were accused of having cruelly murdered their adopted daughter. Elected officers gradually took over the task of keeping order, but as late as 1889 three members of a Colorado band of cattle thieves were informally hanged.

Wyoming minute men were busy at like tasks. Cheyenne, which became a railhead for the winter of 1867–68, attracted so

[53] Leadville *Democrat*, November 14, 16, 20, 1879, January 3, 1880; Certificate of attendance at inquest on the deaths of Frodsham and Stewart, issued by John Law, coroner, to H. W. Gaw, November 20, 1879; *History of the Arkansas Valley, Colorado,* 246–50; John Lord, *Frontier Dust,* 82–91; George F. Willison, *Here They Dug the Gold,* (revised edition), 224–38.

many bandits and assassins that honest citizens had to act. They drove out three thieves in January, 1868, and, later in the same month, caught three gunmen at Dale City, forty miles to the west, and launched them into eternity. On the night of March 20, Cheyenne vigilantes hanged two men, a killer and a horse thief. Others were summarily executed in the next few months.[54]

At Laramie, the next Union Pacific railhead to the west, citizens hanged a young ruffian on the night of August 27, 1868. But as the criminal element remained in control of the town, robbing even in daylight and killing any who resisted, further action had to be taken. A new committee was formed, with more than four hundred members. It was led by Major Thomas B. Sears, a Civil War veteran. On the night of October 18, these citizens, all well armed, met at the railroad roundhouse. Separating into squads, they moved on the saloons and dance halls. The next morning Laramie residents found three desperadoes hanging from crossbeams of a building under construction, while a fourth dangled from a telegraph pole. They also discovered that more than forty other undesirables had hurriedly left town.[55]

Summary action was no less essential in rural areas of Wyoming. In the timber about a mile from Fort Laramie, one night, a committee took from a stagecoach two highwaymen who were being transported from Cheyenne to Deadwood. They hanged the pair from a convenient tree. The most notorious villains in the state were Dutch Charley and George Parrot, better known as Big Nose George. Detected in an attempt to derail and rob a Union Pacific train in 1878, this pair had killed two pursuing officers near the head of Rattlesnake Creek. Later they were arrested in Montana and returned to Wyoming.

Their separate homecomings were well attended. At Carbon, masked men took Dutch Charley off the train and strung

[54] Cheyenne *Leader*, January 11, March 21, 1868; Cheyenne *Argus*, March 22, 1868; J. H. Triggs, *History of Cheyenne and Northern Wyoming*, 24–27; Hubert Howe Bancroft, *History of Nevada, Colorado, and Wyoming, 1540-1888*, 738; Charles Griffin Coutant, "History of Wyoming," *Annals of Wyoming*, Vol. 13, No. 2 (April, 1941), 146–51.

[55] J. H. Triggs, *History and Directory of Laramie City, Wyoming Territory*, 5–15; Charles Griffin Coutant, manuscript notes on the history of Wyoming, Wyoming State Library, Cheyenne.

him from a telegraph pole. Big Nose George, captured later, was tried in a statutory court. He pleaded guilty and, on December 15, 1880, was sentenced to be hanged on April 2, 1881. But after he assaulted his jailer and tried to escape, he was taken by citizens and hanged from a telegraph pole at Rawlins. Dr. John E. Osborne, a young railroad physician at Rawlins, later governor, removed the skin from Parrot's breast and had it tanned and made into a pair of shoes.[56]

Another occasion for informal action came in 1883. A vagabond who had been given a ride by two travelers in a wagon took an ax to his sleeping benefactors while the party was encamped on Crow Creek near Camp Carlin, on the outskirts of Cheyenne. After killing one and almost killing the other, whom he thought dead, he took the wagon and team and drove into northern Colorado. There he was captured and taken back to Cheyenne. Without opposition from the sheriff, vigilantes battered the killer's cell door, took him out, and strung him from the crossbar of a telegraph pole a block from the jail.[57]

In Idaho an influx of desperadoes who stole horses and cattle, held up stagecoaches, and murdered miners and others believed to be carrying money, brought corrective committees into action. As in Montana, the outlaws often were given informal trials; but sometimes these took place before the culprits were taken into custody.[58] After a stagecoach robbery in October, 1863, three highwaymen were taken from the Lewiston jail and hanged.

The Payette vigilance committee, formed to rid its region of horse thieves, adopted three kinds of punishment; banishment, horsewhipping, and death. One act of this group was to send away, on a day's notice, the local agent of a band that had been

[56] Cheyenne *Leader,* August 20, 1881; Kuykendall, *op. cit.,* 227–28; John W. Meldrum, "The Taming of Big Nose George and Others," *Union Pacific Magazine,* November, 1926; John E. Osborne, statement written September 12, 1928, and published in the Rawlins *Republican,* September 27, 1928; Mrs. Charles Ellis, "History of Carbon, Wyoming's First Mining Town," *Annals of Wyoming,* Vol. VIII, No. 4 (April, 1932), 639–41.

[57] Charles A. Guernsey, *Wyoming Cowboy Days,* 89–90.

[58] Cornelius J. Brosnan, *History of the State of Idaho* (revised edition), 175.

making bogus gold dust. It cleared the Payette Valley of horse thieves in three months. In Boise a similar committee, formed in 1864, held several necktie parties, with salutary effects.[59]

In the spring of 1866 these committees went after an Idaho band of horse thieves, highwaymen, and killers. The leader of these outlaws was David Updyke, whose political influence had gained him the post of sheriff of Ada County. On April 3, one of Updyke's men killed a youth of nineteen who had testified against the band. On that night Boise vigilantes took the slayer from the Fort Boise guardhouse and hanged him. Updyke and another of his band fled from Boise on April 12, but were followed by citizens who captured them on the Rocky Bar road. The next morning the captors hanged Updyke in a shed and dangled his companion from a sturdy tree.[60]

Crime that accompanied the building of the Oregon Short Line Railroad through Idaho in the early eighteen eighties gave rise to more vigilance. At one construction camp a pair of saloonkeepers, who had a habit of drugging and sandbagging customers whose money pockets bulged, were hanged from a railroad bridge. Later another liquor dealer who robbed and killed one of the workmen was hoisted to a scaffold made by raising two wagon tongues.[61]

In Nevada, vigilance groups were formed on almost every occasion when officials and courts were not available or were unable to keep crime in check. Hamilton and Treasure City had protective associations for several years, and the frequency of robberies on the road to White Pine led Egan men to join in the Egan Canyon Property Protection Society. These bands had written rules and regulations. Aurora provided, early in 1864, a most noteworthy example of a Nevada committee's work.

There a gang of criminals plotted to kill W. R. Johnson, who kept a station on the Carson road. They were incensed because he refused to let them know the whereabouts of a respectable citizen who had killed a horse thief, one of their confederates.

59 George W. Fuller, *A History of the Pacific Northwest*, 283–86.

60 Langford, *op. cit.*, II, 340–53; Thomas Donaldson, *Idaho of Yesterday*, 165–67.

61 Charles Shirley Walgamott, *Six Decades Back*, 150–53.

When their intended victim came to town to sell some potatoes, they decoyed him into a trap where hidden gunmen killed him and left his body where he fell. This murder aroused Aurora people, who had lost about thirty of their number by violence in the preceding three years. They quickly formed a Citizens' Protective Union and began rounding up the outlaws. Some of the brigands fled on horseback, but four of the ringleaders were jailed.

As the vigilantes began building a scaffold in front of the Armory, someone notified Governor James W. Nye in Carson City. The Governor wired an inquiry to Bob Howland, who recently had been made United States marshal. Howland replied, "Everything quiet in Aurora. Four men to be hanged in fifteen minutes." At midday of February 9, the vigilantes marched to the jail and took the four bandits without any trouble. At the firing of a signal gun, they hanged them before a throng of onlookers.[62]

Nevada had several other informal executions that year. On August 10, about three o'clock in the morning, members of the Dayton vigilance committee bound and gagged the sheriff, took from one of the cells a man accused of killing in a bloody fight on the Truckee River, and hanged him in the jail yard. Later in the year a killer was caught and hanged near the sink of the Carson. In July of the next year, a horse thief who was accused of murder was taken from the sheriff of Lincoln County, was quickly tried by his captors, and was dangled from a timber run out from the upper window of a building[63] At Virginia City and elsewhere in Nevada, sudden deaths from hemp fever continued, on occasions, for another ten or twelve years

In the Pacific Coast states, committees of vigilance were popular from the days of the California forty-niners. Residents along the Walla Walla River formed a vigilance association in the winter of 1864–65. By the last of the following April, they had hanged six horse thieves and cattle rustlers and had caused others to leave. On June 9, this committee addressed a letter to a

[62] Bancroft, *Popular Tribunals,* I, 602–609; Richard G. Lillard, *Desert Challenge,* 203–205.

[63] Bancroft, *Popular Tribunals,* I, 611–13.

Walla Walla newspaper, notifying the people that it had revised its form of organization. The change was aimed to enable the group "to act more expeditiously and with greater certainty in ferreting out the perpetrators of crime."[64]

Any administration of justice as informal and as speedy as that of most of the vigilance committees of the West was bound to be mistaken and unjust in some cases. These informal bands were unfair in that often they allowed accused persons little, if any, opportunity to defend themselves or to produce witnesses who, in a few instances, might have cleared them. In some cases the informal courts executed men who were innocent—at least, innocent of the particular crimes charged against them.

Yet these instances were only a small fraction of the total. As a rule, the vigilantes, especially those in organized groups, got out their ropes only in cases in which guilt was clear. Most of the committees disbanded quickly when law-enforcement officers and formal courts became able to preserve order and to protect lives and property. They had served their purpose in discouraging crime in the interim before statutory law caught up with the frontier. In much of the West, that catching up came in slow and halting steps.

[64] Walla Walla *Statesman,* June 15, 1866.

ARMS OF THE LAW

11. The Texas Rangers

> The Texas Ranger can ride like a Mexican, trail like an Indian, shoot like a Tennessean, and fight like a very devil.—John S. Ford, as quoted by Walter Prescott Webb in the Dallas *Morning News*, March 20, 1921

ARMED with new Colt five-shooters the Republic of Texas had bought for them, Captain John C. Hays and fifteen of his Texas Rangers set out from their camp near San Antonio. On that first day of June, 1844, they rode northward through the wooded hills to scout for Indians who had been committing many depredations. After the Rangers had gone almost as far as Llano and had found signs of Indians, they circled back. They were following instructions made cautious by negotiations then in progress.

While the Rangers were encamped near a creek about fifty miles above Seguin, several Indians appeared and tried to draw Hays out. They pretended to be alarmed at the presence of the Rangers, but the Captain surmised that their intentions were hostile and was too wary to be caught in a trap. He ordered his men to saddle their horses and to prepare for a fight. The Indians used many stratagems to decoy the Rangers into the timber but did not succeed. Hays suspected that warriors were hidden in the woods. His guess proved correct. There was a large band of warriors—Comanches, Wacos, and Mexicans.

After seeing that they could not trick the Rangers, the Indians, who numbered between sixty and seventy, rode boldly out into the prairie and dared the Rangers to fight. As his men wanted to accept the challenge, although outnumbered more than four to one, Hays ordered a charge. After firing their rifles, the Rangers did not stop to reload. They closed in with their five-shooting pistols, which had telling effect as the battle seesawed over three miles of prairie.

The third round from the five-shooters broke the ranks of the Indians. But back they came in several desperate countercharges with arrows and lances. These weapons were no match for the Rangers' guns. When the battle ended, the Indians left twenty warriors dead and had between twenty and thirty wounded. The Rangers had lost one man and had four wounded. Two days later, four Indians appeared on the battleground. The Rangers killed three of them, raising the number of enemy dead to twenty-three.[1]

Having odds against them never deterred the Texas Rangers, whether their foes were Indian marauders, Mexican cattle thieves, or gringo desperadoes. In a period when banditry was commonplace and pioneer life had many hazards, this frontier fighting outfit was one of the longest arms of the law. While the scope of the Rangers was limited to a single state, the vast area of that domain gave them a line of patrol that extended from the mouth of the Río Grande nearly halfway to the Canadian border. As the fringe of settlement pushed westward, the Ranger companies moved in its van to clear the country of predatory bands.

The Rangers were among the earliest and most effective agencies that brought statutory law to the southwestern frontier. Riding into a community where outlaws defied the local sheriff or marshal, a small detail of Rangers could often restore order in a few days. While lawbreakers feared them, honest citizens had the utmost confidence in their ability. In the two decades that followed the Civil War, the Rangers helped immeasurably in making vigilante action no longer necessary.

The Ranger organization had its beginning early in Texas history. While Texas was still a part of Mexico, the Spanish governor, José Trespalacios, received an appeal from the colonists for protection against the Indians. He ordered the recruiting of

[1] Captain John C. Hays, report dated San Antonio, June 16, 1844, in *Texas National Register,* December 14, 1844; John C. Caperton, "Sketch of Col. John C. Hays, Texas Ranger," manuscript in the Bancroft Library, University of California, Berkeley, transcripts in the University of Texas library and the library of the late Dr. William E. Howard, Dallas.

a sergeant and fourteen men. These defenders, who began their service in May, 1823, were stationed near the mouth of the Colorado River. Although poorly equipped and unpaid, they gave effective help. Stephen F. Austin, head of the principal colony, begged General Felipe de la Garza to pay them and to continue their services. Later in that year, Austin announced that he would hire ten men, at his own expense, to serve as Rangers.[2]

In 1826, a band of Tawakonis swooped down on the Colorado River settlements to steal horses but was repulsed. Soon afterward, Austin called a meeting of representatives from six districts to form a plan of defense. The outcome was an agreement to keep twenty to thirty mounted Rangers in service all the time. Each landowner was required to serve a month or to provide a substitute.[3]

As the colonists prepared to break away from Mexican rule, they established a more formally organized corps of Texas Rangers in 1835. In October of that year, a council of the Texans created a temporary corps to guard the frontier. In the following month a larger group, called "the consultation," approved this action and provided for a permanent battalion of 150 Rangers, to serve in addition to the regular army and the militia. These Rangers provided their own horses, saddles, and blankets and received $1.25 a day.[4] With the Indians temporarily pacified in advance and the revolution lasting only a brief time, the Rangers had little opportunity to distinguish themselves in this overturn. One detachment, however, captured three Mexican ships.[5]

During the period of the Republic, the Texas Rangers began the long series of exploits that gave them a global reputation. In protecting the thinly settled frontier against marauders, they engaged in many clashes with Indians and in some with Mexicans. Savages who came to burn cabins or to steal horses soon

[2] Eugene C. Barker, *The Life of Stephen F. Austin,* 102–103.

[3] *Ibid.,* 165–67.

[4] Eugene C. Barker, editor, "Journal of the Permanent Council," *Southwestern Historical Quarterly,* Vol. VII (April, 1904), 249–62; H. P. N. Gammel, compiler, *The Laws of Texas,* I, 513, 526–27, 543–44, 924–25.

[5] Henderson Yoakum, *History of Texas,* II, 180–81.

learned that the Rangers were more than a match for them and tried to keep out of their way. The Rangers were especially effective after they began using the new Samuel Colt revolvers, whose value they were among the earliest to appreciate. Colt called his first successful gun the "Texas" and, about 1842, named an improved military model the "Walker," in honor of Captain Samuel H. Walker of the Texas Rangers, who had suggested some of the changes. The Rangers gave the new revolver the name of six-shooter.[6]

Among the more celebrated Ranger leaders of this period was John C. Hays, better known as Jack Hays. He was a young Tennessean who had settled in San Antonio and had joined the Rangers in time to participate in the battle against a band of Comanches on Plum Creek, August 12, 1840. Before that year ended, he was made a captain. In an 1841 encounter, near the mouth of Uvalde Canyon, he singlehandedly slew ten warriors. For the skill and daring he showed in many encounters, he was promoted to the rank of major.

When several Indian chiefs came to San Antonio to make a treaty, one of them asked Hays why he so often went out alone, running great risks, in places where he could expect no aid. The answer came from Chief Flacco, a celebrated Lipan warrior and an ally of the Texans: "Me and Blue Wing not afraid to go to hell together. Captain Jack, great brave, not afraid to go to hell by himself."[7]

Another romantic figure of the early Ranger companies was a young Virginian, William A. A. (Big Foot) Wallace, who served under Hays and later became a captain. Big Foot was a gigantic fellow with a sense of humor and a fund of anecdotes that made him welcome at any campfire. In and out of the Ranger force, he had a long life as a frontiersman, escaping enemy bullets while he sent many a marauder to the happy hunting ground.[8]

[6] Walter Prescott Webb, "The American Revolver and the West," *Scribner's Magazine,* Vol. LXXXI (February, 1927), 177–78.

[7] Caperton, *loc. cit.*

[8] John C. Duval, *The Adventures of Big-Foot Wallace;* Stanley Vestal, *Bigfoot Wallace.*

Captain L. H. McNelly
No odds deterred him

N. H. Rose Collection

Then, as later, the Texas Rangers wore no uniforms. They dressed in buckskin, corduroy, or khaki, with leather boots and large felt hats. Away from settlements for long periods and forced to sleep in the open much of the time, they had to be resourceful. Of the Ranger's equipment and manner of living in these early days, John C. Caperton, an associate of Jack Hays, wrote:

> Each man was armed with a rifle, a pistol, and a knife. With a Mexican blanket tied behind his saddle and a small wallet in which he carried salt and ammunition and perhaps a little *panola* or parched corn, spiced and sweetened—a great allayer of thirst—and tobacco, he was equipped for a month. The little body of men, unencumbered by baggage wagons or pack trains, moved as lightly over the prairie as the Indians did and lived as they did, without tents, with a saddle for a pillow at night, blankets over them, and their feet to the fire. Depending wholly upon wild game for food, they sometimes found a scarcity and suffered the necessity for killing a horse for food, when all else failed.
>
> The men were splendid riders and used the Mexican saddle, improved somewhat by the Americans, and carried the Mexican *riata,* made of rawhide, the *cabrista,* a hair rope and the lariat, to rope horses. Rangers frequently were divided into small parties and sent to different points for special purposes. When they started after the Indians, if the force was large enough, they never went back until they caught them.[9]

In the war with Mexico, which closely followed the annexation of Texas by the United States, the Rangers performed so valiantly as scouts and guerrilla fighters that they were acclaimed throughout the land. General W. H. King declared that Colonel Jack Hays and his men were "not only the eyes and ears of General Taylor's army but its right and left arms as well."[10] Following the war, the Ranger force was virtually disbanded on the supposition that the federal government had taken over

9 Caperton, *loc. cit.*

10 Dudley G. Wooten, editor, *A Comprehensive History of Texas, 1685 to 1897,* II, 338.

responsibility for protecting the frontier. Some army posts were established along the Río Grande and in the Indian country. But the soldiers sent to man them were untrained in fighting Comanches, and often the cavalrymen were poorly mounted.

The result was a new outbreak of Indian raids and a deluge of petitions to Congress. "Give us one thousand Rangers," Sam Houston thundered in the Senate in 1858, "and we will be responsible for the defense of our frontier. Texas does not want regular troops. Withdraw them if you please."[11]

The army posts remained, but the gradually restored Rangers took over much of the work. They subdued the Indians, curbed Mexican cattle rustlers along the Río Grande, and captured desperadoes on the state's long frontier. Of the period between the Mexican and Civil Wars, General King wrote:

> Many lives were lost, many persons wounded unto death or made cripples for life, many carried into horrible captivity, much property destroyed, and thousands of horses, mules, and cattle driven off by robbers; but still the border kept moving onward and outward, and still the people kept closing upon it, while between these moving and movable frontiers and the outlying wilderness a small but bold and active band of Rangers kept a thin but determined line of defense.[12]

The driving of stolen cattle across the Río Grande in this period was by no means a one-way movement. Yet most of the rustlers in that region were Mexicans. One of the outstanding tasks of the Texas Rangers was to end the raiding of the red-bearded Juan L. Cortinas, a bandit leader who had been terrorizing the border. Cortinas, who sometimes signed his name Cortina, was the black sheep of his family. Although a man of striking appearance, unusual courage, and personal charm, he was a gambler and a horse thief. He plagued many ranchmen by stealing their stock.

[11] Sam Houston, speeches on the increase of the army, United States Senate, February 1, 25, 1858, *Congressional Globe*, Part I, 1857–58, 492–97, 873–75.

[12] Wooten, *op. cit.*, 342.

The most sensational exploit of Cortinas came in 1859, while he was living on his mother's ranch on the Texas side of the river near Brownsville. When he was in that town on July 13, the marshal, Robert Shears, arrested a drunken Mexican who had been a servant of Cortinas. The bandit leader objected to the marshal's unnecessary roughness, and the latter replied with an insult. Cortinas then shot Shears in the shoulder, took the prisoner from him, and galloped out of town. Early on the morning of September 22, he returned with a hundred men and killed three Americans and one Mexican. Some of his followers broke into the jail, released prisoners, and killed the jailer. Others took over Fort Brown, recently evacuated by United States troops.

With their town of more than two thousand in terrorized subjection to armed bandits, Brownsville people stayed behind closed doors. Finally Mexican army officers from across the river persuaded Cortinas to leave. He withdrew to his mother's ranch, where, on July 30, he issued a ringing proclamation that brought him many recruits. Some of the Mexicans believed that Cortinas was about to reannex Texas to their country. Meanwhile, Brownsville people suffered the humiliation of having to call regular Mexican troops from beyond the Río Grande to help civilian patrols protect their town.

A volunteer force known as the Brownsville Tigers set out, with two small cannons, to capture Cortinas. But about the time they arrived within gun range, they turned about and fled headlong for home, leaving their cannons for the bandit leader to capture. Cortinas continued to raid at will until a small force of Texas Rangers under the command of Major John S. (Rip) Ford caught up with him on December 27. In that day's battle the galloping Rangers killed sixteen Mexicans and captured two artillery pieces without losing any of their own men, although sixteen were wounded.

The Rangers continued to pursue Cortinas, even on Mexican soil. Although they did not capture him, they depleted his force and made the Texas towns safe from his terrorism. The Cortinas war had cost the lives of fifteen Americans and eighty friendly Mexicans, while the bandit was believed to have lost 151 men. Claims for American losses from his depredations exceeded one third of a million dollars. In Mexico, Cortinas became a brigadier general and later was governor of Tamaulipas. He piled up a fortune and continued to sponsor raids on Texas ranches.[13]

The outbreak of the Civil War quickly depleted the Ranger companies, as nearly all the men sought more active combat. Many of them achieved high places on the roster of Confederate heroes. After the war, Texas' carpetbag governor, Edmund J. Davis, established a state police force in the summer of 1870. This body, which operated for nearly three years, was unpopular because it was charged with enforcing Reconstruction measures. It had little effect in keeping order on the frontier and often was accused of killing prisoners on the pretense that they were trying to escape. Noting that anyone who killed a state policeman was looked upon as a hero, the Austin *Statesman* viewed the existence of this force as an incentive to crime.[14]

With Indian marauders and white desperadoes on the loose again, the legislature brought the Rangers back by creating two new frontier forces in 1874. Both were made up of men who took pride in the best Ranger traditions. One, a Frontier Battalion, gave its attention to the Indian country in the west. It was headed by Major John B. Jones, a quiet but efficient leader, who was effective in punishing redskin raiders and in settling several bloody feuds. The other, called a "Special Force of Rangers," was entrusted with the suppression of cattle thieving and other banditry on the Mexican border. Its commander was Captain L. H. McNelly, thirty years of age, a Civil War veteran who had served in the state police.

McNelly soon found his hands full. While stationed on the Río Grande, he received, on the morning of November 18, 1875,

[13] John Salmon Ford, "Memoirs," manuscript, IV, 783–809; 36 Cong., 1 sess., *House Exec. Doc. 52*, Serial No. 1,050, *Difficulties on the Southwestern Frontier*, 70–72; 45 Cong., 2 sess., *House Report No. 701*, Serial No. 1,824, *Report and Accompanying Documents of the Committee on Foreign Affairs on the Relation of the United States With Mexico;* Frank C. Pierce, *Brief History of the Río Grande Valley;* Walter Prescott Webb, *The Texas Rangers*, 173–74. Of all the books on the Rangers, Professor Webb's is by far the most comprehensive, the most reliable, and the most useful.

[14] Austin *Daily Statesman*, March 30, 1873.

a dispatch from Río Grande City. The message said that raiders had crossed the river with a herd of cattle near Las Cuevas. This was the ranch of a notorious rustler, Juan Flores. McNelly immediately left for the scene and sent word for his thirty men to follow. When he arrived at noon, he found three troops of United States cavalrymen. The soldiers were debating the safety of crossing after the thieves, who had driven about 250 head of longhorns to the Mexican side on the preceding evening. The rustlers fired over the river at the soldiers every time one showed himself.

Captain McNelly urged a crossing; but the army officers wanted to await further orders, in spite of the fact that they already had an order to follow cattle thieves into Mexico. McNelly said that if they wanted someone to take the lead, he would do so as soon as his men came up. The Rangers arrived at about nine in the evening. Although extremely tired, they were eager for a clash with the rustlers. The army officers agreed to cover the return of the Rangers and to try to rescue them if they were besieged.

At one the next morning McNelly and his men started across. The river was so boggy that they found it almost impossible to get their horses across. After pulling five of the mounts up the opposite bank, they decided to leave the others and to go on afoot. Killing four pickets at the Cucharas ranch on their way, McNelly's men marched to the Cuevas headquarters about three miles from the river.

When he saw the long line of Mexican soldiers he faced—about 100 cavalrymen and 150 to 200 foot soldiers—McNelly feared he never would see his loved ones again. Yet he knew that if he turned back, not one of his men could cross the river alive. So, in a gallant bluff, he marched his Rangers steadily ahead until they were within one hundred yards of the Mexican line, and then retired as if trying to draw the enemy into a trap.

Daybreak showed that the army troops had not followed the Rangers. The thirty Texans stood their ground against repeated attacks by the Mexican troops. In response to a call from McNelly, thirty United States soldiers were sent across the river during the day. But they went back in the evening, saying that the Mexicans would make a night attack and could not be repulsed by so small a force.

The Mexicans were no more eager than the United States soldiers for a real battle. About dark they sent a flag of truce to the Rangers and ordered them to leave Mexican territory. McNelly replied that he would not leave until the soldiers delivered the rustlers and the stolen cattle. When the officers promised to carry out his demands through the proper channels, he said that this meant never. He assured them that he would take the cattle and the thieves.

Next the Mexicans begged for a truce for the night. McNelly granted this on the condition that they would bring in two horses and a gun that some of his men had lost in the fighting that morning. Delivery of these was promised for the next morning. Captain McNelly then allowed the Mexicans to remove the body of one of their officers, who had been killed in one of the morning charges.

During this discussion, McNelly had ten of his little company lined behind him. The others were stationed under the river bank. Then Mexicans had more than two hundred soldiers within a hundred yards and had three or four hundred in reserve.

The next morning the Mexicans had what looked like eight or nine hundred men, but they dared not attack the thirty Rangers. The Texans held their ground without help from the soldiers across the river. The major in command there received that day a telegram from the colonel in command at Fort Brown. "If McNelly is attacked by Mexican forces on Mexican soil," it said, "do not render him any assistance."

In the evening McNelly notified the Mexicans that unless they delivered the stolen cattle and the rustlers within an hour, he would resume hostilities. Within forty minutes they sent two commissioners to his camp with a promise to meet his demands. The Rangers recrossed the Río Grande that night. The next day the Mexicans delivered sixty-five of the stolen beeves, the first ever returned. They had caught one thief, they reported, and had killed him while he was trying to escape.[15] One band of

[15] Captain L. H. McNelly, report to Adjutant General William Steele,

Mexican cattle rustlers had learned to keep out of the way of the Texas Rangers.

For the Rangers the latter eighteen seventies brought many daring exploits. Among the more spectacular of these was Lieutenant John B. Armstrong's singlehanded encounter with one of the state's most wanton killers, John Wesley Hardin. Accused of more than a score of murders, Wes Hardin had a price of four thousand dollars on his head after he had killed a deputy sheriff, Charles Webb, in Comanche on May 26, 1874. Three years later, Lieutenant Armstrong, then recuperating from an accidental pistol wound and using a cane, obtained a special assignment to work on the Hardin case. He had a Dallas detective, John Duncan, assigned to help him.

On hearing that Hardin was living in Alabama under an assumed name, Armstrong went there in August, 1877, taking Duncan along. He was told that the desperado had just gone to Pensacola, Florida. Without waiting for the Texas warrants he had requested, he and Duncan followed. Armstrong learned of Hardin's whereabouts and plans, and then stopped at Pensacola Junction, eight miles from the city. There he engaged local officers in a plan to intercept the bad man on his return.

When Hardin's train pulled in, on the evening of August 23, Armstrong saw the desperado sitting by an open window in the smoking car. He quickly told the local officers to approach Hardin by boarding through the rear door and instructed Duncan to grab the gunman's arm through the window. The lieutenant, still using a cane, entered the car by its forward door. Inside, he faced not only Hardin but four of his friends. Worse, he faced them alone, since neither Duncan nor the local men gave any help.

As Armstrong entered the car, Hardin noticed the six-shooter in his hand, a Colt .45 with a seven-inch barrel. He recognized this at once as a model used on the Texas frontier. Armstrong

November 22, 1875, Adjutant General's papers, Austin; McNelly, letter to his wife, dated Brownsville, Texas, November 29, 1875, in the collection of the late Dr. William E. Howard, Dallas; Galveston *News*, December 12, 1875; manuscript written much later by one of McNelly's men, William Callicott, for Walter Prescott Webb and published in his book, *The Texas Rangers*, 260–78.

ordered the men to surrender, but the desperado reached for his own gun, which caught in his suspenders. One of Hardin's companions put a bullet through the Ranger's hat and received in return a shot in the heart. After jumping through a window and running a few steps, he fell dead.

Armstrong grabbed Hardin's gun and kicked the killer back into his seat. With his six-shooter, he gave him a blow on the head that kept him quiet for two hours. Then he disarmed the other three and added their weapons to his belt. One Ranger had won over five outlaws. After technical delays in Alabama, Armstrong brought Hardin back to Texas. There he was tried, convicted, and sent to prison.[16]

In the following year another bandit, more colorful if less deadly, pitted his skill against that of the Texas Rangers. This was Sam Bass, a young man who had run off from Indiana and had become a cow hand and teamster in Denton County. After acquiring a fleet quarter horse, he had turned to racing and gambling. He and a partner rode north with a herd of longhorns and, after selling the cattle, went on to Deadwood. There they lost their employers' money in games of chance. To recoup their losses, they joined a band of highwaymen, but without much luck. Bigger loot came when the group held up a Union Pacific train in Nebraska and took off $60,000 in gold. Back in Texas, Bass formed a band of his own. After robbing two stagecoaches, he held up four trains—all within thirty miles of Dallas—in the spring of 1878.

To capture Bass, a special company of Texas Rangers was formed in Dallas. This company, led by Captain Junius Peak, kept the outlaw on the run in the late spring and early summer and killed one of his men. But the leader eluded them. He avoided every trap until one of his associates betrayed him. Jim Murphy tipped off Major Jones in Austin that Bass was planning to rob a bank in the village of Round Rock, twenty miles

[16] Lieutenant John B. Armstrong, telegrams to Adjutant General William Steele, August, 1877, Adjutant General's papers, Austin; Galveston *News*, September 8, 1874; *Ibid.*, August 25, October 3, 7, 1877; John Wesley Hardin, *Life of John Wesley Hardin;* Thomas Ripley, *They Died With Their Boots On;* Webb, *The Texas Rangers*, 297–304.

Rangers with Mexican Prisoner
Captain John R. Hughes seated at right

Dallas Morning News

Border Patrol
Rangers on the Río Grande

Dallas Morning News

to the north. In a street battle there on July 19, one man was killed on each side and Bass was wounded by a Ranger bullet. Captured in the brush the next morning, he was brought back to Round Rock. There he died on the following day, his twenty-seventh birthday.[17]

In that turbulent decade, the Rangers often had to strengthen the hands of local officers who were unable to cope with vendettas, range wars, mob action, or bandit depredations. In 1878, after a San Saba attorney had killed a saloonkeeper in a fight over local option, the county judge appealed for a detachment of Rangers. "The lives of the officers of San Saba County are hanging by a thread," he wrote. "Delay would be fatal." Two days later Lieutenant G. W. Arrington arrived to camp in the courthouse and to calm the excited community.[18]

Farther west, other desperadoes were on the prowl. In the spring of 1880 the thinly settled Pecos River and Big Bend regions, much of them mountainous and desolate, were terrorized by a band of outlaws who stole horses and held up crossroads stores. Pleas to the Governor and the Ranger headquarters brought to Fort Stockton on June 6 a squad of ten Rangers from Company D. On the night of July 1, six Rangers began scouting the rough country to the south. Sergeant Ed A. Sieker was in command. On the third they discovered four of the bandits heading for the mountains with pack horses bearing loot from their recent robberies.

The Rangers gave chase but were unable to get within gun range of the robbers, who sped for the protective cover of canyons and trees. Disabled mounts caused two of the Rangers to fall behind while the others continued the pursuit. Once in the wooded mountains, the outlaws were hidden; but Sieker and three of his men tracked them through a narrow canyon. In the mud of the canyon the Spanish ponies of the bandits made better time than the Rangers' larger horses, but finally the superior endurance of the latter enabled them to catch up.

[17] Wayne Gard, *Sam Bass.*

[18] Judge Jonathan Guion, letter to the Texas Rangers headquarters, May 23, 1878; Lieutenant G. W. Arrington, report to Major John B. Jones, March 25, 1878, Adjutant General's papers, Austin.

Soon the four Rangers wore down the ponies of the pursued men and forced the outlaws to stop and fight. The latter dismounted and made their stand on a bit of high ground on which boulders and bushes gave them cover. The Rangers opened fire from behind lower boulders, and the exchange of fusillades filled the air with smoke and echoes. One robber and one Ranger, George R. Bingham, were killed. Finally the three remaining Rangers rushed into the open with their six-shooters and made a direct charge on the desperadoes. In a few minutes, they captured and disarmed all three. That night, after sending a Mexican for a coroner, the Rangers camped by a brush fire in the mountains. They tied the prisoners with ropes and covered with blankets the two bodies.[19]

In 1883 and later the Rangers did much to put down fence cutting, but the fences that enclosed the western ranches were themselves a taming influence. Fenced pastures offered fewer opportunities for outlaws and thus lessened the need for many of the services the Rangers traditionally had given. Only occasionally were they called upon for the kind of fighting that had made their outfit world-famous. One such occasion arose in the fall of 1896, when an outlaw band with a hideout in the Glass Mountains was stealing horses from near-by ranches and was believed to be planning to rob a train.

Captain John R. Hughes, with two other Rangers, several cattlemen, and an expert trailer, traced the thieves to their lair. The captain and his men charged into the protected position at full speed. "We ran our horses almost to the top of the mountain," Captain Hughes reported, "when the fight was so hot that we dismounted. Here W. C. Combs got a bullet through his left ear. We drove them off the mountain top to the side, where two of them were killed." The Rangers recovered five stolen horses, and those bandits who got away did not return.[20]

19 Sergeant Ed A. Sieker, report to Captain Dan W. Roberts, embodied in report of Captain Roberts to Major John B. Jones, July 12, 1880, Adjutant General's papers, Austin; J. P. Cranke, article in Dallas *Morning News,* October 4, 1895; Dan W. Roberts, *Rangers and Sovereignty,* 111–15.

20 Captain John R. Hughes, report to Adjutant General W. H. Mabry, October 4, 1896, Adjutant General's papers, Austin.

One of the force's more popular officers of this period was Captain W. J. (Bill) McDonald. In addition to being as courageous as the next one, he had a flair for the dramatic. When, in 1895, Dallas people feared that a fight between Jim Corbett and Bob Fitzsimmons might be held in their city despite a law just passed to prevent it, the mayor appealed for a company of Rangers.

The next day, when Captain McDonald got off the train alone, the mayor was disappointed. "Where are the others?" he asked.

"Hell! ain't I enough?" was the response. "There ain't but one fight, is there?"[21]

In 1897 trouble came to a head in San Saba County, where forty-three killings had taken place in a decade. Most of these were attributed to a clandestine band of the county's lawless elements that pretended to vigilante functions. This organization, said to number three hundred, held monthly meetings at Buzzards' Water Hole, usually when the moon was full. The mobsters had sentinels, passwords, and calls. Most, if not all, of the county officials were honorary members. Victims of this organization were not lawbreakers but respectable citizens. Usually they were killed from ambush. The latest victim was James Brown, who was shot one Sunday night while riding home from church with his wife and her brother.

Captain Bill, soon after his arrival in San Saba with three of his Rangers, learned that the leader of the assassin group and the chief instigator of this latest crime was Will Ogle. Unable to get any co-operation from local officers, he confronted Ogle in a hardware store. He dared him to get his crowd together and fight and, before the outlaw could leave town, had his men arrest him. With the judge and most of the other county officials on Ogle's side, it was hard to get an indictment. Yet McDonald managed to find enough members of the band whom he could induce to turn state's evidence. Tried in another county, Ogle was sent to prison for life. Buzzards' Water Hole became just another puddle, and San Saba turned a new leaf. One of Mc-

[21] Albert Bigelow Paine, *Captain Bill McDonald, Texas Ranger,* 220.

Donald's Rangers was elected sheriff, and another was chosen as constable.[22]

In March, 1899, McDonald went alone to Columbus, where a feud of the Reece and Townsend families had brought several killings and finally had caused the death of a boy who belonged to neither faction. When the Captain arrived, men of the two factions were gathered on opposite sides of the courthouse square, armed and ready for action. After talking with the county judge, who advised him to wait until he had a whole company of Rangers, McDonald went alone to the Townsend crowd and called out the sheriff, who was a member of that faction. When the sheriff said he was powerless to disarm the men, McDonald undertook the job himself.

"Here, boys," he drawled, "come and stack your guns in this wardrobe. It's a good, safe place for 'em. They won't be likely to go off and hurt anybody here."

With the Townsend men disarmed, to their own and the sheriff's surprise, McDonald strode over to the Reece crowd, carrying his Winchester. In a friendly manner, he told them that the Governor had sent him to stop the trouble and that they would have to disarm and go home, as the other party had done. When one husky fellow burst out, "Well, you'll play hell getting my gun!" Captain Bill shoved his Winchester under the man's nose and threatened to put him in jail. The frightened feudist dropped his gun, and the leader of the Reece faction told his men to obey McDonald. The Captain then marched them into a store, where they left their guns in charge of a clerk. One man had restored peace to a community that had been on the verge of battle.[23]

As the new century opened, however, the Rangers began to find themselves in a less heroic light. While there still were occasional bandits to be chased in the Big Bend region and elsewhere along the Río Grande, the old frontier was gone. The Rangers most of the time were mere state policemen, with such unpopular assignments as keeping order in labor strikes, enforcing prohibition laws, and raiding night clubs. Some sheriffs resented them as meddlers, and many people regarded their

[22] *Ibid.*, 221–42. [23] *Ibid.*, 243–49.

methods as highhanded. It became increasingly hard to recruit the kind of men who had given the force its earlier reputation. Meanwhile, the state failed to modernize the force to enable the Rangers to cope with new criminal methods.

The organization reached its lowest ebb in the era of James E. and Miriam Ferguson, who made its personnel a field for political patronage. Tough, trigger-fingered Rangers were dismissed to make room for drugstore cowboys who happened to be on the right side of the political fence. The prestige of the force was further weakened by the wholesale issuance of special Ranger commissions to liquor dealers, night-club bouncers, gambling-house operators, barbers, dentists, and wrestling referees. In Ma Ferguson's last year in office, more than two thousand persons had these special Ranger commissions, while the paid force dwindled to about thirty men.[24]

The low state of the Ranger organization was a subject of common jest in the spring of 1934. Clyde Barrow, the notorious bank robber and killer, and his companion, Bonnie Parker, cruised back and forth across the state, almost openly, without molestation. Ironically, these two finally were shot down, on the morning of May 23, by a party led by a former Ranger captain, Frank Hamer, who had dropped out of the force in the Ferguson era.[25]

Further disaffection arose a year later. Governor James V. Allred's use of the Rangers in an onion strike in the Río Grande Valley and his sending them to break up liquor and gambling resorts, especially in cities on the Gulf Coast, came under fire. In Corpus Christi public feeling against the Rangers became so strong that county and city officials demanded on April 1, 1935, that the Rangers be withdrawn. The sheriff and the district attorney complained of an assault against a citizen by a Ranger and declared that these outsiders were not needed. They warned that blood might be shed if the Rangers remained. On the same day, in the interior city of Corsicana, a district judge, in impaneling a grand jury, declared, "We don't want the Rangers here, and I hope they don't come."

[24] Dallas *Morning News*, February 9, 1935.
[25] *Ibid.*, May 24, 1934.

On the day these statements were made, while the Rangers were looking for petty bootleggers and gamblers along the coast, one of Texas' most dangerous criminals, Ray Hamilton, drove unmolested through the northern part of the state.

With the reputation of the Rangers down almost to that of the state police of Reconstruction days, Governor Allred acted. He canceled all the special Ranger commissions and reappointed veteran Rangers to their old jobs. Then he pushed through the legislature in May an act to reorganize and modernize the force. Without erasing the identity of the Rangers, the new law placed them and the highway patrol in a Department of Public Safety. This new agency was given a crime laboratory, bureaus of identification and records, and communication facilities for the detection of crime and the catching of lawbreakers.

The statute limited the number of special Rangers to three hundred. Those obtaining the special commissions were required to make a $2,500 bond, and their authority was limited to enforcing laws for the protection of life and property. The new measure frowned upon the recent ax-swinging of the Rangers by forbidding the destruction of any property seized without a court order.[26] This reorganization gave a fitting occasion for Walter Prescott Webb's accurately detailed and graphically presented history of the Ranger force through a century of frontier defense.

The Texas Ranger who wore pressed pants and sped along the highway in a streamlined car could hardly compete in romance with his colorful predecessor of pioneer days. It was hardly enough that sometimes a trailer brought along saddle horses for use in tracking fugitives in the mountains. Yet the Ranger continued to do effective, if little publicized, work in running down motorized cattle thieves, bank robbers, killers, and other lawbreakers with whom local officers were unable to cope. For many Texans he was also a symbol. He was a living reminder of the heroic men who rode and fought to tame the state's long frontier and to make safe for settlement vast sections of the southern plains.

[26] *Acts, 44th Legislature,* 444; *Vernon's Texas Statutes,* 835–39; Dallas *Morning News,* May 4, 1935.

12. Marshals and Sheriffs

> They usually were quiet men. They served society fearlessly and with inadequate reward. Their resort to the six-shooter was always in reluctant self-defense.
>
> —William MacLeod Raine, in *Helldorado*, by William C. Breakenridge

ABILENE was celebrating in its usual boisterous manner one Saturday night in the summer of 1870. Sweat-stained belts were heavy with guns and knives. Cow hands had shot to bits a posted notice that the carrying of fire-arms was prohibited. Few men in the saloons doubted the boast that Abilene had more desperadoes and cutthroats than any other town on the continent.

No marshal had lasted more than a few weeks in this Kansas cow town at the end of the Chisholm Trail. No one supposed that the new marshal, Thomas James Smith, who had been sworn in on June 4, would last any longer. Smith was a New Yorker who had come to Abilene by way of Nebraska, Wyoming, and Colorado.

That Saturday night, Big Hank, one of the town rowdies, decided to show Smith up. With his six-shooter conspicuously in his belt, he swaggered up to the new officer, a well-built Irishman with a light mustache. "Are you the man who thinks he's going to run this town?" he asked.

"I've been hired as marshal," Smith replied. "I'm going to maintain order and enforce the law."

"What are you goin' to do about that gun ordinance?" the bully demanded.

"I'm going to see that it's obeyed—and I'll trouble you to hand me your pistol now."

When Hank refused, the marshal sprang at him and felled him with a terrific blow on the jaw. He then took the gun from the ruffian and ordered him to leave town at once—which he was glad to do rather than to face the jibes of his fellows.

News of this encounter created a sensation in the saloons and the cow camps. On a branch of Chapman Creek, northeast of town, burly Wyoming Frank made a bet that he could defy the new marshal. The next morning he rode into town. After downing a few drinks, he encountered Smith in the middle of the street. Failing to engage the marshal in a quarrel, he insolently refused the demand that he give up his gun. As Smith advanced toward him, Wyoming Frank backed into a saloon, where again he refused to turn over his pistol. Smith then pounced on him with the speed of a gamecock and, with two blows, sent him to the floor. After removing his gun, Smith gave him five minutes to leave town.

The crowd which had gathered about the pair was electrified and, for a moment, speechless. Then the saloonkeeper broke the silence by handing Smith his gun and saying, "That was the nerviest act I ever saw. That coward got what he deserved. Here's my gun. I reckon I'll not need it as long as you're marshal here." Others also offered their pistols to Smith. He told them to leave their weapons with the bartender for safekeeping.

Thus Tom Smith quickly won over the town's permanent residents. His pay was raised from $150 a month to $225, and he was given a policeman to help patrol the town. The marshal himself spent much of his time in the saddle; and his gray horse, Silverheels, became a familiar figure in the streets. Among early law officers in the West, Smith was unusual in his abstinence from drinking and gambling and in his ability to carry out his official duties without killing anyone. Occasionally he had trouble with Texas cow hands who had not learned that law had come to Abilene; but they soon discovered that Tom Smith was boss, and the fame of the new marshal spread quickly and far.[1]

[1] Theodore C. Henry, "Thomas James Smith of Abilene," *Kansas Historical Collections*, Vol. IX (1905–1906), 526–32; Stuart Henry, *Conquering Our Great American Plains*, 123–61; Floyd Benjamin Streeter, *Prairie Trails and Cow Towns*, 82–90.

Booming Abilene owed its eminence as a cow town to the enterprise of an Illinois livestock shipper, Joseph G. McCoy. Early in 1867, Abilene had been a wind-swept village of about a dozen log huts, most of them with dirt roofs. McCoy, seeking to connect Texas cattle trails with the railroads then pushing west, built stockyards at Abilene and invited Texas cattlemen to bring up their longhorns. As the cattle arrived, the town suddenly came to life.

In Tom Smith's day, Abilene had several hundred inhabitants. Its sod-roofed log cabins were giving way to more pretentious frame buildings. In the preceding year the town had shipped out 150,000 longhorns driven up the trail from Texas and had carried on a business of three hundred million dollars.[2] Sometimes a thousand or more cow hands would be paid off there in a single week. Supplying these men with provisions and entertainment provided lucrative occupations.

Abilene boasted board sidewalks on its main streets and had four hotels. There were ten boardinghouses, nine or ten saloons, and five clothing stores. The town's red-light district contained more than twenty-five houses of ten to twenty rooms each. A courthouse and a jail were being built. Recently enlarged stockyards spread along the railroad tracks at the east edge of town.

Tom Smith kept Abilene in hand for five months. But trouble was never far away. On October 23, Andrew McConnell, a Scot who lived on Chapman Creek, about ten miles northeast of Abilene, was out hunting deer. On his return to his dugout, he saw an Irish neighbor, John Shea, driving cattle across his land and noticed that the cattle had destroyed some of his corn. In an argument that followed, Shea snapped his pistol twice at McConnell, but it failed to go off. While he was cocking it a third time, McConnell shot him through the heart.

McConnell went for a doctor and later gave himself up, but was released on his plea of self-defense. Some of his neighbors, not satisfied with this outcome, obtained a warrant for his arrest on a charge of murder. The sheriff, Joseph Cramer, was un-

[2] Joseph G. McCoy, *Historic Sketches of the Cattle Trails of the West and Southwest*, 202–204.

able to arrest McConnell and went back to Abilene for help. Tom Smith, who by this time had added to his coat the badge of a deputy United States marshal, volunteered to arrest McConnell. He rode out on the afternoon of November 2, with his deputy, James H. McDonald. At the dugout they found McConnell and with him a friend, Moses Miles, who lived on a neighboring farm.

Smith entered the dugout and told McConnell he had a warrant for his arrest. At this, McConnell instantly shot the marshal in the chest with his Winchester. Smith took one shot at McConnell, piercing his hand, and then—though seriously wounded himself—grappled with him. The marshal dragged McConnell outside the dugout, where Miles was holding off the deputy. At this, Miles struck Smith on the head with his gun, then picked up an ax and chopped his head almost completely from his body.

McDonald, instead of battling these killers, left his horse tied there and ran to another claim, half a mile away. There he found a mount and hastened back to Abilene with the tragic news. Miles and McConnell fled, but later were caught and given prison terms. Tom Smith received an elaborate funeral two days after his death. In 1904, Abilene citizens marked his grave with a granite boulder. To this was fastened a bronze plate which noted that Smith died as a martyr to duty and described him as "a fearless hero of frontier days who, in cowboy chaos, established the supremacy of law."[3]

Abilene's next marshal, although destined to gain much greater fame than Tom Smith, was a man of less admirable character. This was James Butler Hickok, better known as "Wild Bill." Those who knew both men testified that Wild Bill's bravery was of a much lower type. Most Abilene people never saw Tom Smith's guns; they could not miss seeing Wild Bill's. J. B. Edwards, who called Smith "the most efficient officer of the frontier," noted that

Wild Bill did not use his bare hands as his luckless predecessor had done; he used his hardware instead. His bravery has been de-

[3] Theodore C. Henry, *loc. cit.*, 531; Stuart Henry, *op. cit.*, 199–210; Streeter, *op. cit.*, 90–93.

scribed by old-timers in Abilene as cruder than Tom Smith's. Many believed that Wild Bill without his guns would have been tame.[4]

Wild Bill, who hailed from Illinois, had served in the Civil War and in some Indian fighting and had been marshal of Hays. He was made marshal of Abilene on April 15, 1871, the peak year of Abilene cattle trade. Joseph G. McCoy, founder of the town's cattle business, had just been elected mayor. Phil Coe and Ben Thompson had just opened their Bull's Head Saloon. A new novelty theater was about to open near the railroad. The new mayor was moving the red-light district to a new site at the east edge of town, which some called McCoy's Addition and others the Devil's Half-Acre.

Hickok could perforate the brim of a hat while it spun in the air or, with a gun in each hand, could keep a tin can dancing in the dust. A six-footer, he had piercing eyes and a droopy mustache. He allowed his brown hair to brush his shoulders. He had given up the fringed and beaded buckskins of his scouting days for a Prince Albert coat, checked trousers, and an embroidered vest. Ordinarily he carried a pair of double-action army pistols; but when dressed up, he sported silver-mounted, pearl-handled revolvers. He received $150 a month, plus one-fourth of the fines.

Wild Bill made his headquarters at the Alamo Saloon, in the section known as Texas Abilene, south of the railroad. Instead of patrolling the streets, as Tom Smith had done, he spent most of his time in saloons and gambling halls. Yet he did keep order fairly well, thanks to the start Smith had made, the activities of three deputies, and the fear inspired by his fame as a marksman and a killer. Extravagant tales were told of the number of notches in his guns and how they were merited, but only two more notches were added in Abilene. In the fall a feud developed between Hickok and Phil Coe. On the night of October 5, the two engaged in a shooting fray in which Hickok mortally wounded Coe and a bystander, Mike Williams. On December 12 the city council discharged Hickok, effective the next day.

Wild Bill returned to Hays, where he served another brief

[4] Kansas City *Star*, November 15, 1925.

term as marshal. Then he joined a theatrical troupe and toured the country. Tiring of this, he went to Cheyenne. There, on March 5, 1876, he married Mrs. Agnes Lake, a circus equestrienne he had met at Hays. After a honeymoon in Cincinnati, he left his bride with her relatives there and went to Deadwood, Dakota Territory, which was enjoying its gold boom. On August 12, while playing poker in a Deadwood saloon, he was shot in the back and killed by Jack McCall. Bill was thirty-nine years old.[5] Abilene remembered him as a colorful figure and as a dextrous pistoleer, but saved its honors for Tom Smith.

Tom Smith's name belongs near the head of a long list of courageous marshals and sheriffs who helped to bring order and law to the frontier. In a county adjoining Smith's was another outstanding Kansas officer who tamed many bullies with his fists. This was Irish-born Thomas Allen Cullinan, marshal of Junction City from 1871 almost continuously until his death in 1904.[6] Many local enforcement officers, while as daring as Smith, were less punctilious in their personal conduct. Some lapsed or backslid into crime, as did John Henry Brown, marshal of Caldwell, Kansas, who tried to rob a bank at Medicine Lodge and was shot while seeking to escape, and John M. Larn, who, after serving as a sheriff in Texas, was executed by vigilantes as a cattle rustler. Others, such as Henry Plummer in Montana and David Updyke in Idaho, used sheriffs' badges to hide their leadership in crime—until each criminal weighted down a hangman's rope.

As the Kansas cattle business moved westward, Dodge City became the principal market for longhorns trailed up from Texas. With its saloons, gambling rooms, and dance halls in full blast, Dodge City offered plenty of excitement for cow hands who had just been paid off and wanted to celebrate. Six-shooters blazed without much interference until Wyatt Earp was made chief deputy marshal on May 17, 1876. Born in Illinois and

[5] Frank J. Wilstach, *Wild Bill Hickok;* Wilbert E. Eisele, *The Real Wild Bill Hickok;* William Elsey Connelley, *Wild Bill and His Era;* Stuart Henry, *op. cit.*, 271–89; Streeter, *op. cit.*, 96–104.

[6] George W. Martin, "Thomas Allen Cullinan of Junction City," *Kansas Historical Collections*, Vol. IX (1905–1906), 532–40.

reared in Iowa, Earp had wandered about much of the West. He had worked as a stagecoach driver, a railroad construction hand, a surveyor, a buffalo hunter, and a Wichita policeman.

Earp, who was over six feet tall, was expert at poker and quick with his guns; but he drank nothing stronger than coffee. Paid $250 a month and $2.50 for every arrest he made, he enforced the ordinance against gun toting and helped the town to begin living down its reputation as the "Gomorrah of the Plains." But on September 9, with the cattle rush over, he quit his job to take a look at the excitement over gold at Deadwood.[7]

For 1877, Dodge City entrusted its law enforcement to two trigger-fingered brothers who had been deputies of Earp. William Barclay Masterson, better known as "Bat," was elected sheriff; and Edward J. Masterson, who was older, became deputy marshal. Ed, though a courageous officer, had bad luck. On November 5, while trying to break up a gun fight at the Lone Star Dance Hall, he was hit by one of the bullets.[8] He recovered; but, on the following April 9, when he went to arrest two desperadoes, he was shot again. This wound proved mortal.[9]

Bat Masterson, as a youth of eighteen, had come to Dodge City in 1872 and had gained experience as a railroad subcontractor, a buffalo hunter, and a scout. He had become a dandified gunman and an even more foppish dresser than Wild Bill Hickok. His suit was of the latest cut, and he usually wore a pearl-gray bowler hat and a diamond stickpin. Often he carried a cane. But his mannerisms were overlooked by those who knew him to be one of the deadliest gunmen of the frontier.[10]

The spring of 1878 brought complaints that the ban against carrying firearms was not being enforced and that, with the arrival of another season's herds, street fights were becoming frequent again.[11] On May 12, five weeks after the death of Ed Masterson, Wyatt Earp returned to Dodge City as marshal.[12]

[7] Stuart N. Lake, *Wyatt Earp, Frontier Marshal,* 2–155.
[8] Dodge City *Times,* November 10, 1877.
[9] Robert M. Wright, *Dodge City, the Cowboy Capital,* 304–307.
[10] *Ibid.,* 300–304.
[11] *Ford County Globe,* March 5, May 7, 1878.
[12] *Ibid.,* May 14, 1879; Lake, *op. cit.,* 201–202.

Soon the situation was in hand again, but dapper Bat Masterson failed to be re-elected sheriff.

Elsewhere on the frontier, outlawry and the measures taken to suppress it were not always as spectacular as in the rampaging Kansas cow towns. But in many localities quiet officers, with courage to back their badges, risked their lives at frequent intervals to make their communities safe. Early Denver had in David J. Cook an officer who made that city's climate bad for horse thieves and desperadoes. As an army detective, beginning in 1863, he broke up an organized gang of bandits and recovered more than ten thousand dollars' worth of loot. As marshal, 1866–69, and as sheriff, 1869–73, Cook made such an outstanding record for strategy and daring that lawbreakers tried to keep out of his path.[13]

Leadville in its boom days had as marshal roughshod Mart Duggan, who rid the mining town of some of its worst outlaws. Residents of the Black Hills looked up to Seth Bullock and his successor, A. M. Willard, two Deadwood sheriffs who drove out or captured many desperadoes. The Dakotans did not quickly forget Jack Davis, a deputy marshal who defied an angry crowd to obtain a fair trial for a gunman he had brought back from Fort Laramie.

After local service, some of the men with badges took up federal tasks. The citizens of Wyoming remembered Nathaniel K. Boswell, a deputy United States marshal, who, riding out alone from Laramie, trailed two desperate horse thieves, single-handedly captured them, induced them to put handcuffs on each other, and brought them back safely.[14] In the Indian Territory another federal deputy, Benjamin F. Williams, held at bay a band of horse thieves and later returned with help to capture them.[15]

Frontier Texas had many fearless law officers. Most of them

[13] *Rocky Mountain News,* Denver, March 30, 1867, October 19, 1868; David J. Cook, *Hands Up;* William Ross Collier and Edwin Victor Westrate, *Dave Cook of the Rockies.*

[14] Edwin L. Sabin, *Wild Men of the Wild West,* 276–78.

[15] Topeka *Commonwealth,* July 14, 1875; Hubert E. Collins, *Warpath and Cattle Trail,* 70–74.

received scant recognition for their work in quieting feuds, checking cattle rustling and horse thieving, and capturing those who too easily reached for their guns. One who stood out was James B. Gillett, who, after six years with the Texas Rangers, became marshal of El Paso and helped to tame that border town.[16] Another was A. J. Spradley, who, as sheriff of Nacogdoches County for thirty years, was relentless in bringing lawbreakers to justice.[17]

In the Texas Panhandle, John Henry Brown, the first constable of Tascosa, put fear into some of the more impetuous cow hands. When one of them, hauled into court for shooting up the town, referred to Tascosa as a mere pile of adobe huts, Brown took offense. The constable slammed his pistol on a chair, stepped back until he was as far from it as was the loudmouthed culprit, and suggested that the two grab for the gun. At this the blusterer quailed, reddened, and—after paying his fine—left town in disgrace.[18]

The most celebrated local law officer of Texas belonged to the more dubious tradition of Wild Bill Hickok rather than to that of Tom Smith. Ben Thompson, notorious gambler and gunman of the western frontier, served part of a term as marshal of Austin. Born in Nova Scotia in 1843, of English parents, he grew up in Austin, entered school there, and, at an early age, began getting into scrapes. He learned the printer's trade on the *Southern Intelligencer* in Austin and on the *Picayune* in New Orleans but soon quit work to live by gambling. In New Orleans he became involved in a duel that resulted in the first of many killings attributed to him.

Thompson made a show of fighting for the Confederacy, but the only persons he shot were a lieutenant and a sergeant on his own side. He ran whiskey into camp for his friends and spent much of his time in the guardhouse. After the war he killed two Mexicans in Laredo and John Coombs in Austin. He escaped

[16] James B. Gillett, *Six Years With the Texas Rangers* (revised edition), 232–38.

[17] Henry C. Fuller, *A Texas Sheriff*.

[18] John L. McCarty, *Maverick Town, the Story of Old Tascosa*, 97, 99–100.

from jail in Austin and served as an adventurer under one of Maximilian's officers. On his return to Austin, he was tried, convicted, and imprisoned for the killing of Coombs. Released in 1870, he went to Abilene, Kansas, the next spring, where he operated as a professional gambler.

With nearly $2,600 in his pocket from his gambling, Thompson joined his Austin friend, Phil Coe, in a business venture. On Texas Street in Abilene, the pair opened the Bull's Head Saloon, with an expensive faro bank and other fancy equipment. Thompson dressed as a dandy and always had his hair carefully parted. From Abilene, after his partner's death, he drifted to Kansas City. Later he turned up in Ellsworth, Kansas, where he and his younger brother, Billy, made precarious living as gamblers. In August, 1873, the two Thompsons left Ellsworth hurriedly after a shooting affray in which Sheriff C. B. Whitney was killed by a bullet from Billy's gun.

Ben operated for the next few years in Wichita, Dodge City, Leadville, and other lively places. Then he returned to Austin, where he opened a gambling house. He soon became politically ambitious and, after an initial defeat, was elected marshal. He kept order fairly well, but only by his prowess as a gunman. He was well behaved while sober but overbearing when intoxicated. He spent much of his time in gambling, drinking, and quarreling. On a trip to San Antonio, he killed Jack Harris, the owner of a gambling house there, and was clapped into jail. This ended his career as marshal of Austin, although his trial, in January, 1883, resulted in his acquittal.[19]

From that time on, Thompson became wilder than ever. He shot up parts of the town, broke up a cattleman's banquet, and whipped a man in a courtroom while court was in session. On other occasions he emptied a theater during a performance by firing shots from a box seat and drove editors and printers from the *Statesman's* office and pied all its forms.[20] On the night of March 11, 1884, he became involved in a gun fight in a variety theater in San Antonio and was killed.[21]

[19] W. M. Walton, *Life and Adventures of Ben Thompson, the Famous Texan;* Streeter, *op. cit.*, 93–142, 166.

[20] Albany *Echo,* February 8, 1884.

Tom Smith
He taught manners to a cow town

Kansas State Historical Society

While Ben Thompson was still flashing his guns about the Iron Front Saloon in Austin, local law enforcement was gaining headway, to the accompaniment of much gun smoke, in southern Arizona. The boom silver-mining town of Tombstone had attracted many desperadoes. Tall, mustached Wyatt Earp, who had been a marshal in Kansas and had gone to Arizona to start a stage line, was persuaded to drop his plan and to go to Tombstone as deputy sheriff. He arrived in the mining town on December 1, 1879, to find himself in one of the toughest communities on the frontier.

One of the first tasks of the new deputy was to stop the robbing of outgoing stagecoaches carrying bullion shipments. He either rode with the treasure shipments to Tucson or Benson or sent an armed assistant, and soon the holdups stopped. Earp next went after the cattle rustlers, with good results. His fees brought him a large income, which he invested in local real estate.

Tombstone organized a town government soon after Earp's arrival and, on January 6, 1890, elected Fred White marshal. In the fall of that year, White was killed while trying to arrest some outlaws who had been carousing for two days with their guns in their belts. Virgil Earp, Wyatt's brother, was appointed for the remainder of the term but refused to be a candidate in the election of the following January.

By this time Wyatt Earp had resigned as deputy sheriff, but he continued as a law officer with the badge of a deputy United States marshal. In addition, he served as a guard for the Wells-Fargo Express Company. Soon he also took over the job of protecting the town's leading gambling house, the Oriental, from outlaws who were trying to break up its business. For this work he received a one-fourth interest in the establishment, an interest that sometimes brought him a thousand dollars a week.

Early in 1881, Tombstone found itself in a newly formed county. Its first sheriff was a political appointee who seemed

[21] Austin *Daily Statesman,* March 13, 1884; San Antonio *Daily Express,* February 19, 1911; Frank H. Bushick, *Glamorous Days,* 182–96; Paul Adams, "The Unsolved Mystery of Ben Thompson," *Southwestern Historical Quarterly,* Vol. XLVIII, No. 3 (January, 1945), 321–29.

more interested in the rewards of his office than in law enforcement. Horse thieving, stagecoach robbing, and the hijacking and killing of Mexican smugglers increased. Many of these activities were attributed to a band headed by the four Clantons who had a ranch on the San Pedro River a few miles above Charleston. Among their friends were Frank and Tom McLowery, whose ranch in Sulphur Springs Valley, about twenty-five miles east of Tombstone, was said to be a hangout for outlaws. Members of the Clanton band escaped from the Tombstone jail so easily that some citizens began to suspect the sheriff of complicity. Wyatt Earp, who worked only on those cases in which federal laws or the express company's interests were involved, soon clashed with the Clantons and incurred their enmity.

Determined to rid Tombstone of this band, despite the laxity of the sheriff, a Citizens' Safety Committee called for the resignation of the ineffective marshal. They put Virgil Earp in his place, with Wyatt and Morgan Earp and John H. (Doc) Holliday as his deputies. The showdown came soon. On the evening of October 25, 1881, Ike Clanton made the rounds of the saloons on Allen Street, boasting that he would kill Wyatt Earp and Doc Holliday before another sunset. But when he encountered Holliday, who had been informed of the threat, he begged off from a fight by saying that he was unarmed. Wyatt and Virgil Earp came along in time to separate the two. Half an hour later, Wyatt Earp ran into Ike Clanton again. Ike said he would have friends with him the next day and would fight it out with Holliday and the Earps.

The next day Ike had reinforcements. Besides Tom McLowery, who had come in with him from Antelope Springs, he found William Clanton, Frank McLowery, and Billy Claiborne, who had just ridden in from Charleston. Ike resumed his boasting that he would wipe out the Earps and Holliday. These officers soon received warnings and began keeping an eye out for the visitors.

On Fourth Street, between Frémont and Allen, Morgan and Virgil Earp came up behind Ike Clanton, who was carrying a Winchester. As Ike swung around and raised his rifle, Virgil

Earp seized it with his left hand. With his right, he grabbed the braggart's Colt and used it to give his captive a blow on the head. The two Earps took the outraged Clanton to the town court, where he was fined twenty-five dollars for disturbing the peace. Virgil Earp told Clanton he could pick up his rifle and his six-shooters at the Grand Hotel as he left town.

Meanwhile, outside the courtroom, Wyatt Earp encountered Tom McLowery. After an exchange of words, Earp slapped McLowery in the face and, before the latter could reach his gun, hit him over the head with a pistol and knocked him flat in the gutter. While the Earps and some of the vigilantes watched from various posts, Ike Clanton joined his friends at Spangenberg's gun shop, where he bought a six-shooter to replace one of those he had given up. All five loaded their cartridge belts.

The ranchmen visited several saloons, where they repeated their threats to wipe out the Earps. Then, in the early afternoon, they went to the O K corral where they had left their horses. There they were joined by Wes Fuller, who served them as a lookout. After more threats were relayed to the Earps and Holliday, these four policemen started on foot for the corral. Virgil Earp, the marshal, told the sheriff he was going to arrest the troublemakers and let them cool off. He asked the sheriff to come along, but the latter—who had tried ineffectually to disarm the men—declined.

The marshal and his deputies spread out as they approached the corral. As they rounded a corner and faced the outlaws, Wyatt Earp called on them to surrender. At this, some of the Clanton group reached for their guns and the shooting began. When the smoke cleared away, Billy Clanton and the two McLowerys were dead. Virgil and Morgan Earp were wounded, although not seriously. Doc Holliday had a superficial scratch. Tombstone had been made unsafe for blustering lawbreakers.[22]

Many in and about Tombstone, however, refused to grant

[22] Tombstone *Epitaph*, October 27, November 1, 1881; Walter Noble Burns, *Tombstone*, 179–219; Lorenzo D. Walters, *Tombstone's Yesterday*, 52–93; Breakenridge, *op. cit.*, 139–53; Lake, *op. cit.*, 231–311; Jack Ganzhorn, *I've Killed Men*, 16–37.

halos to the Earps for their part in the fight at the O K corral—or the massacre, as some called it. While the Earps and Holliday were freed in court, the magistrate, Wells Spicer, censured Virgil Earp as injudicious and incautious for calling on Wyatt Earp and Doc Holliday to help him arrest men with whom they had been quarreling.

The Earps, viewed more as feudists than as law officers, became increasingly unpopular in Tombstone. Jack Ganzhorn, who was there at the time, later referred to Wyatt Earp and his followers as "cold-blooded murderers."[23] C. L. Sonnichsen, there later, reported, "The people I talked to were definitely against the Earps."[24] Frank Waters concluded that Wyatt Earp was "little more than a tin-horn outlaw operating under the protection of a tin badge until he was run out of Arizona."[25]

A clearer case of heroism in law enforcement in early Arizona was that provided by an Apache County sheriff, Commodore P. Owens. At Holbrook on September 4, 1887, he went to a house to arrest a horse thief who was involved in the Graham-Tewksbury feud. A few minutes later he had killed three outlaws and had wounded and captured a fourth.

Meanwhile, courageous officers were at work elsewhere in the Southwest. A little more than three months before the battle in Tombstone, a New Mexico sheriff had struck a resounding blow against frontier crime. This officer was Patrick Floyd Garrett, sheriff of Lincoln County, who was doing much to make the fine arts of cattle rustling and horse thieving dangerous in his bailiwick.

Born in Alabama in 1850, Garrett spent most of his boyhood in Louisiana, worked as a cow hand in northern Texas, hunted buffalo in the Texas Panhandle, and drifted to Tascosa. From there, in 1878, he went to Fort Sumner, on the Pecos River in New Mexico. Garrett was six feet four in his socks and made an imposing figure in cowboy boots and high-crowned sombrero. An expert in riding, roping, and shooting, he had no trouble

23 Ganzhorn, *op. cit.*, 23.
24 Sonnichsen, letter to the author, September 6, 1946.
25 Frank Waters, *The Colorado*, 225.

in finding work along the Pecos, where his height led the Mexicans to call him "Juan Largo."

Garrett married a local *señorita* and, in the fall of 1880, ran for sheriff. He made an active campaign, promising to break up the bands of thieves who were preying on herds of cattle and horses and to fight it out with the county's most notorious outlaw. This was young William H. Bonney, better known as "Billy the Kid." Garrett was elected in spite of Billy's efforts for his opponent, and he quickly found that he had his hands full.

At the Greathouse and Kuch ranch in November, 1880, between the election of Garrett and the time he took office, a White Oaks posse tried to capture Billy the Kid and two of his fellows. But the outlaws escaped, killing the leader of the posse, James Carlyle. In the same month they ran off stock from many ranches and engaged in a second battle with a posse at Coyote Springs. In this skirmish, two of the outlaws had their horses shot from under them, but all three escaped.[26] Governor Lew Wallace offered a reward of five hundred dollars for the delivery of Bonney to the sheriff of Lincoln County.[27]

Lincoln County ranchmen knew that his youth made Billy the Kid a no less dangerous desperado. Born to Irish parents on New York's East Side, November 23, 1859, he and his younger brother were taken to Kansas in 1862. There the father soon died and the mother took the youngsters to Colorado. After a short time she remarried and moved to Santa Fé, where she helped her husband run a boardinghouse. In Santa Fé, and later in Silver City, Billy had an almost normal boyhood but became much more interested in dealing monte than in playing with toys. At twelve, after a fight, he ran away from home on a stolen horse and entered upon a career of crime in which many killings were attributed to him.

Garrett knew Billy the Kid well and often had drunk and gambled with him. Billy had been jailed several times, but never for long. Now that a price had been put on his head, he became more wary. But Garrett, as sheriff-elect, made the capture of the outlaw leader his main objective and kept posses hot on his trail.

[26] Las Vegas *Gazette*, November 30, 1880.
[27] *Ibid.*, December 24, 1880.

Late in December, Garrett and others beseiged Billy the Kid and four of his companions after they had taken refuge in a stone hut that sheepherders had abandoned near Stinking Spring. The posse killed one of the outlaws when he appeared in the doorway. The others soon were starved into surrender. Bonney and the three other prisoners were taken to Las Vegas, and from there by train to Santa Fé.

The Kid remained in jail there until April, when he was taken to Mesilla for trial. He was convicted of murder and sentenced to be hanged on May 13 at Lincoln. On April 21 he was turned over to Sheriff Garrett for safekeeping. As Lincoln County had no jail worthy of the name, Garrett kept Bonney under guard in a room on the second floor of the county building. There, on the evening of the twenty-eighth, while shackled with handcuffs and leg irons, he shot and killed his two guards. Then he removed his shackles and escaped on horseback.

This sensational break put Garrett on the spot. He set out to track down the young killer, who boasted that he had slain a man for every year of his life. Garrett caught up with Bonney on the night of July 14, in a large home on the grounds of Fort Sumner. About midnight, while the sheriff was talking with his host in a dark bedroom, the desperado appeared in the doorway. Without warning, Garrett fired two shots, the first of which killed the Kid instantly.

Some persons criticized the sheriff for not giving Bonney a chance to surrender, but most New Mexicans were relieved to be rid of the outlaw. Las Vegas citizens raised several hundred dollars as a purse for Garrett. Later the legislature passed an act which enabled him to collect the reward offered for Billy the Kid's capture. Garrett did not run again for sheriff. He turned his attention back to his cattle business, which he interrupted with service as a Texas Ranger, as sheriff of Doña Ana County, New Mexico, and as collector of customs at El Paso. On February 29, 1908, on a road near his ranch in the Organ Mountains, he was shot and killed.[28]

[28] Report of the coroner's jury on the death of William Bonney, July 15, 1881, files of the Secretary of State, Santa Fé; Garrett, *The Authentic Life of Billy the Kid;* Charles A. Siringo, *The History of Billy the Kid* (re-

In the Indian country which became Oklahoma, outlawry persisted longer than in the surrounding states. That region became a bailiwick for one of the most successful of frontier peace officers—William Tilghman, who spent fifty-one years in taming the wild men of the plains. Born at Fort Dodge, Iowa, in 1854, Tilghman was taken by his parents to Kansas two years later. When he was sixteen, he went to the southwestern part of the Sunflower State and became a buffalo hunter and Indian fighter. In 1874 he was a government scout in the Cheyenne and Arapaho war. Four years later he fought in the campaign against Dull Knife, who had left the reservation at Fort Sill to plunder in Kansas and Nebraska.

In Dodge City, where he was a deputy sheriff for four years under Bat Masterson and others, Tilghman became known as a fearless officer. Later he was marshal there for three years and captured several of the town's more troublesome desperadoes.

Pushing into Oklahoma with the 1889 Boomers, Tilghman became the first marshal of Perry and did much to rid that town of outlaws. Soon thereafter he became a deputy United States marshal. Later he held other posts, including that of chief of police of Oklahoma City. For thirty-five years, mustached Bill Tilghman, with Windsor tie and derby hat, was a familiar figure in the Oklahoma plains and hills. An expert gunman, he never killed anyone he could take alive. Nor did he ever hesitate to risk his own life in making a capture. His efforts brought doom to several bands of outlaws.

The most famous exploit of Tilghman was his single-handed encounter with William Doolin, who had been one of the notorious Dalton band of bank and train robbers. After the breaking up of that outfit, dark, mustached Doolin had formed his own outlaw band. In January, 1895, Tilghman unwittingly entered a dugout where Doolin and his men were hiding. He was covered with their guns, although he did not see the bandits.

But Bill Doolin, who had a spark of chivalry in his make-up, refused to allow his men to shoot. "Bill Tilghman's too good a

vised edition); Walter Noble Burns, *The Saga of Billy the Kid;* Coe, *Frontier Fighter,* 146–57; John W. Poe, *The Death of Billy the Kid;* Sophie A. Poe, *Buckboard Days,* 97–118; Keleher, *The Fabulous Frontier,* 57–82.

man to be shot in the back," he said. Because of this incident and because he knew that Doolin had a wife and child, Tilghman was determined to capture the desperado leader alive if possible.

A year later he heard that Doolin was in Eureka Springs, Arkansas, taking baths for his rheumatism. Tilghman went to that resort and, disguising himself in a long coat and a high hat, found Doolin in the lobby of a bathhouse. The outlaw was sitting in a corner reading a newspaper. He had placed himself where he could see everyone in the room, but he did not recognize Tilghman in his disguise. After ordering a bath, the officer confronted Doolin. He pressed the muzzle of his six-shooter against the abdomen of the bandit and ordered him to put up his hands.

Doolin sprang to his feet and reached for his gun. Tilghman tried to grab Doolin by the wrist but missed and caught his coat sleeve. While others fled, the two men struggled about the lobby. Doolin tore his sleeve and pushed his hand nearer the gun under his left arm. Tilghman told the bandit he would have to kill him if he did not give up. Finally Doolin realized that Tilghman meant what he said. Unable to reach his gun, he surrendered and allowed himself to be disarmed. Tilghman delivered Doolin to the Guthrie jail without using handcuffs. The prisoner escaped on the evening of July 5, 1896, but soon afterward was killed in a gun duel with another officer.

The long career of Bill Tilghman took him into many tight places. Often he barely escaped desperadoes' bullets. In September, 1924, against the advice of friends, to took the post of marshal of Cromwell, a lawless oil town. "I want to go out in the smoke and die with my boots on," he said. Less than two months later, on the night of November 1, he heard a shot and went out into the street. He seized the man with the gun and had a bystander wrench the weapon from him. But the disorderly man—a tipsy prohibition officer—drew a second gun and shot his captor. Tilghman died a few minutes later—in his boots.[29]

[29] Zoe A. Tilghman, *Outlaw Days,* 1–5, 82–103; A. B. McDonald, *Hands Up!,* 64–65, 200–24, 301–303; William MacLeod Raine, *Famous*

Wild Bill Hickok
A handy man with a pistol

Kansas State Historical Society

Not all of the stern men who carried guns in the interest of order and law on the frontier were in public employ. Some were shotgun messengers seated beside the stagecoach drivers or guards who worked for the pioneer railroads and the express companies. Others were range detectives of the livestock associations who followed the trails of thieves across the plains and through the mountain passes. Occasionally one of these men cast his lot with the outlaws he was paid to exterminate. A few became too free with their guns, as did Tom Horn, a cattlemen's gunman who took one too many lives and was hanged in Cheyenne in 1903.[30]

Yet nearly all of the pioneer enforcement officers, public or private, gave a good account of themselves. They risked their lives to make the West safe, and more than a few carried desperadoes' bullets to their graves. Only through their work could the emerging courts gain the confidence of law-abiding citizens and the respect of wrongdoers.

Sheriffs and Western Outlaws, 210–16; Sabin, *op. cit.,* 283–90; E. D. Nix, *Oklahombres,* 165–230.

[30] Jay Monaghan, *Last of the Bad Men.*

13. Without Benefit of Blackstone

At best, much of the court procedure of frontier days was little better than that of the vigilance committee.

—CARL COKE RISTER, *Southern Plainsmen*

PEDDLING peanuts on the streets of San Francisco in the booming days of 1849 had put comfortable sums in the pockets of William B. Almond. Yet his money seemed to make this popular vendor ambitious for easier work and still larger income. So, with the aid of political friends, he induced the governor to authorize a new court, superior to that of the alcalde, and to appoint him judge. In a shanty on the southwest corner of the Plaza, on the Clay Street side of the Monumental engine house, Judge Almond opened his court on December 12, 1849. He was determined that his fees should keep him in affluence.

The new court, which was confined to civil cases, did not disappoint the judge. With his chair tipped back and his feet planted against the wall, Judge Almond habitually trimmed his finger nails as he listened to lawyers and witnesses. He seldom tolerated juries or long speeches that might cut down the number of cases tried in one day. His fees ran high for those able to pay, and such minor items as motions and postponements regularly cost an ounce of gold dust. These payments became so frequent that on some days the judge's table was half-covered with the yellow dust.

In the sleepy days of 1847, some had criticized an alcalde for smoking while holding court, halting his rulings every half-minute to take a puff or two.[1] Such sticklers found even more to complain of in the lack of decorum in Judge Almond's court. On one occasion, when atmosphere and argument were unusually arid, the judge rose from his chair and announced: "The court's dry. The court's adjourned. Let's take a drink!"[2]

Judge Almond's type of court, in which decisions were based as much on instinct as on evidence, was not unusual in early California. Often statutory justice afforded little real advance over that of the miners' court or the committee of vigilance. One man who became a judge had come to the Golden Gate after being sentenced to a Pennsylvania prison for robbing the Chester bank.[3] Another was habitually drunk, consorted with lewd women, and—despite the bribes he accepted—failed to pay his bills.[4]

Especially informal in procedure and free from statutory restraints were the justices of the peace. Usually they were men who worked at other occupations most of the time. As late as 1877, Vallejo had a sign that read: "C. W. Riley, Dealer in Imported Wines and Liquors and Choice Cigars—also Justice of the Peace."[5]

Drinking in and about the early local courts was common. In one instance, near Placerville, the trial of a miner charged with assaulting a claim jumper did not begin until eleven at night. In this case, the presiding justice of the peace adjourned the court every few minutes. The recesses were made to allow the court officers, jurors, prosecutor, defendant, witnesses, and spectators to quench their thirst at the bar of a near-by saloon. When morning came, reported a contemporary historian, "a drunken lawyer addressed a drunken jury on behalf of a drunken prosecutor. A drunken judge having delivered an inebriated charge, a fuddled verdict of acquittal was delivered."[6]

Yet, in other instances, common sense and grass-roots fair-

[1] *California Star,* Yerba Buena, January 9, 1847.

[2] Hubert Howe Bancroft, *California Inter Pocula,* 591–600.

[3] *Ibid.,* 602–604.

[4] *Ibid.,* 605–607.

[5] *Ibid.,* 622.

[6] George Frederic Parsons, *Life and Adventures of James W. Marshall, the Discoverer of Gold in California.*

ness went far to make up for lack of decorum and legal training. Charles Howard Shinn, social historian of the early California diggings, commented:

The men who were chosen justices of the peace in these mining camps were often eccentric and illiterate, but as a rule their honesty and good judgment were unquestionable. They had the full confidence of the people and were conscious of the responsibilities of their office. In many a town of the mining region, the pioneers still remember their names with respect and still smile over their eccentricities. One of them, when dying, left all his money, after paying funeral expenses, to the boys for a treat; and it was duly spent in the saloons of the camp. Yet he is said to have dealt out justice with firmness and good sense; his official conduct was satisfactory.[7]

In general, sagebrush justice was scarcely less fair than that based upon hairsplitting of legal phrases. Sometimes the frontiersman on the bench had to resort to drastic means to make his decisions stick. On the Stanislaus, an unlearned miner serving as justice of the peace was challenged to a fight by a blustering itinerant lawyer. Immediately the miner stepped down from his bench and gave the arrogant attorney a thrashing.[8]

Later a similar instance of judicial nerve was given by Charles E. Clay, who was appointed justice of the peace at Douglas, Wyoming, in 1886. One of the first men brought before him was Joe Bush, a bouncer for Bill Tucker's dance hall. Bush had given a cow hand a cruel beating.

"I guess I'm guilty, Your Honor," the culprit answered after the complaint had been read.

"The court fines you a hundred dollars—"

"Here it is, Judge," the bouncer interrupted, throwing the money on the grocery counter that served as a bench.

"—And six months in the county jail. Have you got that in your pocket, too?"

This took the wind out of Bush. That evening Tucker and

[7] Charles Howard Shinn, *Mining Camps: a Study in American Frontier Government,* 205.

[8] Bancroft, *California Inter Pocula,* 613–14.

some of his gambler friends came to intercede with the judge. "Look here, Clay," said one, "you've got to suspend that jail sentence. If you don't, we'll tar and feather you and ride you out of town on a rail."

The new justice said nothing, but walked back of the bench and pulled out a gun containing a double charge of powder and shot. Placing it in front of him, he reminded the gamblers that he was running the court. The gun, he assured them, "will always be here to make that sentence good."[9]

In some of the more isolated frontier communities, public opinion was the court of final appeal. Traveling in Oregon in 1865, Albert D. Richardson was told of this incident that had occurred in an earlier period:

> In the early days, the miners of Jacksonville elected an alcalde. A party to a contested claim case, thinking himself wronged, posted this notice: "Whereas, the alcalde has given an unjust and corrupt decision against me, on Sunday next I shall take an appeal to the Supreme Court."
>
> Sunday saw a hundred miners convened, from curiosity to learn what the Supreme Court was. They themselves were that august tribunal! The aggrieved party organized them into a mass meeting; they retried the case and rendered a verdict reversing the alcalde's decision. All acquiesced in this assize of original and final jurisdiction.[10]

In new settlements and remote outposts throughout the West, many of the early courts of law had little in common with the more formal ones which followed. They were more closely akin to the committees of vigilance, miners' courts, or people's courts that often preceded them. The presiding judge or justice of the peace had scant legal training, if any. He relied mainly on common sense or accepted custom for his decisions. Much depended on the fairness and intelligence of the judge, which

[9] Robert B. David, *Malcolm Campbell, Sheriff*, 132; Douglas *Budget*, June 4, 1936.

[10] Albert D. Richardson, *Beyond the Mississippi*, 407–408.

might vary greatly from one tribunal to another. But usually the informality of the court made its decisions no less binding on the unlucky culprits hauled in for judgment.

In many frontier courts, written law was encountered only on rare occasions. Early Arizona had a roughshod dispenser of law in Jim Burnett, a justice of the peace on the San Pedro. With the aid of a double-barreled shotgun, he bossed the mining town of Charleston—and pocketed the fines. Acting as coroner, Burnett once ruled that "it served the Mexican right for getting in front of a gun." On another occasion, after losing all his money in a poker game, he arrested the proprietor of the gambling hall and fined him fifty dollars. With this money he bought another stack of chips and resumed his game. Burnett, who held court wherever he happened to be, once collected from a desperado, Jack Harrer, a fine of twenty head of three-year-old steers.[11]

Frontier Tucson gave heed to an unconventional justice of the peace in Charles H. Meyer, a druggist of German birth. He sent lawbreakers and vagrants to a local chain gang that kept the town's streets cleaner than they ever had been. Once a defense lawyer told Meyer that his client demanded trial by jury. "Oh, he does, does he?" said the justice. "Well, I sentence him to two weeks on the chain gang, and I sentence you to one week for disrespect of the court."[12]

In the Kansas towns at the end of the cattle trails, the handing out of justice was scarcely more formal. From an early account of a proceeding in the Dodge City police court comes this item:

> "The marshal will preserve strict order," said the judge. "Any person caught throwing turnips, cigar stumps, beets, or old quids of tobacco at this court will be immediately arraigned before this bar of justice." Then Joe looked savagely at the mob in attendance, hitched his ivory handle a little to the left, and adjusted his mustache. "Trot out the wicked and unfortunate, and let the cotillion commence," said the judge.
>
> "City versus James Martin"—but just then a complaint not on file had to be attended to, and the Reverend John Walsh of Las

[11] Burns, *Tombstone*, 85; Lockwood, *Pioneer Days in Arizona*, 266–67.
[12] Lockwood, *op. cit.*, 263–64.

Animas took the throne of justice while the judge stepped over to Hoover's for a drink of old rye to brace him for the ordeal to come.[13]

The pine woods of eastern Texas, in the days of the Republic, had a highly informal justice of the peace in Jonas Phelps. In front of the village hotel in Shelbyville one sunny June morning, Phelps was leaning back in his chair, smoking his pipe before taking up his official duties. As he sat there, a lanky farmer appeared before him in yellow jeans and a coonskin cap. In his hand was a basket containing half a dozen chickens.

"Want to buy any fowls?" he inquired.

"What do you want for 'em?" demanded Phelps.

"Only a dollar for the lot," said the man from the country. "Mighty cheap!"

"Well, take 'em up to my house, and come back and I'll pay you for 'em," said the justice, pointing to a dilapidated cabin of hickory poles and oak boards at the edge of the village.

For a few moments after the visitor left, Phelps was lost in thought, wondering how he could pay for the chickens. Then he suddenly got up and went into his temple of justice, a dingy ten-by-twelve room containing a greasy table, a single chair, and—for the jurors—a plank supported at each end by a chunk of firewood. A few loungers dropped in, and by the time the farmer returned for his money the justice was in the midst of a suit. The plaintiff sought compensation for a mule which a neighbor had shot for breaking into his corn field, although the fence was only four rails high.

Unimpressed by the dignity of this proceeding, the poultryman, with his coonskin cap still in place and his hands deep in his pockets, strode into the courtroom and up to the bench. "Squire," he began, "I've—"

"I fine you one dollar for contempt of court," Phelps interrupted, giving the intruder a look of severe and offended dignity.

"Me! Fine me?" exclaimed the surprised farmer.

"Yes, sir, you," said the judge decisively.

Finding that he could neither demur nor appeal, the dis-

[13] Quoted from an unnamed source by Robert M. Wright in *Dodge City in Cowboy Capital,* 184.

gusted farmer retreated to the door but turned there to ask, "Does that make us even, Squire?"

"Yes, sir, it does," Phelps replied quickly.

At this the farmer departed in despair, but not until he had assured His Honor, "Them's the last chickens you'll get from me."[14]

Sometimes informality was far from synonymous with equity. One such instance came up in the Texas village of Callisburg, in Cooke County, on February 23, 1875. There a local settler accused a man from neighboring Grayson County of stealing a cow and haled him before a justice of the peace. The defendant showed a bill of sale attested by two witnesses who had seen him pay the money for the cow. Nevertheless, the expounder of law and justice held the accused for trial and refused to take anyone from outside Cooke County on his bond. The justice said he was satisfied that the defendant had bought the cow and paid for her. Yet he maintained that, since there had been many unpunished cow thefts, he was forced to take action.[15]

One elderly justice of the peace in the arid Texas plains was called "Old Necessity" because he knew no law. He had a mail-order catalog bound in sheepskin so that it looked like a law book. He kept the catalog on his bench and consulted it diligently before giving his verdicts. On one occasion a man brought before him for some misdemeanor pleaded guilty. The defendant's lawyer mentioned a mitigating circumstance and asked the court to be lenient. The justice put on his spectacles, opened his bound volume at random, looked at it a moment, and announced, "I fine you $4.88."

The accused man jumped up to protest, but his attorney caught him by the coat and yanked him back to his seat. "Sit down," he ordered. "Be thankful he opened it at pants instead of at pianos."

Occasionally bluffing was a resort to hide ignorance of laws and procedure. In a case before a justice of the peace in the

[14] Levi Henderson Ashcroft, "The History of the War Between the Regulators and Moderators of Shelby County," MS. See Chapter II, note 3.

[15] Austin *Intelligencer-Echo,* March 29, 1875.

Roy Bean
Law West of the Pecos

prairie-dog country of western Texas, the prosecutor was outraged when his opponent quoted the law to the court. Unable to disprove the citation, the prosecutor nevertheless declared boldly, "Your Honor, that ain't the law."

When the defending lawyer refused to give in, the prosecuting attorney asserted with finality, "I'll bet you ten dollars it ain't the law," and threw a ten-spot on the table.

The opposing lawyer, who didn't have a ten with him, received no sympathy from the court. "Yes, money talks," said the justice. "If you ain't got the nerve to cover his ten, I guess you're wrong. The court rules against you."[16]

Yet informality in procedure did not always denote ignorance on the bench. Sometimes a judge well versed in the law would resort to brusque methods when these seemed to suit the occasion. Such a jurist was Judge Robert M. Williamson, one of the first district judges of the Republic of Texas. This salty frontiersman was better known as "Three-Legged Willie," since, from a childhood illness, he walked with a peg leg below one knee, with his withered limb sticking out behind.

In 1837, Three-Legged Willie went into the backwoods of Shelby County to establish the first district court there. Some of the citizens in that paradise for fugitives made it plain that they wanted no court. When the visiting judge seated himself behind a dry-goods box to open court, one of these opponents appeared before him. An assembly of citizens, he announced, had resolved that no court should be held. "What legal authority," asked Williamson, "can you give for such procedure?"

The ruffian's answer was to draw a bowie knife from his belt and slam it on the improvised bench. "This, sir," he snarled, "is the law of Shelby County."

As quickly, the judge whipped out a long-barreled pistol and placed it beside the knife. "If that is the law of Shelby County," he thundered, "this is the constitution that overrules your law."[17]

[16] Thomas F. Turner, "Prairie Dog Lawyers," *Panhandle Plains Historical Review*, Vol. II (1929), 117–18.

[17] Duncan W. Robinson, *Judge Robert McAlpine Williamson, Texas' Three-Legged Willie*, 160–61. A Texas county was named for Judge Williamson.

By far the most widely publicized of the frontier oracles was Roy Bean. Conscious of tourist interest, Texas has restored that landmark of the plains, the weather-beaten shack in which Bean used to dispense liquor with one hand and justice with the other. This forlorn, boxlike building, wearing a film of alkali dust, stands at the edge of the Big Bend region, a mountain wilderness that for generations has been a hide-out for bandits and a hunting ground for lone prospectors.

After his day, Bean's procedure and decisions became subjects for levity and ridicule. But in the eighties and nineties he helped to establish order in his neck of the greasewood country and to disprove the cowboy saying that there was "no law west of the Pecos." His was one of those primitive courts that marked the transition from vigilante rule to statutory justice. Bean's verdicts had scant foundation in law, but were based on common sense tinged occasionally with the judge's self-interest. Usually they suited the patrons of his court, who were better acquainted with gun smoke than with legal verbiage.

Bean had had a lively and checkered career before he settled in Langtry and assumed his judicial air. He grew up in the hills of Mason County, Kentucky, on the Ohio River, where he had been born in an obscure cabin in the late eighteen twenties. When he was about sixteen, he joined a party going down the river to New Orleans but hastened home after getting into trouble in the Crescent City. In the summer of 1847, an elder brother, Sam, came home with tales of his adventures as a teamster on the Santa Fé and Chihuahua trails and as a Mexican fighter. Roy decided to join him on his next expedition.

The pair reached Independence, Missouri, in the spring of 1848. They acquired a wagon, mules, and a stock of trading goods and set out for Chihuahua, where they established a trading post. Roy acquired a liking for chili *con carne,* tequila, cockfights, and *señoritas.* But the next spring he shot a drunken Mexican in self-defense and had to leave town hurriedly. He went to San Diego, where his eldest brother, Joshua, was a successful trader and the town's alcalde. In the next spring, 1850, Josh was named major general of the state militia.

Roy enjoyed his brother's affuence and hospitality by wearing the gay trappings of a *caballero* and dashing about on a fine horse. He patronized the taverns, the race tracks, and the cocking pits and became a favorite of the *señoritas.* But when his brother moved north in 1851, Roy stayed in San Diego and encountered bad luck again. On February 24, 1852, he and another blade engaged in a pistol duel on horseback, for which both were jailed. In April, Bean escaped and rode off to find Josh, who was operating the Headquarters Saloon in the mission village of San Gabriel, nine miles from Los Angeles.

Roy put on a bartender's apron and helped his brother—until Josh was killed by a night assassin in the following November. Roy continued the saloon for some time, but again fortune was against him. He had only a limping horse and the clothes on his back when he arrived at Mesilla, New Mexico. There he found his brother Sam, who was doing well with a combination store, hotel, café, saloon, and gambling room, with a freighting business on the side.

Roy quickly made himself useful, and in 1861 the brothers established a branch in Pinos Altos, a bonanza mining camp in the mountains. Early in the Civil War, Roy helped organize some Confederate sympathizers into an informal company. These men named themselves the "Free Rovers" but were called the "Forty Thieves" by some of their critics. Without achieving anything, they disbanded after the failure of the Texas campaign in New Mexico. Many years later, Bean claimed he had been attached to the command of General John R. Baylor as a spy and scout.[18]

A backwash of Confederate sympathizers took Bean to San Antonio, Texas. He spent the remainder of the war there, except for profitable trips to Mexico as a freighter running the Yankee blockade. His business dealings got him into several lawsuits, but usually he managed to outwit his opponents. After the war, he moved to South Flores Street, in a shabby neighborhood that came to be known as Beanville. On October 28, 1866, he mar-

[18] Horace Bell, *Reminiscences of a Ranger* (1927 edition), 368–69; Horace Bell, *On the Old West Coast,* 233–36; C. L. Sonnichsen, *Roy Bean.* Of the three biographies of Bean, Sonnichsen's is by far the best and is the only one which has a detailed and reliable account of Bean's early life.

ried an eighteen-year-old Mexican girl, Virginia Chávez. For sixteen years he lived in Beanville. He marketed firewood cut from others' property without permission, peddled watered milk, sold meat from stray cows, and engaged in other dubious but not too strenuous activities. In this period, he acquired children, took on weight, and grew a beard.[19]

As he did not get on well with either his wife or his neighbors, Bean welcomed a chance to follow the Southern Pacific Railroad westward in the early eighties. He took along a tent in which he sold whiskey to the hard-drinking Irishmen of the construction crews. This business took him into a desolate country where thirst called for frequent quenching. By midsummer of 1882, Bean had established himself in the dusty railroad tent village of Eagle's Nest, on the bank of the Río Grande, where he sold food, cigars, and liquor.[20] His tent, with its portable bar and gambling tables, became a mecca for tired workmen and was the scene of much roistering.

In a dreary country of cactus, brush, and rattlesnakes, this and near-by railroad camps held eight thousand workmen. Many of them were foreigners who spoke little English, and all were isolated from normal social life and amusements. Other crews were building eastward from El Paso, mainly with Chinese labor, bringing a threat of racial clashes. Quarrels and shootings were inevitable, and many of these received scant attention. "Everything is perfectly peaceful here," Bean told one visitor. "There hasn't been a man killed in four hours."

Although Bean had little schooling, his generous beard, his imperious bearing, and the cool manner in which he handled his six-shooters when occasion arose marked him as a leader in the camp. Often he was called on to settle a dispute or to decide what disposal should be made of a man who had died of lead poisoning. Soon, since there was no court nearer than Fort Stockton, nearly two hundred miles away, the Texas Rangers stationed at Eagle's Nest began bringing their prisoners to Bean for judgment.

At first, Bean's informal court had no authority except that of

[19] Franklin Hall in the San Antonio *Express,* December 31, 1933.

[20] San Antonio *Express*, July 27, 1882.

common consent, backed by the Rangers' guns. But that did not keep him from passing judgment on minor offenses and on at least one case of aggravated assault. Soon this lack of authority was remedied. At the request of the Rangers, who were tired of marching prisoners across the dusty plains, the commissioners court appointed Roy Bean as justice of the peace on August 2, 1882. He did not qualify by providing a thousand-dollar bond until December 6; but a minor detail such as that did not keep him from conducting court.

In September the Rangers and Judge Bean moved to another tent town, the biggest and wickedest of them all. This was Vinegaroon, named for a kind of spider. The new place provided plenty of grist for Judge Bean's mill. He impressed spectators with the dignified bearing he could assume on occasion and with the smattering of legal jargon he had picked up in courts in which he had been a defendant. And he had the support of the Rangers to make his decisions stick. By stepping up the fines of those who talked back, he quickly taught offenders not to question his verdicts.

Late in 1882, when the population of Vinegaroon began to dwindle, Bean moved his business to near-by Strawbridge, which later became the town of Sanderson. Driven from there by the trickery of a rival liquor dealer, who had kerosene put in his whiskey barrel, Bean settled near a water tank where lots were being marked off for sale. This was about the time of the ceremonial joining of the tracks in Dead Man's Canyon, January 12, 1883. Bean named the budding place Langtry, in honor of the famous English actress, Lily Langtry, who had come to America a few months earlier. He induced the Post Office Department to adopt this name officially on December 8, 1884.

Although the railroad builders had gone, Bean had confidence in the future of this sagebrush country and decided to stick. The railroad gave him an annual pass, and he obtained enough lumber to build a one-room cabin with a porch across the front. Soon he impressed an itinerant painter to provide signs that read: "Judge Roy Bean, Notary Public—Justice of the Peace—Law West of the Pecos—Ice Beer." He was elected justice of the peace for two years more in 1884, and his place of business was made the precinct polling place. His court business remained profitable, despite the exodus of construction workers. Part of the money collected in fines found its way to the county treasury.

Bean had strong opposition in some later elections but, by one means or another, he usually managed to keep in office. To add dignity to his court, he obtained a blank book in which he wrote his "statoots" as well as his poker rules. "Cheating and horse theft," he recorded, "is hanging offenses if ketched." On another page he wrote, "A full beats a straight unless the one holding the full is not straight or is himself too full."[21] Soon he expanded his law library with a copy of the *Revised Statutes of Texas,* but this was more for show than for reference.

This law book figured in Bean's celebrated decision on the slaying of a Chinese railroad hand in a brawl in 1884. The culprit, a brawny Irishman, was haled before the court but brought along a squad of equally husky friends. These rough workers, none too delicately, gave the justice of the peace to understand that the wrong decision might result in boycott of his liquor bar and even wrecking of the building. Perplexed a bit by his dilemma, Bean studiously thumbed through the statutes and then announced:

"Gentlemen, the court finds that the law is explicit on the killing of a fellow man, but nothing at all is said about knocking off a Chinaman. Case dismissed." The drinks, he hastened to add, would be on the impetuous Irishman.[22]

Bean used his public office regularly to stimulate his tavern business. Every trial opened and closed with a round or two of drinks, and long sessions were interrupted by recesses for refreshments at the bar. Any juror who failed to take full advantage of this opportunity would find his name dropped from the list of eligibles—if indeed he escaped a fine for contempt of court.

[21] Charles Merritt Barnes, "The Halcyon Days of Vinegaroon," San Antonio *Express,* August 20, 1905. Years later a Southern Pacific official, G. S. Waid, disputed the claim that Bean had named the town of Langtry for the actress. Waid said the station was named in honor of a railway construction foreman.

As there was no jail for many miles, Bean kept prisoners chained to a near-by mesquite tree. They slept in the open, with gunny sacks for pillows, and worked at whatever jobs Bean wanted done. Although he sometimes tried men for capital offenses, he never had a death penalty carried out. Once he threw a scare into a young thief by having a noose placed about his neck but allowed him to escape. In another case, the story goes, he sentenced a horse thief to be hanged. But a few minutes later, on discovering that the prisoner had $400 in his pocket, he reopened the case. He fined the defendant $300—explaining that it wasn't much of a cayuse he had tried to steal—and advised him to leave town in a hurry.

Cases bringing fines were much preferred, since most of the money collected went into the judge's pocket. Whenever Bean knew that an accused person had money with him, he found some pretext for slapping on a fine to take most of his bankroll. Even a dead man, on one notable occasion, was not immune from this rule. In 1892, the body of Pat O'Brien, killed by falling from the high railroad bridge over Myers Canyon, was brought before Bean. The judge quickly discovered in the dead man's pockets a six-shooter and forty dollars in currency. He thereupon confiscated the gun and fined the culprit forty dollars for having carried a concealed weapon.[23]

At one time the Attorney General of Texas wrote Bean to inquire why he failed to send to the capital the state's share of the fines he collected. The judge replied that he never received any money from the state and that he had to make his court self-sustaining—and with that the matter was dropped. Equally emphatic was Bean's defense of his granting of divorces. When a district judge reminded him that a justice of the peace was not authorized to grant divorces, the Langtry sage had a ready answer. He said that since he was allowed to perform marriage ceremonies, he necessarily had the power to undo the knots he tied, thus rectifying his errors; and he kept on doing so.

Judge Bean's legal duties did not prevent him from playing

[22] *Ibid.*

[23] El Paso *Daily Times,* June 2, 1884; San Antonio *Express,* March 18, 1903.

poker on his front porch, attending an occasional cockfight, or carrying on a flourishing liquor business. Indeed, he often used drastic methods to increase the dollars and pesos in the money drawer of his bar. Much of his business came from selling drinks, at fifty cents each, to Southern Pacific passengers who got off the train long enough to stretch their legs and quench their thirst. To such customers, Bean's rule was never to give change—not even for a twenty-dollar bill or gold piece.

If a customer, hearing the train's whistle, called for his change, Bean merely ignored him. At this, the visitor, worried by fear of missing his train and being stranded, usually would become louder in his demand and perhaps would throw in a few cuss words. This would be the cue for Bean to assume his judicial dignity and to declare the customer guilty of abusive language, disturbance of the peace, and contempt of court. The judge would fine him the amount of the change due and advise him to vamoose if he wanted to catch his train.[24]

Bean took special delight in defrauding the beer and whiskey salesmen who stopped off at Langtry. It was customary for these visitors to treat the crowd on their arrival, and Bean saw to it that their bills ran high. Since the amount was compiled by counting the empty glasses, Bean got out all he had. When the salesman's back was turned, he poured liquor from one glass into another to give each the appearance of having been used.

Early in 1896, Judge Bean had a hand in bringing to Langtry the biggest crowd it ever had. The Dallas fight promoter, Dan Stuart, had planned a match at El Paso. His contenders were the Irish champion, Peter Maher, and the Australian, Bob Fitzsimmons, who was destined to wrest the championship from Jim Corbett a year later. But with Texas Rangers present to enforce the state law against prize fights and with Mexican officials equally adamant at Juárez, across the river, another place had to be found.

Desperate for a site, Stuart accepted a telegraphic invitation from Bean and packed fighters and fans on a special train headed east. At Langtry, Rangers were on hand, ready for trouble. Bean,

[24] San Antonio *Express*, March 18, 1903.

too, was ready. He had Mexicans build a pontoon bridge across the Río Grande, and, on February 21, the fight was held in a natural bowl on the other side, far from the reach of Mexican officials. Lanky Bob knocked out Maher in less than two minutes. This outcome left the fans time to drink—at a dollar a bottle—the extra shipment of beer that Bean had imported from San Antonio.[25]

Bean continued to be a strong admirer of Lily Langtry, whose picture adorned the *Police Gazette* and other literature that found its way to his bailiwick. He wrote to the actress, telling her that he had named the place in her honor. Pleased at this, she offered to present the town with an ornamental drinking fountain; but Bean declined the gift. He explained that the only drink Langtry people did not relish was water. He was proud of her letter and added to the front of his tavern a misspelled sign—"The Jersey Lilly." He wanted the actress to visit him, as Jay Gould had done in 1890. She finally stopped off in Langtry, while her train waited; but by this time Bean had been gone for ten months.[26]

The end came quietly, before daybreak, on March 16, 1903, a few days after the Judge had returned from a trip to San Antonio.[27] He was buried at Del Río, a larger town down the Río Grande. Mexicans said his ghost haunted the badlands of the Big Bend, and Texans retold and embellished the stories of his judicial antics. Judge Bean had made good his promise to bring law west of the Pecos.

For a long time after Roy Bean's passing, the dubious sort of justice he brought was the only kind available in many isolated communities on either side of the Pecos. As late as 1932, a survey showed that fewer than 5 per cent of the active justices of the peace in six typical counties of a Midwestern state had any legal training. These justices, who obtained their compensation in costs collected from guilty defendants, gave ver-

[25] Dallas *Morning News*, February 22, 1896.

[26] Lillie Langtry, *The Days I Knew*, 195–200.

[27] Dallas *Morning News*, March 17, 1903; San Antonio *Express*, March 18, 1903.

dicts of guilty in 99.2 per cent of the the cases.[28] Kent Sagendorph told in 1939 of one justice who, after trying cases for twenty years, boasted that he had not opened a law book yet. Another was so deaf that he could not hear any of the testimony or argument. Sagendorph added:

> Most justices hold court anywhere they happen to be at the time some judicial business pops up. I saw a justice delay a hearing because he was up on the roof of his barn laying some shingles. Another holds court in the village grain elevator, where he is the bookkeeper. And one fairly well known justice can invariably be found in a village poolroom, forever trying to make a combination shot for the side pocket, and nobody has ever seen him do it yet. He grumblingly leaves the game, sits enthroned in an ancient chair in the front window, and dispenses justice and sarcasm in equal parts.
>
> Another justice I know of is a barber in a small community. Not long ago a prominent businessman was brought before him on a charge of speeding. The businessman was in a hurry, trying to get to a distant point to keep an important engagement. But, before hearing his case, the minion of the law kept the defendant cooling his heels for the better part of an hour while he shaved several stubble-bearded customers.[29]

As the office itself became obsolete, many justices of the peace became wealthy by operating marriage marts and motorist speed traps. In some instances, their courts became rural rackets that would have made Roy Bean green with envy.

Bean and his kind had some excuse in the uncouth times and the isolated posts in which they lived. Although many of their decisions were open to question, they established local precedents for judicial action. They showed that disputes could be settled without the use of six-shooters and that crimes could be punished without resort to vigilante hanging ropes. Their loose procedure was a steppingstone to the more formal courts that followed.

[28] Edson R. Sunderland, "The Efficiency of Justices' Courts in Michigan," *Fourth Report of the Judicial Council of Michigan* (May 1934), 169–72.

[29] Kent Sagendorph, "Jack-Rabbit Justice," *Country Home Magazine*, July, 1939.

14. Order in the Court

> Little formality was evidenced at a frontier court session. The judge disliked fog-raising disputations which would cloud the issue and drag out the case. He knew little law but preferred to do business on the basis of equity.
>
> —EVERETT DICK, *The Sod-House Frontier, 1854–1890*

WILLIAM Z. COZENS, who in 1862 became the second sheriff of Gilpin County, Colorado, picked up a couple of husky horse thieves one afternoon but did not know what to do with them. Court would not open until the next morning, and the county did not yet have a jail. His equipment was limited to a Sharp's rifle, a pair of Colts, and a few handcuffs and legirons. The only solution he could think of was to take the prisoners to his home, handcuff them to a post at the foot of a bed, and allow them to sleep on the floor. He did this in spite of the fact that his wife was confined to the bed with a new baby. But what she had to say about his action sent him scurrying the next morning to round up enough Central City loafers to build a primitive jail.[1]

Lack of safe jails was one of the chief impediments to the enforcment of statutory law on the frontier and often delayed the effectiveness of early courts. In California, where the gold rush brought a sudden surge of adventurers, the jail problem was especially acute. At Yerba Buena, which was later to become San Francisco, a hungry prisoner appeared before the

[1] *History of Clear Creek and Boulder Valleys, Colorado,* 447; Lynn Irwin Perrigo, "A Social History of Central City, Colorado," 203, Ph.D. dissertation, University of Colorado; Lafayette Hanchett, *The Old Sheriff,* 9-12.

alcalde one morning, carrying on his back the door of the calaboose, to which he was chained, and demanding his breakfast.[2] In 1849, desperate San Franciscans bought a dismantled brig, the *Euphemia,* and used it as the boom town's hoosegow.[3] At Sacramento in the following year, the bark *La Grange* was acquired for the same purpose.[4]

Other California towns were in like straits. Los Angeles kept wrongdoers in an old adobe dwelling on the hill in the rear of the Lafayette Hotel. This house was so insecure that the jailer, George Whitehorn, chained his prisoners—like fish on a string—to a big pine log that extended the length of the room.[5] Contra Costa County built a stone jail in 1850, but prisoners continued to escape.[6] Placer County's jail in 1851 was a log cabin at Auburn.[7] In the next year W. B. Ide, a justice of the peace at Monroeville, in Colusa County, built an iron cage and placed it in the shade of a tree, thus keeping lawbreakers in the fresh air.[8]

Early emigrants noted the frailty of California's jails in a ballad called "Seeing the Elephant" and sung to the tune of "The Boatman's Dance." It ended:

Because I would not pay a bill,
They kicked me out of Downieville.
I stole a mule and lost the trail
And fetched up in the Hangtown jail.

Canvas roof and paper walls,
Twenty horse thieves in the stalls—
I did just like I'd done before—
Coyoted out from 'neath the floor.

Throughout the plains country, especially where building

[2] J. H. Brown, *Reminiscences and Incidents of the Early Life of San Francisco,* 30.

[3] Bancroft, *Popular Tribunals,* I, 107.

[4] George F. Wright, editor, *History of Sacramento County,* 87–88.

[5] Horace Bell, *Reminiscences of a Ranger,* 51.

[6] *Illustrations of Contra Costa County,* 12.

[7] *History of Placer County,* 97.

[8] Justus H. Rogers, *Colusa County,* 77–78.

materials were scarce, jail troubles were similarly common. In Stephen F. Austin's colony in Texas, which had no jail, some prisoners were held in chains for months.[9] Decades later, arrested men sometimes were placed in dry cisterns to sober up or to await bail or trial.[10] At Sherman, Texas, in 1857, the first Grayson County jail was built on the south side of the square. It was made of heavy logs, and its walls had no window or door. Prisoners were lowered and lifted through a trap door in the roof. This device was supposed to keep prisoners from escaping. It worked except when the prisoners had friends outside.

In western Texas, bearded Roy Bean was not the only one who had prisoners fastened to a tree and forced to sleep on the ground.[11] At Fort McKavett, Texas, late in December, 1886, another justice of the peace, John Fleutsch, had a drunken Mexican chained by his neck to a live oak in the public square. He left the culprit there during a blizzard until, nearly frozen, he was rescued by outraged citizens.[12]

There were many such improvizations. At Seymour, where even trees were scarce, Texas Rangers who arrested riotous cow hands in the early eighteen eighties sometimes left them overnight handcuffed to stakes in the prairie.[13] At Warner, Kansas, a prisoner was handcuffed to a telephone pole until sober enough to appear in court.[14] In 1906, a Texas Ranger, Frank Hamer, took a trouble-making, drunken cow hand from a Christmas Eve dance at Marathon, at the edge of the Big Bend country. For the rest of the night, Hamer left him chained to a nearby windmill.[15]

Occasionally sheriffs boarded their prisoners in the jails of

[9] Noah Smithwick, *The Evolution of a State,* 84–85.

[10] Arthur G. Harral, "Arthur G. Anderson, Pioneer Sheep Breeder of West Texas," *Southwestern Sheep and Goat Raiser* (Now *Sheep and Goat Raiser*), November, 1935; Dick, *The Sod-House Frontier, 1854–1890,* 133.

[11] Barnes, "The Halcyon Days of Vinegaroon," San Antonio *Express,* August 20, 1905.

[12] Charles Warren Hunter, "John Fleutsch, a Frontier Justice," *Frontier Times,* February, 1924.

[13] Mrs. Lenora Bandy of Dallas, who lived at Seymour in the early eighteen eighties, to the author, 1947.

[14] Dick, *The Sod-House Frontier, 1854–1890,* 133.

[15] Bert Griffith, "Texas Ranger," *Today,* December 15, 1934.

adjoining counties[16] or had to keep them in their own homes until court opened.[17] In many instances they used places built for other purposes. At Lincoln, Nebraska, the milk house of the county treasurer served as a lockup. Elsewhere on the frontier, prisoners were chained in a stall in a livery stable or kept in a newspaper office.[18]

Such jails as did exist on the outer fringe of settlement usually were unsafe. Officers hesitated to lock up those accused of major crimes. It was too easy for prisoners to bribe a deputy, to dig themselves out, to tear a hole through the shingle roof, or to have confederates batter down the door when the jail was left unguarded at night. In 1842, Sheriff David Rusk of Nacogdoches County, Texas, refused to accept from another county men accused of murder. He explained that his jail was "unsafe and insufficient to detain prisoners with security and safety and could easily be broken open, either by prisoners within or by persons without."[19]

To the north, Abilene, Kansas, began building a stone jail in 1870. Before the structure could be completed, its walls were demolished by exuberant cow hands. After that incident, work was resumed under guard. The jail's first prisoner was a lamp-shooting Negro cook from one of the trail drivers' camps on Mud Creek. He was quickly rescued by his camp companions, who chased away the peace officers and shot the lock off the jail door.[20] In tumultuous Deadwood, during the Black Hills gold rush in 1877, the jail was a log cabin about fifteen by twenty feet. It sometimes had as many as twenty-five occupants, who took turns lying on the floor.[21] In Wyoming, Cheyenne's first jail was a small log cabin back of the Dyer Hotel.[22]

[16] R. C. Crane, "Early Days in Fisher County," *West Texas Historical Association Year Book,* Vol. VI (June, 1930), 145.

[17] *Texas Pioneer Magazine,* 1880, 215; Carl Coke Rister, *Southern Plainsmen,* 199.

[18] Dick, *The Sod-House Frontier, 1854–1890,* 132–33.

[19] *Lewis* v. *Ames,* No. 44, *Texas Reports,* 319–51; Louis Wiltz Kemp, *The Signers of the Texas Declaration of Independence,* 276.

[20] Theodore C. Henry, "Thomas James Smith of Abilene," *Kansas Historical Collections,* Vol. IX (1905–1906), 528–29.

[21] Omaha *Herald,* June 22, 1877, quoting the Deadwood *Champion.*

[22] I. S. Bennett, editor, *History of Wyoming,* 554.

Early Texas newspapers contained frequent notices of escapes from jail. At Boerne, in 1877, a young scamp locked up for stealing the sheriff's horse removed his handcuffs and tore a board off the floor of his cell. He used this to open a window shutter and bend the iron bars enough to allow him to slip through. Once outside, he appropriated a fine horse, with saddle and bridle, and rode off in style.[23] At Jacksboro, in the same year, three prisoners charged with theft escaped after sawing out two of the jail's ceiling timbers and making a large hole through a weatherboarded gable end of the roof.[24]

Weeks earlier, Jacksboro's newspaper, the *Frontier Echo,* had lamented the frequent jail deliveries of the preceding two years. It demanded a jail "that will securely hold all evil-doers who may be put in it, one from which prisoners cannot escape without complicity of the keeper."[25] Such pleas were made often in the new towns of the Great Plains. Several years after the Jacksboro appeal, the *Frontier,* at O'Neill, in northern Nebraska, asserted: "The crying need of O'Neill is a safe place to put the many drunken wretches that disgrace our streets day and night continually. Let us have a jail at any cost."[26]

Lack of secure jails had been one of the chief incentives to vigilante action. The vigilance committees dared not disband until there was reasonable assurance that local prisoners could be held behind bars. Lack of courthouses in which criminal records could be kept safely was another handicap in the enforcement of statutory laws. Often the first courthouse was a log cabin or a crude structure built for other purposes. Sometimes court records were kept in homes. In 1878 the tax funds of Holt County, Nebraska, were kept in a hollowed cottonwood board in the roof of a dwelling.[27] In Adams County, in the same state, a contractor agreed to build a log courthouse for thirty dollars and to have it ready in ten days, the county to provide all materials except the windows and the door.[28]

23 Galveston *News,* May 1, 1877.
24 *Frontier Echo,* Jacksboro, Texas, September 7, 1877.
25 *Ibid.,* July 27, 1877.
26 Dick, *The Sod-House Frontier, 1854–1890,* 133.
27 *Nebraska History and Record of Pioneer Days,* Vol. I, No. 7, 4.
28 Dick, *The Sod-House Frontier, 1854–1890,* 461.

Such makeshifts were common in the frontier West. In most Iowa counties the first court met in the log cabin of some pioneer settler. A mill served this purpose in one county, and saloons in two others.[29] In northeastern Texas, the first Smith County courthouse, built in 1847, was made of pine logs, with a plank floor. The first in Cooke County, built of scotched logs and boards, cost a $29 note.

In frontier Texas the stealing of criminal records and the burning of courthouses to destroy such records were frequent practices. The Parker County courthouse at Weatherford was burned by an incendiary in March, 1874.[30] Early the next month a roaring blaze consumed the Milam County courthouse and all the records it housed. A kerosene jug was found under the courtyard fence. A Negro arrested for setting the fire was believed to have been hired by an indicted white man who wanted to destroy the records in his case.[31] The courthouse and records at Rockwall met a similar fate in March, 1875.[32]

This wave of arson continued for several years. In the spring of 1876, the district court in Fort Worth was thrown into confusion by the destruction of all its records.[33] In adjoining Denton County, incendiaries burned the courthouse in Christmas week of that year. When the district court began holding its sessions in the Denton Presbyterian Church, this building was burned during the first week of March. Its loss did away with the indictments of men awaiting trial for cattle rustling.[34]

Several other Texas courthouses were burned within a few months. On the night of April 10, 1877, four horsemen galloped into Castroville. They poured coal oil on the records in the courthouse, set the building ablaze, and fired sixteen shots at citizens

[29] Benjamin F. Gue, *History of Iowa,* III, 296–436.

[30] Weatherford *Times,* March 28, 1875; Dallas *Weekly News,* April 3, 1875.

[31] Galveston *News,* April 14, 1874; San Antonio *Herald,* April 16, 1874.

[32] Dallas *Weekly News,* March 27, 1875.

[33] Austin *Weekly Statesman,* April 6, 1876, quoting the Fort Worth *Democrat.*

[34] [Thomas E. Hogg], *Authentic History of Sam Bass and His Gang;* Wayne Gard, *Sam Bass,* 100.

JUDGE ISAAC C. PARKER
Lawbreakers called him "Hell on the Border"

Daily Oklahoman

who rushed out to try to stop the flames and save the records.[35] In May, vandals burned the courthouse at Frio.[36] On the night of June 11, the records of all pending criminal cases were stolen from the courthouse at Lampasas, where participants in the bloody Horrell-Higgins feud were under indictment.[37] One night later the district clerk at Llano County, John C. Oatman, who kept the court records in his home, had his residence burned by an arsonist but managed to save the records.[38] In the spring of 1879 the district court was unable to meet in Refugio because the courthouse and its records had been burned.[39]

Even where jails and courthouses were adequate, there was often difficulty in finding jurors who would vote convictions. Many jurors preferred to let their neighbors off, while some recalled shady activities of their own or feared retaliation by friends of the accused. Most of the early sheriffs and other local enforcement officers did their best, while working under difficulties. Occasionally one was found to be in collusion with lawbreakers. Few, however, went as far as the Montana and Idaho sheriffs who were hanged by vigilantes, the Kansas marshal who tried to rob a bank, or the Texas sheriff who was careless of the brands on the cattle he sold.

Often it required a long time for the frontier court to make itself feared by outlaws, or even to be taken seriously by law-abiding citizens. When Judge William B. Ochiltree came to the log-cabin town of Dallas, Texas, in early December, 1846, soon after Dallas County had been formed, he set up court in one of the cabins. He impaneled a grand jury that deliberated under a tree and, between sessions, played poker or held mock trials. In one of the mock trials, the grand jury convicted the prosecuting attorney, Thomas W. Blake, of letting down bars by beginning at the top instead of at the bottom. The jury assessed him, as a fine, a gallon of whiskey that cost him five dollars. The jurors then began celebrating and fined Judge Ochiltree two

35 Austin *Weekly Statesman,* April 19, 1877.
36 *Ibid.,* May 24, 1877.
37 Galveston *News,* June 15, 1877.
38 Austin *Weekly Statesman,* June 28, 1877.
39 *Western Chronicle,* May 1, 1879.

gallons of like refreshment for refusing to obey a summons to attend their party.[40]

Nearly three decades later, Dallas still heard complaints that its courts were not as effective as they were intended to be. In its issue of June 5, 1875, the *Weekly Herald* lamented:

> It is fearful to feel that we are living in a community where the courts and juries set no higher value upon human life, to feel that any day you may be shot down without cause and that tomorrow your murderer may be walking abroad in search of other victims. But is this not true of the people of Dallas today?
>
> There is a remedy and a sure one. It is the stern and unfaltering execution of the laws.

Three months later the *Herald* editor was still disheartened. In the issue of September 4 he wrote: "The people—the bone and sinew of the country—are losing confidence in the courts and justice. This leads to mob violence and lynch law."

Decorum in the frontier court was not easily achieved. Some of the early judges were careless in appearance and informal in procedure. An Englishman who visited Texas in the latter days of the Republic was a bit shocked at the conduct of a Galveston judge. He found this jurist chewing his quid and resting his feet on his desk while the lawyers, "ready of speech and loads of references, from Magna Charta upwards," chewed, smoked, and whittled.[41] In a later day, Zack Miller of the Oklahoma 101 Ranch recalled the official crier at the federal court at Guthrie, Dick Plunkett. Dick used to open the proceedings by shouting, "Hear ye! Hear ye! Now all you mully-grubs in the back of the courtroom keep your traps shut and give these swell guys up in front a chance to talk!"[42]

Most frontier judges were less interested in hair-splitting

[40] Thomas W. Blake, letter to E. S. Brown of Lynchburg, Virginia, August 5, 1898, in archives of Dallas Historical Society; J. R. Bradfield, Jr., "When the Law First Came to Dallas," Dallas *Morning News*, April 18, 1926.

[41] William Bollaert, "Personal Narrative of a Residence and Travels in the Republic of Texas, 1840–44," 191, manuscript in the Ayer Collection, Newberry Library, Chicago.

[42] Fred Gipson, *Fabulous Empire*, 143.

arguments and citations of decisions than in horse sense and grass-roots rhetoric. Some of them, even in statutory courts, recessed occasionally to allow everyone present to quench his thirst at a near-by bar or to enable a pair of belligerent lawyers to continue their fist fight outdoors. Other judges tried, with varying degrees of success, to bring formality and dignity into their courts. They banned tipsy lawyers and required spectators to leave their six-shooters outside. One jurist was miffed when confronted at the door of his hotel room by the sheriff and twelve jurors ready to give their verdict in a criminal case. He had them marched into the courtroom, where he heard their decision read with full formality.[43] In Arizona a territorial judge, who was a stickler for decorum, required all jurors to wear coats. Once, on noticing a juror in shirt sleeves, he sent the offender home after his coat. After three days the juror returned with the required garment. His home, the judge discovered, was at Quijotoa, eighty miles away.[44]

Many of the frontier judges worked hard. Some, like the circuit-riding preachers, covered broad areas on horseback or in jolting buggies. Writing of the northern Great Plains in the sod-house era, Everett Dick told of one especially energetic judge. In 1866 he "left home on Sunday evening, drove his team eighty miles, and held court on Monday, during which he sent two men to the penitentiary with the aid of a grand jury and trial jury. He also cleared the docket of twenty-seven civil cases and reached home at Tuesday noon."[45]

As the frontier courts became better established and met at regular intervals, their sessions often became social events. They competed, to a mild degree, with horse races, circuses, and community fairs. Farm and ranch families timed their visits to the county seat to coincide with the court session and thus picked up more news and occasionally listened to legal forensics. "District court meets a week from Monday, and we look for music and fun then," said the Tascosa (Texas) *Pioneer* of May 4, 1889. "Lawbreakers will need to look wary on that day, and so will

[43] Dick, *The Sod-House Frontier, 1854–1890,* 457–58.
[44] Richard E. Sloan, *Memories of an Arizona Judge,* 80.
[45] Dick, *The Sod-House Frontier, 1854–1890,* 458.

the state, because we look to see the bar represented by nearly all the illustrious lights of the Panhandle."

In the mountain states, where disputes over mining claims often were brought into court for settlement, judges sometimes were tempted to accept favor that might have influenced their decisions. These offers generally were spurned, and rumors of bribery went unproved. In territorial Idaho, prior to 1870, one mining company gained its end by less direct means. It induced an unfriendly district judge to resign by paying him the equivalent of his salary for the three remaining years of his four-year term.[46]

Some jurists were especially careful to avoid taint. In Deadwood, Dakota Territory, a United States judge, Granville G. Bennett, turned down in 1877 a friend's offer of two thousand shares of mining stock on unlimited credit, with no strings attached. The judge spurned the stock because he did not want to find himself entangled in case he should be called upon to make a decision in which the mining company was involved. Although he lived to see this stock multiply incredibly in price and pay enormous dividends, he never regretted his decision.[47]

Federal judges, who had the advantage of being free from local politics, played a large part in bringing statutory law to the frontier. In many respects, the most outstanding of these jurists was Judge Isaac Charles Parker of the Western District of Arkansas, with jurisdiction over the Indian Territory. In the twenty-one years in which he presided over the court at Fort Smith, Judge Parker became one of the most influential individuals in putting down outlawry in the West. Unlike Judge Bennett, who would rather have resigned than to inflict capital punishment,[48] Judge Parker sent eighty-eight men to the gallows that stood within view of the window of his first courtroom. Severity of sentences, however, was by no means the only factor that made his court a landmark in the bringing of formal justice to the western frontier.

[46] Thomas Donaldson, *Idaho of Yesterday*, 199–200.
[47] Estelline Bennett, *Old Deadwood Days*, 41–42.
[48] *Ibid.*, 42–43.

Born in Belmont County, Ohio, on October 15, 1838, Parker was reared on a farm. With intervals of teaching, he attended Barnesville Academy and later studied law. He was admitted to the Ohio bar in 1859 but later in that year moved to St. Joseph, Missouri. There he opened a law office and in 1860 was elected city attorney. He married Mary O'Toole in 1861, retained his city post four years, and in 1864 served as a presidential elector, voting for Abraham Lincoln. He was a corporal in the Home Guard during the war and in 1864 became prosecuting attorney for the Twelfth Judicial Circuit. Four years later he was elected judge of this court. In October, 1870, he resigned to run for Congress. In his two terms in Congress, Parker showed a strong interest in the territories and in the Indians and advocated numerous measures for the advancement of each.

Early in 1875, President Ulysses S. Grant named Parker to become chief justice of Utah, and the Senate promptly confirmed the nomination. But two weeks later the President withdrew the appointment and asked Parker to take the more difficult post at Fort Smith.[49] This proved to be one of Grant's wisest appointments and one that gave almost universal satisfaction after the new judge began his work.

This Arkansas assignment was one of the toughest in the country. Parker succeeded a weak and incompetent jurist who had allowed the court to slide into disrepute. He came to Fort Smith at a time when the Indian Territory was infested with renegades and cutthroats—white and black as well as bronze—many of them fugitives from other parts of the nation or even from foreign countries. People called it "Robbers' Roost" and "the Land of the Six-Shooter." Current statements that the territory was under a reign of terror were not exaggerated.

"It is sickening to the heart," wrote the editor of Fort Smith's *Western Independent*, "to contemplate the increase of crime in the Indian country." He went on to mention that in the sparsely settled territory travelers were waylaid, shot, and robbed. He noted that the cattle trail from Texas to Kansas was "infested

[49] William S. Speer, managing editor, *The Encyclopedia of the New West;* Fort Smith *Times-Democrat*, November 17, 1896; Van Buren *Press*, November 21, 1896; S. W. Harman, *Hell on the Border*, 83–84.

with murderers, robbers, and horse thieves gathered from all parts of the country. It is time Congress should take this matter in hand and organize a territory, for if crime increases there so fast, a regiment of deputy marshals cannot arrest the murderers."[50]

In a later issue he added:

> We have lived in and around the Indian country since the spring of 1834 but have never known such a state of terror. Now it is murder throughout the length and breadth of the Indian country. It has been the rendezvous of the vile and wicked from everywhere, an inviting field for murder and robbery because it is the highway between Texas, Missouri, Kansas, and Arkansas.
>
> A few years ago a deputy marshal could travel anywhere unmolested, but now they have to go in squads for self-protection from bands of desperadoes roaming through the country, seeking persons to murder and plunder. A company of forty men, known as Gallagher's band, bid defiance of law and are fearless of the United States cavalry. This band infests the cattle trail, and its members have friends everywhere that keep them posted as to the movements of the marshals and the military. Stealing horses is an everyday occurence, and murder and robbery seem to equal that sin. It is dangerous to travel alone where villains from the four quarters of the United States congregate to murder, rob, and steal.[51]

A big man physically, Parker at thirty-six was the youngest man on the federal bench when he arrived at Fort Smith and took up his new duties. Prior to his arrival, some misgiving had been expressed there, especially by Democrats. The *Western Independent* had been disgusted with most of Grant's appointments and had been much displeased with some of Parker's Congressional votes on bills embodying party and sectional issues. Its editor extended only a guarded welcome.[52]

Within a few weeks, however, this coolness gave way to enthusiastic support. Judge Parker showed from the start that

50 *Western Independent*, Fort Smith, Arkansas, August 21, 1873.
51 *Ibid.*, August 28, 1873.
52 *Ibid.*, April 8, 1875.

he did not intend to use his new post for political purposes. More than that, he gave evidence of unbounded energy and fearlessness in enforcing the laws and in bringing criminals to justice. One of his early moves was to appoint two hundred deputy marshals to patrol the areas under his jurisdiction and to bring in lawbreakers and witnesses.

The *Western Independent* was quick to recognize Judge Parker's outstanding merits. It observed on May 19 that the new judge was "giving entire satisfaction to both the bar and the public" and had brought with him a higher appreciation of his duties than his predecessor had shown. The Fort Smith *Herald* was likewise appreciative of the almost revolutionary improvement wrought by Judge Parker. Three months after his arrival, this paper noted, in its issue of August 14, 1875: "Just now, for the first time in years, confidence is being restored. The moneys appropriated are being properly applied, and the court and the several departments are being run in perfect order and harmony." On February 12, 1878, this paper referred to Judge Parker as "a man of coolness, calmness, and great deliberation."

The courtroom in which Judge Parker took up his gavel, on May 10, 1875, was on the first floor of a two-story brick building, situated inside the military garrison and previously used as a barracks. Offices of the court attachés were on the same floor. The musty, dungeon-like basement served as a jail. By the time his first term ended, late in June, Parker had tried ninety-one criminal cases. Of eighteen murder cases, fifteen had resulted in conviction. The judge sentenced eight of the killers to be hanged on September 3. The number dropped to six when one was killed while trying to escape and another, because of his youth, had his sentence commuted to life imprisonment and later was pardoned.[53]

The multiple hanging made a big day in Fort Smith. Newspaper reporters from Little Rock, Kansas City, and St. Louis were on hand. Farmers and their families began pouring into town early in the morning, crowding the streets by ten o'clock. Many brought their lunches and went early to the courtyard to have a favorable spot from which to view the major event. The

[53] Harman, *op. cit.*, 71–72, 90, 171, 176.

Western Independent, which issued an extra edition with a history of the condemned men and their crimes, estimated that five thousand witnessed the hanging.[54]

The six who played stellar roles on that day were three white men, two Indians, and a Negro. One of the whites, Daniel Evans, twenty years old, had killed a Texas youth to get his boots. John Whittington, thirty, had clubbed an elderly neighbor and slit his throat to take the money from his pocket. James Moore, twenty-eight, had stolen two horses from a crippled farmer and had killed one of his pursuers—his eighth victim. One of the Indians, Samuel Fooy, twenty-six, a half-white Cherokee, had shot a barefoot white school teacher to rob him. Smoker Man-killer, twenty-six, another Cherokee, had borrowed a neighbor's gun, used it to kill him, and boasted of his deed. The Negro, Edmund Campbell, had killed a Negro neighbor and a young Negro woman.[55]

At 9:30 in the morning the six condemned men were escorted to the gallows, which had been built big and strong enough to drop a dozen at the same moment. After the sentences had been read, there were hymns, prayers, and farewell statements. Then black hoods were drawn over the faces of the prisoners, and the nooses were adjusted. At 10:55 the trap fell. All six men dropped to receive broken necks and almost instant death. The first performance was over.[56]

The next was not long in coming. On April 21, 1876, five more men went to the gallows in the presence of an orderly throng estimated at six to seven thousand. The *Western Independent,* whose extra edition devoted two pages of six columns each to the five murderers and their crimes, concluded:

> The certainty of punishment is the only sure preventive of crime, and the administration of the laws by Judge I. C. Parker has made him a terror to all evil doers in the Indian country. The determination shown by the judge that the laws shall be faithfully and fearlessly administered and the firmness he has displayed dur-

[54] *Western Independent,* September 8, 1875.
[55] Harman, *op. cit.,* 199–211.
[56] *Western Independent,* September 8, 1875.

ing the less than twelve months he has sat on the bench have won for him the confidence and respect of the members of the bar and our citizens, as well as of the law-abiding men of all races in the Indian Territory.

Judge Parker had to contend with unusual difficulties. Sixty-five of his deputy marshals were killed while trying to carry out their duties.[57] Often prosecution witnesses feared to testify lest they be the victims of bloody reprisal. But Parker did not allow such obstacles to deter him from his course. In his twenty-one years on the federal bench at Fort Smith, during fourteen of which no appeal could be taken from his decisions, he tried more than thirteen thousand persons. More than nine thousand of them were convicted. Of 344 men convicted of crimes punishable by death, the judge sentenced 172 to be hanged.[58] Fewer than half of the latter escaped the noose by dying in jail or by obtaining commutation or presidential reprieve.

Judge Parker's docket was always heavy. There were local courts in the Indian Territory, but these could try only Indians and could try them solely for crimes against members of their own race. Indians who robbed or killed whites had to be brought to Fort Smith. Along with them came the white and black renegades—"criminal intruders" Judge Parker called them[59]—who infested the Indian country and lived by plunder and murder.

Judge Parker gave every defendant a scrupulously fair trial. Whenever an Indian had trouble in understanding the questions of the lawyers, the judge had the lawyers speak more simply. Often he intervened to explain something himself. Yet he never hesitated to impose sentences designed to make the Indian Territory safe for law-abiding citizens of all races.

The overcrowded basement jail from which Judge Parker's first prisoners were brought into court was a disgrace even to a rough frontier town. It was so packed with filth, vermin, and

[57] Harman, *op. cit.*, 87.
[58] *Ibid.*, 89.
[59] *Ibid.*, 86.

stench that members of grand juries hardly dared enter. In 1877 a new, three-story brick jail was built adjoining the courthouse. The new structure had seventy-two cells designed to hold two prisoners each; but before many years it, too, was overcrowded.[60]

To Blue Duck, Cherokee Bill, and other brigands of the Indian country Judge Parker's court was "Hell on the Border;" but to honest frontier people it was a rock of security. In its issue of July 31, 1878, the *Western Independent* commented:

> The quiet and systematic working order in which this court conducts its business has been the subject of frequent remarks by visitors. Everything seems to work like well oiled machinery. Every officer and employee is found at his post, alert and efficient in his peculiar calling. There is no tumult, no nervousness, and no vexatious delay unless it be from tardy jurors or the occasional long-winded chin music that attorneys have to indulge in to satisfy a client or to interpret to a jury the evidence they have listened to.
>
> Not infrequently the contending parties slide into encounters, on which the court at once bids them hold their prancing steeds. Nor does the court hesitate to come to the rescue of a bewildered witness when he is being borne to the earth by an over-zealous effort to invalidate his testimony or to fasten the crime of perjury on him because he is on the wrong side.
>
> To realize that a presiding officer is master of the situation inspires respect and confidence. Where a calm and unimpassioned dignity characterizes his patient and untiring earnestness of purpose to give the most trivial cases the same attention as those of momentous import, the prisoner at the bar feels that he will receive that justice to which he may be legally entitled.
>
> If a juryman has been inattentive or gets lost in a fog which the lawyers are often able to invoke and relies upon getting his cue from any bias in the charge by the court, he is gone beyond redemption. If the court has one faculty pre-eminent, it is that of so evenly balancing its charge on points to be considered by the jury that the feather that is to tip the canoe and swamp it must be placed by the juryman himself—it cannot be had from the court unless in cases where there is but one side.

[60] *Ibid.*, 72–75.

It was apparent that the approbation which it pleased the court to express toward the jurymen was reciprocated, without a shade of qualification, by every juror present.

News of the multiple hangings at Fort Smith was played up in many newspapers over the country. Soon the reports gave Parker the name of "the Hanging Judge" and—in distant states—an undeserved reputation for being heartless and bloodthirsty. Nothing could have been further from the truth. Judge Parker was as eager to protect the innocent as to punish the guilty, and his charges to juries were noted among lawyers and laymen alike for their fairness and their freedom from bias. If he was more severe than some in his sentences, his sternness came from his having to deal with exceptionally hardened criminals. He realized that many innocent people might suffer if he freed the guilty men before him to continue their careers as looters and assassins. His human sympathy often went to the defendants and their families but was not reserved for them alone.

Perhaps the most noted wrongdoer to be sentenced by Judge Parker was a white woman. Belle Starr, of Missouri birth and Texas escapades, had been widowed early in life by the shooting of her horse-thief and killer husband, Jim Reed. Later she went to the Indian Territory, married a Cherokee, Sam Starr, and became the leader of a band of thieves and cutthroats who operated on the Canadian River. Usually she kept herself in the background of her outlaw band, satisfying her exhibitionism with feats of horsemanship in the streets of Fort Smith. But in the spring of 1882 she and her husband stole two horses from a corral. For this pilfering the pair were arrested in October and brought before Judge Parker on February 15, 1883. After four days of testimony and argument, they were found guilty and were sentenced to a year in the House of Correction in Detroit.[61]

For judicial purposes, Congress divided the Indian Territory in 1883, shifting cases from certain areas to courts in Kansas and Texas. But offenders in large numbers still were brought to

[61] Records of the United States District Court, District of Western Arkansas, Fort Smith, February 15–19, 1883; Fort Smith *New Era,* February 22, 1883; Burton Rascoe, *Belle Starr, the Bandit Queen.*

Judge Parker in Fort Smith. In 1889, Congress established a federal court at Muskogee. However, this new court did not have jurisdiction over felonies punishable by death or imprisonment at hard labor. The more serious offenses still had to be tried in courts in adjoining states.[62]

In 1889, the court of Judge Parker was moved into more commodious quarters in a new, three-story federal building.[63] Even after his hair and beard turned white, he remained one of the hardest-working jurists on the federal bench. He continued to open his court at eight in the morning and seldom adjourned it before dark. Sometimes the court was not in recess more than ten days in a whole year. Outside the courtroom, the judge avoided political entanglements, contributed liberally to charitable and civic causes, and was a strong supporter of the public schools. For more than four years he was a member of the Fort Smith school board.

Judge Parker frequently gave vent to humor on the bench. Often there was a twinkle in his eye and a smile on his lips. Yet he had scant patience with the technicalities and delays that began to impede the court in his latter years. Some of these prevented the punishment of vicious killers.

One such case irked him deeply. On the evening of July 26, 1895, a notorious outlaw, who had been kept in jail a month past his execution date because he had appealed his case, attacked one of the guards. With a pistol he had obtained from the outside, he succeeded in killing the guard. At that time Judge Parker was in St. Louis on a brief vacation. His comment, as it appeared in an interview published in the St. Louis *Globe-Democrat* of July 30, included sharp criticism of the handling of appeals.

The Fort Smith jail, he said, held more than fifty convicted murderers, with insufficient guards. These criminals were waiting to have their appeals heard by the Supreme Court of the United States. The judge asserted that, while crime in general had decreased sharply in the Indian Territory in the preceding

[62] Harman, *op. cit.*, 48–57; Grant Foreman, *A History of Oklahoma*, 279–82.

[63] Harman, *op. cit.*, 75.

twenty years, murders had risen in the last two years. He went on:

> I attribute the increase to the reversals of the Supreme Court. These reversals have contributed to the number of murders in the Indian Territory. First of all, the convicted murderer has a long breathing spell before his case comes before the Supreme Court. Then, when it does come before that body, the conviction may be quashed. And whenever it is quashed, it is always upon the flimsiest technicalities. The Supreme Court never touches the merits of the case.

When Judge Parker died, on November 17, 1896, the Indian Territory was almost ready to take over its own enforcement of justice. The establishment of order and justice over the whole western frontier was virtually complete. Feuds, range wars, and vigilante activities had given way to fairly regular application of statutory law. True, there still were sporadic outbreaks of violence, as in the clashes between cattlemen and sheepmen in Oregon and Wyoming. But westerners in general had put aside their six-shooters and their hanging ropes. Most of them had settled down to growing meat and grain and husky youngsters.

The West still held its spirit of freedom and individualism, its boundless energy and initiative. It was confident that it could feed half the world or repel any foe. Yet the days of its own conquest were past. Its pioneers had subdued not only deserts and mountains and raging streams but the destructive elements within their own ranks. The tomahawk and the bowie knife were buried. The West's rampaging era of war whoops and gun smoke had become the province of the historian and the storyteller.

Bibliography

MANUSCRIPTS

Ames, Harriet A. "The History of Harriet A. Ames During the Early Days of Texas." Transcript in the University of Texas Library, Austin.

Ashcroft, Levi Henderson. "The History of the War Between the Regulators and Moderators of Shelby County." Transcripts in the Texas State Library, Austin, and the libraries of the University of Texas, Austin, and Southern Methodist University, Dallas.

Benson William Ralganal. "The Facts of the Stone and Kelsey Massacre in Lake County." Bancroft Library, University of California, Berkeley.

Blake, Thomas W. Letter to E. S. Brown of Lynchburg, Virginia, August 5, 1898. Archives of Dallas Historical Society.

Bollaert, William. "Personal Narrative of a Residence and Travels in the Republic of Texas, 1840–44." Ayer Collection, Newberry Library, Chicago.

Campbell, W. S. (Stanley Vestal). Letter to the author, October 24, 1946.

Caperton, John C. "Sketch of Col. John C. Hays, Texas Ranger." Bancroft Library. Transcripts in the University of Texas Library and the library of the late Dr. William E. Howard, Dallas.

Clerk of the court at Mansfield, Louisiana, to Sam Asbury, undated. Asbury Papers, University of Texas Library.

Coutant, Charles Griffin. Notes on the history of Wyoming. Wyoming State Library, Cheyenne.

Daggett, Ephraim M. "Recollections of the War of the Moderators and Regulators." Library of the late Dr. William E. Howard, Dallas.

Davis, Ross W. Letter dated Waxahachie, Texas, December 3, 1945.

Eilers, Kathryn Burford. "A History of Mason County." M. A. thesis, University of Texas, 1939.

Fish, Joseph. "History of Arizona." Arizona State Historian, Phoenix.

Ford, Captain John Salmon. "Memoirs." Texas State Library, Austin.

Gibson, C. E., Jr. "The Original Settler at Medano Springs." Library of the State Historical Society of Colorado, Denver.

Irvine, William C. Letter dated Ross, Wyoming, December 6, 1913, to Dr. Charles B. Penrose, Philadelphia. Penrose Papers, University of Wyoming Library, Laramie.

Law, John, coroner. Certificate of attendance at the inquest on the deaths of Edward Frodsham and Patrick Stewart, issued at Leadville, Colorado, to H. W. Gaw, November 20, 1879.

McNelly, Captain L. H. Letter to his wife, dated Brownsville, Texas, November 29, 1875. Collection of the late Dr. William E. Howard, Dallas.

Penrose, Dr. Charles Bingham. "The Rustler Business," 1914. Penrose Papers, University of Wyoming Library.

Perrigo, Lynn Irwin. "A Social History of Central City, Colorado." Ph.D. dissertation, University of Colorado, 1936.

Sonnichsen, C. L. "I'll Die Before I'll Run: A History of Feuding in Texas."

———. Letter to the author, September 6, 1946.

Vigilantes of San Francisco, statements by members of the committees of 1851 and 1856. Bancroft Library.

Vigilantes of Virginia City, Montana Territory, oath and signatures. Library of the Historical Society of Montana, Helena.

Wyoming Stock Growers' Association, minute books, University of Wyoming Library.

PUBLIC RECORDS

Montana Territory. Minutes of the Bannack election of May 24, 1863, D. H. Dillingham, secretary. Library of the Historical Society of Montana, Helena.

New Mexico. Report of the coroner's jury on the death of William Bonney, July 15, 1881. Files of the Secretary of State, Santa Fé.

Texas. Harrison County, court proceedings, 1841, Minute Book A.

Texas Rangers, reports and correspondence. Adjutant General's Papers, Texas State Library, Austin.

Texas. Shackelford County, minutes of the Commissioners Court, 1876–77, I.

United States District Court, District of Western Arkansas, Fort Smith, records for February 15–19, 1883.

Wyoming. Johnson County, coroner's report on the death of John A. Tisdale, district court, Second Judicial District, Buffalo, 1891.

Wyoming. Johnson County, amended information, *State of Wyoming* v. *Frank M. Canton et al.,* district court, Second Judicial District, filed May 9, 1892, Doc. 3, No. 365.

Wyoming. Laramie County, dismissal order in case of *State of Wyoming v. Frank M. Canton et al.,* district court, First Judicial District, January 23, 1893, Crim. Doc. 3, No. 363, J. 13.

Wyoming. Laramie County, injunction order of district court, First Judicial District, in case of *United States* v. *Alexander H. Swan et al.,* August 30, 1883, No. 45, J. 7.

Wyoming. Big Horn County, indictment and trial records in Tensleep cases, district court, Fifth Judicial District, 1909.

PUBLIC DOCUMENTS

Michigan. Sunderland, Edson R., "The Efficiency of Justices' Courts in Michigan," *Fourth Report of the Judicial Council of Michigan,* May, 1934.

Texas. *Acts of the 44th Legislature.*

Texas. *Cases Argued and Adjudged in the Court of Appeals of the State of Texas, 1880,* VIII.

Texas. Gammel, H. P. N., (compiler), *The Laws of Texas,* 1898.

Texas Reports, 44, *Lewis* v. *Ames.*

Texas. *Vernon's Texas Statutes,* 1936.

United States. *Annual Report of the Commissioner of the General Land Office, 1869, 1896.*

United States. *Condition of the Indian Tribes,* report of the joint special committee appointed under the joint resolution of March 3, 1865, 1867.

United States. *Difficulties on the Southwestern Frontier,* 36 Cong., 1 sess., *House Exec. Doc. No. 52,* Serial No. 1,050.

United States. *El Paso Troubles in Texas,* 45 Cong., 2 sess., *House Exec. Doc. No. 93,* Serial No. 1,809.

United States. Report and accompanying documents of the committee on foreign affairs on the relation of the United States with Mexico, 45 Cong., 2 sess., *House Report No. 701,* Serial No. 1,824.

United States. Report of the Indian Peace Commissioners, 40 Cong., 2 sess., 1868, *Exec. Doc. No. 97.*

United States. Report of the Secretary of War, communicating evidence taken by a military commission ordered to inquire into the Sand Creek Massacre, 39 Cong., 2 sess., *Exec. Doc. No. 26.*

United States. Richardson, James D., compiler, Messages and Papers of the President, 1899.

United States. "Massacre of the Cheyenne Indians," in report of the joint committee on the conduct of the war, 38 Cong., 2 sess., 1865.
United States. Report by Colonel Thomas Moonlight in War of the Rebellion records, Series 101.
Wyoming. Constitution of the state of Wyoming.

NEWSPAPERS

Albany *Echo,* 1883–84.
Albany *Star,* December 12, 1883.
Alta California, San Francisco, 1851–56.
Arizona Silver Belt, Globe, February 12, October 1, 1887.
Austin *Intelligencer-Echo,* March 29, 1875.
Austin *Republican,* November 1, 1870.
Austin *State Gazette,* November 25, 1865.
Austin *Statesman,* 1874–84.
Big Horn County Rustler, 1908–1909.
Buffalo *Bulletin,* 1891–92.
California Courier, San Francisco, June 14, 16, July 14, 1851.
California Star, Yerba Buena, January 9, 1847.
Carbon County Journal, January 8, 1887.
Casper *Weekly Mail,* April 7, July 26, 1889.
Cheyenne *Argus,* March 22, 1868.
Cheyenne *Leader,* 1868–95.
Cheyenne *Sun,* December 9, 1886.
Chicago *Herald,* April 15, 1892.
Coconino *Sun,* September 10, 17, 24, 1887.
Cody *Enterprise,* August 24, 1905.
Craig *Courier,* 1894–99.
Crook County Journal, Prineville, Oregon, 1904.
Dallas *Daily Herald,* March 25, 1874, April 23, 1876, August 19, 1877.
Dallas *Morning News,* 1885–1949.
Dallas *Weekly News,* March 27, April 3, 1875.
Denison *Daily News,* January 4, March 22, 1874, June 4, 1876.
Denver *Post,* November 21, 1899, February 15, 1902.
Denver *Republican,* 1893–1910.
Denver *Times,* 1899–1902.
Dodge City *Times,* November 10, 1877.
Douglas *Budget,* June 4, 1936.
El Paso *Daily Times,* June 2, 1884.
Flagstaff *Champion,* 1887–88.
Ford County Globe, March 5, May 7, 1878, May 14, 1879.

Fort Smith *New Era,* February 22, 1883.
Fort Smith *Times-Democrat,* November 17, 1896.
Fort Worth *Gazette,* 1883–84.
Frontier Echo, Jacksboro, Texas, 1876–78.
Galveston *News,* 1869–1907.
Golden Era, White Oaks, New Mexico, June 18, 1885.
Helena *Daily Gazette,* April 30, 1870.
Hoofs and Horns, Prescott, Arizona, February 10, 1887.
Houston *Morning Star,* October 7, 1841, February 5, 1842.
Houston *Telegraph and Register,* February 9, 1842, October 3, 1872.
Kansas City *Star,* November 15, 1925.
Laramie *Boomerang,* 1886–89.
Las Animas *Leader,* October 9, 1874.
Las Vegas *Gazette,* November 30, December 24, 1880.
Leadville *Democrat,* 1879–80.
Lincoln County Leader, June 6, August 1, 1885.
Lovell *Chronicle,* May 4, 1907, May 8, October 23, 1909.
Matagorda County Tribune, August 23, 1945.
Mineral Argus, 1884.
Montana Post, September 23, November 4, December 30, 1865.
National Intelligencer, Washington, D. C., October 31, 1844.
Natrona County Tribune, August 25, 1905, April 6, May 20, 1908.
Natrona Tribune, December 9, 1891.
New Orleans *Daily Picayune,* March 19, 1842, November 1, 1844.
New York *Times,* June 11, 1867.
New York *Tribune,* December 3, 1886.
Omaha *Herald,* June 22, 1877.
Phoenix *Gazette,* August 20, 1892.
Phoenix *Herald,* 1887–88.
Portland *Oregonian,* 1899–1905.
Prescott *Courier,* November 7, 1887.
Rawlins *Republican,* September 27, 1928.
Red-Lander, San Augustine, Texas, 1841–44.
Rocky Mountain News, Denver, 1860–1901.
Sacramento *Transcript,* February 12, 1851.
Saint Johns *Herald,* August 18, September 9, 29, 1887.
St. Paul *Phonograph,* February 15, 29, 1884.
San Antonio *Express,* 1873–1911.
San Antonio *Herald,* 1873–75.
San Antonio *Light,* June 29, 1913.

San Francisco *Bulletin,* November 20, December 12, 1855, June 23, 1856.

San Francisco *Chronicle*, October 3, 1915.

San Francisco *Herald,* 1851–56.

Santa Fé *New Mexican,* January 14, 1883.

Semi-Weekly Farm News, Dallas, April 4, 1924.

Tempe *News,* August 20, 1892.

Texas National Register, December 14, 1844.

Thermopolis *Record,* 1903–1909.

Tombstone *Epitaph,* October 27, November 1, 1881.

Topeka *Commonwealth*, July 14, 1875.

Trinity *Advocate,* May 20, 1857.

Tucson *Star,* August 13, 20, 1892.

Van Buren *Press,* November 21, 1896.

Waco *Examiner,* August 26, 1883.

Walla Walla *Statesman,* June 15, 1866.

Weatherford *Times,* March 28, 1875.

Western Chronicle, May 1, 1879.

Western Independent, Fort Smith, Arkansas, 1873–75.

Wichita *Vidette,* November 10, December 8, 1870.

Winfield *Censor,* December 3, 1870.

Wyoming Derrick, Casper, June 25, December 10, 1891; June 16, 1892.

Yellowstone Journal, Miles City, October 9, 1880.

PERIODICALS

Adams, Paul. "The Unsolved Mystery of Ben Thompson," *Southwestern Historical Quarterly,* Vol. XLVIII, No. 3 (January, 1945), 321–29.

Barker, Eugene C. (editor). "Journal of the Permanent Council," *Southwestern Historical Quarterly,* Vol. VII, No. 4 (April, 1904), 249–78.

Barnes, Will C. "The Pleasant Valley War of 1887," *Arizona Historical Review.* Part I in Vol. IV, No. 3 (October, 1931), 5–34. Part II in Vol. IV, No. 4 (January, 1932), 23–45.

Botkin, J. T. "Justice Was Swift and Sure in Early Kansas," *Kansas Historical Collections,* Vol. XVI (1923–25), 488–93.

Coutant, Charles Griffin. "History of Wyoming," *Annals of Wyoming,* Vol. XIII, No. 2 (April, 1941), 146–51.

Crane, R. C. "Early Days in Fisher County," *West Texas Historical Association Year Book,* Vol. VI (June, 1930), 124–69.

Davidson, Levette J. "A Ballad of the Wyoming Rustler War," *Western Folklore,* Vol. VI, No. 2 (April, 1947).

Ellis, Mrs. Charles. "History of Carbon, Wyoming's First Mining Town," *Annals of Wyoming,* Vol. VIII, No. 4 (April, 1932), 639–41.

———. "Robert Foote," *Annals of Wyoming,* Vol. XV, No. 1 (January, 1943), 50–62.

Griffith, Bert. "Texas Ranger," *Today,* December 15, 1934, 5, 22.

Harger, Charles Moreau. "Sheep and Shepherds of the West," *Outlook,* Vol. LXXII, No. 12 (November 22, 1902), 689–93.

Hatcher, Curley. "Got Fifty Dollars for an Indian Scalp," *Frontier Times,* July, 1924.

Havins, T. R. "Sheepmen-Cattlemen Antagonisms on the Texas Frontier," *West Texas Historical Association Year Book,* Vol. XVIII (October, 1942), 10–23.

Harral, Arthur G. "Arthur G. Anderson, Pioneer Sheep Breeder of Texas," *Southwestern Sheep and Goat Raiser* (now *Sheep and Goat Raiser*), November, 1935.

Henderson, Harry B., Sr. "Wyoming Territorial Governors," *Annals of Wyoming,* Vol. XI, No. 4 (October, 1939), 250.

Henry, Theodore C. "Thomas James Smith of Abilene," *Kansas Historical Collections,* Vol. IX (1905–1906), 526–32.

Holden, William Curry. "Law and Lawlessness on the Texas Frontier," *Southwestern Historical Quarterly,* Vol. XLIV, No. 2 (October, 1940), 188–203.

Holt, Roy D. "C. C. Doty, West Texas Pioneer," *Sheep and Goat Raiser,* Vol. XXII, No. 2 (November, 1941).

———. "The Introduction of Barbed Wire Into Texas and the Fence-Cutting War," *West Texas Historical Association Year Book,* Vol. VI (June, 1930), 65–79.

———. "The Saga of Barbed Wire in the Tom Green Country," *West Texas Historical Association Year Book,* Vol. IV (June, 1928), 32–49.

———. "Sheepmen and Cattlemen Had Only Mild War on Texas Frontier," *Sheep and Goat Raiser,* Vol. XXVIII, No. 3 (December, 1947), 28–29, 52–54.

———. "The Woes of a Pioneer Texas Sheepman," *Sheep and Goat Raiser,* Vol. XXI, No. 3 (December, 1940).

Houston, Sam. Speeches on the increase of the army, United States Senate, February 1, 25, 1858, *Congressional Globe,* Part I, 1857–58, 492–97, 873–75.

Hunter, John Warren. "John Fleutsch, a Frontier Justice," *Frontier Times,* February, 1924.

Love, Clara M. "History of the Cattle Industry in the Southwest," II, *Southwestern Historical Quarterly,* Vol. XX, No. 1 (July, 1916), 1–18.

Martin, George W. "Thomas Allen Cullinan of Junction City," *Kansas Historical Collections,* Vol. IX (1905–1906), 532–40.

McKinney, Joe T. "Reminiscences," *Arizona Historical Review.* Part I in Vol. V, No. 1 (April, 1932), 33–54. Part II in Vol. V, No. 2 (July, 1932), 141–45. Part III in Vol. V, No. 3 (October, 1932), 198–204.

McLean, John H. "Bob Potter and Old Rose," *Texas Methodist Historical Quarterly,* Vol. II, No. 1 (July, 1910), 1–11.

Meldrum, John W. "The Taming of Big Nose George and Others," *Union Pacific Magazine,* November, 1926.

Rister, Carl Coke. "Outlaws and Vigilantes of the Southern Plains, 1865–1885," *Mississippi Valley Historical Review,* Vol. XIX (March, 1933), 537–54.

Roberts, Oran M., "The Shelby War, or the Regulators and Moderators," *Texas Magazine,* Vol. III (August, 1897).

Sagendorph, Kent. "Jack-Rabbit Justice," *Country Home,* July, 1939, 7, 26–27.

"Swapped His Beard for Indian Scalps," *Frontier Times,* January, 1924.

Travis, Edmunds. "Austin's Premier Gun Fighter," *Bunker's Monthly,* Vol. II (September, 1928), 314–23.

Turner, Thomas F. "Prairie Dog Lawyers," *Panhandle Plains Historical Review,* Vol. II (1929), 104–22.

Webb, J. R. "Henry Herron, Pioneer and Peace Officer During Fort Griffin Days," *West Texas Historical Association Year Book,* Vol. XX (October, 1944), 21–50.

Webb, Walter Prescott. "The American Revolver and the West," *Scribner's Magazine,* Vol. LXXXI, No. 2 (February, 1927), 171–78.

Wentworth, Edward Norris. "Sheep Wars of the Nineties in Northwest Colorado," *Brand Book,* Vol. II, No. 7 (July, 1946), 1–22.

Wilber, Ed. P. "Reminiscences of the Meeker Country," *Colorado Magazine,* Vol. XXIII, No. 6 (November, 1946), 273–83.

PAMPHLETS

Day, Jack Hays. *The Sutton-Taylor Feud.* N. p., 1937.

Dosch, Henry Ernst. *Vigilante Days at Virginia City.* Portland, Oregon, Fred Lockley, 1924.

Middleton, John W. *History of the Regulators and Moderators and the Shelby County War in 1841 and 1842 in the Republic of Texas.* Fort Worth, Loving Publishing Company, 1883.

BOOKS

Adams, Ward R. *History of Arizona.* Phoenix, Record Publishing Company, 1930.

Anderson, Ed H. (compiler). *History of Sherman and Grayson County.* Sherman, Texas, Lewis Printing Company, 1947.

Andrews, C. C. (editor). *Minnesota in the Indian and Civil Wars.* St. Paul, State of Minnesota, 1890–93. 2 vols.

Arrington, A. W. *Desperadoes of the Southwest.* New York, W. H. Graham, 1847.

———. *The Rangers and Regulators of the Tanaha.* New York, R. M. Dewitt, 1856.

Atherton, Gertrude. *California, an Intimate History.* New York, Harper and Brothers, 1914.

Baber, D. F. *The Longest Rope.* Caldwell, Idaho, The Caxton Printers, 1940.

Bade, William Frederick. *Life and Letters of John Muir.* Boston, Houghton Mifflin Company, 1924. 2 vols.

Bancroft, Hubert Howe. *California Inter Pocula.* San Francisco, The History Company, 1888.

———. *History of Nevada, Colorado and Wyoming, 1540–1888.* San Francisco, The History Company, 1889.

———. *Popular Tribunals.* San Francisco, The History Company, 1887. 2 vols.

Banditti of the Rocky Mountains and Vigilance Committee in Idaho, The. Chicago, 1865.

Barker, Eugene C. *The Life of Stephen F. Austin.* Nashville and Dallas, Cokesbury Press, 1925.

Barnes, Will C. *Apaches and Longhorns.* Los Angeles, The Ward Ritchie Press, 1941.

Barrows, John R. *Ubet.* Caldwell, Idaho, The Caxton Printers, 1934.

Beadle, J. H. *Western Wilds.* Cincinnati, Jones Brothers and Company, 1877.

Bell, Horace. *On the Old West Coast.* New York, William Morrow and Company, 1930.

———. *Reminiscences of a Ranger.* Los Angeles, Yarnell, Caystile and Mathes, 1881. Santa Barbara, Wallace Hebberd, 1927.

Bennett, Estelline. *Old Deadwood Days.* New York, J. H. Sears and Company, 1928. New York, Charles Scribner's Sons, 1935.

Biggers, Don Hampton. *Shackelford County Sketches.* Albany, Texas, Albany News office, 1908.

Birney, Hoffman. *Vigilantes.* Philadelphia, Penn Publishing Company, 1929.

Breakenridge, William M. *Helldorado.* Boston and New York, Houghton Mifflin Company, 1928.

Briggs, Harold E. *Frontiers of the Northwest.* New York, D. Appleton-Century Company, 1940.

Brosnan, Cornelius J. *History of the State of Idaho.* New York, Charles Scribner's Sons, 1918. Revised editions, 1926, 1935.

Brown, Jesse, and A. M. Willard. *The Black Hills Trails.* Rapid City, South Dakota, Journal Publishing Company, 1924.

Brown, John Henry. *Reminiscences and Incidents of the Early Life of San Francisco.* San Francisco, Mission Journal Publishing Company, 1886.

Bruce, John. *Gaudy Century.* New York, Random House, 1949.

Bryant, Charles M., and Abel B. Murch. *A History of the Great Massacre by the Sioux Indians in Minnesota.* Cincinnati, 1863.

Buffum, Edward Gould. *Six Months in the Gold Mines.* Philadelphia, Lea and Blanchard, 1850.

Burnham, Frederick R. *Scouting on Two Continents.* Garden City, New York, Doubleday, Page and Company, 1926.

Burns, Walter Noble. *The Saga of Billy the Kid.* Garden City, New York, Doubleday, Page and Company, 1925.

———. *Tombstone.* Garden City, New York, Doubleday, Page and Company, 1927.

Burt, Struthers. *Powder River: Let 'er Buck.* New York, Farrar and Rinehart, 1938.

Bushick, Frank. *Glamorous Days.* San Antonio, The Naylor Company, 1934.

Butcher, Solomon D. *Pioneer History of Custer County.* Broken Bow, Nebraska, S. D. Butcher, 1901.

Cady, John Henry. *Arizona's Yesterday.* Los Angeles, privately published, 1916.

Canton, Frank M. *Frontier Trails.* Boston and New York, Houghton Mifflin Company, 1930.

Clay, John. *My Life on the Range.* Chicago, privately printed, 1924.

Clover, Samuel Travers. *On Special Assignment.* Boston, Lothrop Publishing Company, 1903.

Clum, Woodworth. *Apache Agent.* Boston and New York, Houghton Mifflin Company, 1936.

Coblentz, Stanton A. *Villains and Vigilantes.* New York, Wilson-Erickson, 1936.

Cody, William Frederick. *The Life of the Hon. William F. Cody, Known as Buffalo Bill.* Hartford, F. E. Bliss, 1879.

Coe, George W. *Frontier Fighter.* Boston and New York, Houghton Mifflin Company, 1934.

Collier, William Ross, and Edwin Victor Westrate. *Dave Cook of the Rockies.* New York, Rufus Rockwell Wilson, 1936.

Collins, Hubert E. *Warpath and Cattle Trail.* New York, William Morrow and Company, 1928.

Connelley, William Elsey. *Wild Bill and His Era.* New York, Press of the Pioneers, 1933.

Cook, David J. *Hands Up.* Denver, Republican Print, 1882. Denver, W. F. Robinson Printing Company, 1897.

Cranfill, James Britton. *Dr. J. B. Cranfill's Chronicle.* New York and Chicago, Fleming H. Revell Company, 1916.

Crawford, Lewis F. *Rekindling Camp Fires.* Bismarck, North Dakota, Capital Book Company, 1926.

Crockett, George Louis. *Two Centuries in East Texas.* Dallas, The Southwest Press, 1932.

David, Robert B. *Malcolm Campbell, Sheriff.* Casper, Wyoming, Wyomingana, 1932.

Dewees, W. B. *Letters From Texas.* Louisville, New Albany Tribune plant, 1852.

Dick, Everett. *The Sod-House Frontier, 1854–1890.* New York, D. Appleton-Century Company, 1937.

———. *Vanguards of the Frontier.* New York, D. Appleton-Century Company, 1941.

Dimsdale, Thomas Josiah. *The Vigilantes of Montana.* Virginia City, Montana Territory, Montana Post Press, 1866. Other editions in 1915 and 1921.

Dobie, James Frank. *A Vaquero of the Brush Country.* Dallas, Southwest Press, 1929.

Donaldson, Thomas. *Idaho of Yesterday.* Caldwell, Idaho, The Caxton Printers, 1941.

Douglas, Claude Leroy. *Famous Texas Feuds.* Dallas, The Turner Company, 1936.

Dunn, J. P. *Massacres of the Mountains.* New York, Harper and Brothers, 1886.

Duval, John C. *The Adventures of Big-Foot Wallace.* Philadelphia, Claxton, Remsen and Haffelfinger, 1871. Facsimile reproductions, Austin, The Steck Company, 1935 and 1947.

Eisele, Wilbert E. *The Real Wild Bill Hickok.* Denver, William H. Andre, 1931.

Farish, Thomas Edwin. *History of Arizona.* San Francisco, The Filmer Brothers Electrotype Company, 1915–18. 8 vols.

Featherston, Edward Baxter. *A Pioneer Speaks.* Dallas, Cecil Baugh and Company, 1940.

Folwell, William Watts. *A History of Minnesota.* St. Paul, Minnesota Historical Society, 1921–30. 4 vols.

Foreman, Grant. *A History of Oklahoma.* Norman, University of Oklahoma Press, 1942.

Forrest, Earle R. *Arizona's Dark and Bloody Ground.* Caldwell, Idaho, The Caxton Printers, 1936.

Freeman, G. D. *Midnight and Noonday, or Dark Deeds Unraveled.* Caldwell, Kansas, G. D. Freeman, 1890. Second edition, with illustrations, 1892.

[French, George H., compiler.] *Indianola Scrapbook.* Victoria, Texas, Victoria Advocate, 1936.

Fuller, George W. *A History of the Pacific Northwest.* New York, Alfred A. Knopf, 1931.

Fuller, Henry C. *A Texas Sheriff.* Nacogdoches, Texas, Baker Printing Company, 1931.

[Gamel, Thomas W.] *The Life of Thomas W. Gamel.* N. p., n. d.

Ganzhorn, Jack. *I've Killed Men.* London, Robert Hale, n. d.

Gard, Wayne. *Sam Bass.* Boston and New York, Houghton Mifflin Company, 1936.

Garrett, Pat F. *The Authentic Life of Billy the Kid.* Santa Fé, New Mexican Printing and Publishing Company, 1882. Revised edition, New York, The Macmillan Company, 1927.

Gillett, James B. *Six Years With the Texas Rangers.* Austin, Von Boeckmann–Jones Company, 1921. Revised edition, New Haven, Yale University Press, 1925.

Gipson, Fred. *Fabulous Empire.* Boston, Houghton Mifflin Company, 1946.

Graves, Richard S. *Oklahoma Outlaws.* Oklahoma City, State Printing and Publishing Company, 1915.

Grinnell, George Bird. *The Fighting Cheyennes.* New York, Charles Scribner's Sons, 1915.

Gue, Benjamin F. *History of Iowa.* New York, The Century History Company, 1903. 4 vols.

Guernsey, Charles A. *Wyoming Cowboy Days.* New York, G. P. Putnam's Sons, 1936.

Hafen, LeRoy R., and Francis Marion Young. *Fort Laramie and the Pageant of the West.* Glendale, California, The Arthur H. Clark Company, 1938.

Haley, J. Evetts. *Charles Goodnight, Cowman and Plainsman.* Boston and New York, Houghton Mifflin Company, 1936.

Halsell, H. H. *Cowboys and Cattleland.* Nashville, Parthenon Press, 1937.

Hanchett, Lafayette. *The Old Sheriff.* New York, Margent Press, 1937.

Hanson, Joseph Mills. *The Conquest of the Missouri.* Chicago, A. C. McClurg Company, 1909. New York, Rinehart and Company, 1946.

Hardin, John Wesley. *The Life of John Wesley Hardin.* Seguin, Texas, Smith and Moore, 1896.

Harman, S. W. *Hell on the Border.* Fort Smith, Arkansas, The Phoenix Publishing Company, 1898.

Henry, Stuart. *Conquering Our Great American Plains.* New York, E. P. Dutton and Company, 1930.

Hill, Alice Polk. *Tales of the Colorado Pioneers.* Denver, Pierson and Gardner, 1884.

History of Napa and Lake Counties, The. San Francisco, Slocum Bowen and Company, 1880.

History of Placer County. Oakland, Thompson and West, 1882.

Hogan, William Ransom. *The Texas Republic.* Norman, University of Oklahoma Press, 1946.

[Hogg, Thomas E.] *Authentic History of Sam Bass and His Gang.* Denton, Texas, printed at the Monitor job office, 1878.

Hough, Emerson. *The Story of the Cowboy.* New York, D. Appleton and Company, 1897.

House, E. *A Narrative of the Captivity of Mrs. Horn and Her Two Children, With That of Mrs. Harris, by the Comanche Indians.* St. Louis, C. Keemle, 1839.

Illustrations of Contra Costa County. Oakland, Smith and Elliott, 1878.

Jennings, Napoleon Augustus. *A Texas Ranger.* New York, Charles Scribner's Sons, 1899. Dallas, The Turner Company, 1930.

Keleher, William A. *The Fabulous Frontier.* Santa Fé, The Rydal Press, 1945.

Kemp, Louis Wiltz. *The Signers of the Texas Declaration of Independence.* Houston, The Anson Jones Press, 1944.

Kupper, Winifred. *The Golden Hoof.* New York, Alfred A. Knopf, 1945.

Kuykendall, William Littlebury. *Frontier Days.* N. p., J. M. and H. L. Kuykendall, 1917.

Lake, Stuart N. *Wyatt Earp, Frontier Marshal.* Boston and New York, Houghton Mifflin Company, 1931.

Langford, Nathaniel Pitt. *Vigilante Days and Ways.* Boston, J. G. Cupples Company, 1890. 2 vols. New York and St. Paul, D. D. Merrill Company, 1893. Chicago, A. C. McClurg and Company, 1912.

Langtry, Lillie. *The Days I Knew.* New York, George H. Doran Company, 1925.

Le Sueur, Meridel. *North Star Country.* New York, Duell, Sloan and Pearce, 1945.

Lillard, Richard G. *Desert Challenge.* New York, Alfred A. Knopf, 1942.

Lindsay, Charles. *The Big Horn Basin.* Lincoln, Nebraska, 1932.

Lockwood, Frank C. *Pioneer Days in Arizona.* New York, The Macmillan Company, 1932.

Lord, John. *Frontier Dust.* Hartford, Edwin Valentine Mitchell, 1926.

MacLeod, William Christie. *The American Indian Frontier.* New York, Alfred A. Knopf, 1928.

McCarty, John L. *Maverick Town, the Story of Old Tascosa.* Norman, University of Oklahoma Press, 1946.

McCoy, Joseph. *Historic Sketches of the Cattle Trails of the West and Southwest.* Kansas City, Ramsey, Millett and Hudson, 1874.

McDonald, A. B. *Hands Up!* Indianapolis, The Bobbs-Merrill Company, 1927.

McLean, John H. *Reminiscences.* Nashville, Smith and Lamar, 1918.

McNeal, T. A. *When Kansas Was Young.* New York, The Macmillan Company, 1922.

Mercer, Asa Shinn. *The Banditti of the Plains.* Cheyenne, 1894. San Francisco, printed for George Fields by the Grabhorn Press, 1935.

Mokler, Alfred James. *History of Natrona County, Wyoming, 1888–1922.* Chicago, R. R. Donnelley and Sons Company, 1923.

Monaghan, Jay. *Last of the Bad Men.* Indianapolis, The Bobbs-Merrill Company, 1946.

Nelson, Bruce. *Land of the Dacotahs.* Minneapolis, University of Minnesota Press, 1946.

Nix, Evett Dumas. *Oklahombres.* St. Louis and Chicago, Eden Publishing House, 1929.

Olmsted, Frederick Law. *A Journey Through Texas.* New York, Mason Brothers, 1857.

Osgood, Ernest Staples. *The Day of the Cattleman.* Minneapolis, University of Minnesota Press, 1929.

Otero, Miguel Antonio. *The Real Billy the Kid.* New York, Rufus Rockwell Wilson, 1936.

Paine, Albert Bigelow. *Captain Bill McDonald, Texas Ranger.* New York, J. J. Little and Ives Company, 1909.

Parsons, George Frederick. *Life and Adventures of James W. Marshall, the Discoverer of Gold in California.* Sacramento, J. W. Marshall and W. Burke, 1870.

Paxson, Frederic L. *History of the American Frontier, 1763–1893.* Boston and New York, Houghton Mifflin Company, 1924.

Peake, Ora Brooks. *The Colorado Range Cattle Industry.* Glendale, California, The Arthur H. Clark Company, 1937.

Pelzer, Louis. *The Cattlemen's Frontier.* Glendale, California, The Arthur H. Clark Company, 1936.

Pierce, Frank C. *Brief History of the Río Grande Valley.* Menasha, Wisconsin, George Banta Publishing Company, 1917.

Piper, Edwin Ford. *Barbed Wire and Wayfarers.* New York, The Macmillan Company, 1924.

Poe, John W. *The Death of Billy the Kid.* Boston and New York, Houghton Mifflin Company, 1936.

Poe, Sophie A. *Buckboard Days.* Caldwell, Idaho, The Caxton Printers, 1936.

Priest, Loring Benson. *Uncle Sam's Stepchildren.* New Brunswick, New Jersey, Rutgers University Press, 1942.

Raht, Carlysle Graham. *The Romance of the Davis Mountains and the Big Bend Country.* El Paso, The Rahtbooks Company, 1919.

Raine, William MacLeod. *Famous Sheriffs and Western Outlaws.* Garden City, New York, Doubleday, Doran and Company, 1929.

Raine, William MacLeod, and Will C. Barnes. *Cattle.* Garden City, New York, Doubleday, Doran and Company, 1930.

Rascoe, Burton. *Belle Starr, the Bandit Queen.* New York, Random House, 1941.

Raymond, Dora Neill. *Captain Lee Hall of Texas.* Norman, University of Oklahoma Press, 1940.

Richardson, Albert D. *Beyond the Mississippi.* Hartford, American Publishing Company, 1867.

Richardson, Rupert Norval. *The Comanche Barrier to South Plains Settlement.* Glendale, California, The Arthur H. Clark Company, 1933.

Ripley, Thomas. *They Died With Their Boots On.* Garden City, New York, Doubleday, Doran and Company, 1935.

Rister, Carl Coke. *Southern Plainsmen.* Norman, University of Oklahoma Press, 1938.

Roberts, Dan W. *Rangers and Sovereignty.* San Antonio, Wood Printing and Engraving Company, 1914.

Robinson, Duncan W. *Judge Robert McAlpin Williamson, Texas' Three-Legged Willie.* Austin, Texas State Historical Association, 1948.

Robson, William A. *Civilisation and the Growth of Law.* New York, The Macmillan Company, 1935.

Rogers, Justus H. *Colusa County.* Orland, California, Justus H. Rogers, 1891.

Rollins, Philip Ashton. *The Cowboy.* New York, Charles Scribner's Sons, 1922. Revised edition, 1936.

[Rose, Victor M.] *The Texas Vendetta, or the Sutton-Taylor Feud.* New York, J. J. Little and Company, 1880.

Royce, Josiah. *California From the Conquest in 1846 to the Second Vigilance Committee in San Francisco.* Boston and New York, Houghton Mifflin Company, 1886.

Rye, Edgar. *The Quirt and the Spur.* Chicago, W. B. Conkey Company, 1909.

Sabin, Edwin L. *Wild Men of the Wild West.* New York, Thomas Y. Crowell Company, 1929.

Scherer, James A. B. *The First Forty-Niner.* New York, Minton, Balch and Company, 1925.

Schmitt, Martin F. (editor). *General George Crook: His Autobiography.* Norman, University of Oklahoma Press, 1946.

Seagle, William. *The Quest for Law.* New York, Alfred A. Knopf, 1941.

Seymour, Flora Warren. *Indian Agents of the Old Frontier.* New York, D. Appleton-Century Company, 1941.

———. *The Story of the Red Man.* New York, Longmans, Green and Company, 1929.

Shinn, Charles Howard. *Mining Camps: a study in American Frontier Government.* New York, Charles Scribner's Sons, 1885. New York, Alfred A. Knopf, 1948.

Siringo, Charles A. *The History of Billy the Kid.* [Santa Fé, New Mexico, the author], 1920.

Sloan, Richard E. *Memories of an Arizona Judge.* Stanford University, California, Stanford University Press, 1932.

Smith, Frank Meriweather (editor). *San Francisco Vigilance Committee of '56.* San Francisco, Barry, Baird and Company, 1883.

Smithwick, Noah. *The Evolution of a State.* Austin, Gammel Book Company, 1900.

Sonnichsen, C. L. *Roy Bean.* New York, The Macmillan Company, 1943.

Speer, William S. (managing editor). *The Encyclopedia of the New West.* Marshall, Texas, The United States Biographical Publishing Company, 1881.

Streeter, Floyd Benjamin. *Prairie Trails and Cow Towns.* Boston, Chapman and Grimes, 1936.

Stuart, Granville. *Forty Years on the Frontier.* Cleveland, The Arthur H. Clark Company, 1925. 2 vols.

Sutley, Jack T. *The Last Frontier.* New York, The Macmillan Company, 1930.

Taylor, Bayard. *Eldorado, or Adventures in the Path of Empire.* New York, G. P. Putnam, 1850.

Taylor, William. *Seven Years' Street Preaching in San Francisco, California.* New York, published for the author, 1856.

Tilghman, Zoe A. *Outlaw Days.* Oklahoma City, Harlow Publishing Company, 1926.

Towne, Charles Wayland, and Edward Norris Wentworth. *Shepherd's Empire.* Norman, University of Oklahoma Press, 1945.

Triggs, J. H. *History and Directory of Laramie City, Wyoming Territory.* Laramie City, Daily Sentinel Print, 1875.

———. *History of Cheyenne and Northern Wyoming.* Omaha, Herald Printing House, 1876.

Turner, Frederick Jackson. *The Frontier in American History.* New York, Henry Holt and Company, 1920.

Vestal, Stanley (W. S. Campbell), *Bigfoot Wallace.* Boston, Houghton Mifflin Company, 1942.

———. *Sitting Bull.* Boston and New York, Houghton Mifflin Company, 1932.

———. *Warpath and Council Fire.* New York, Random House, 1948.

[Vickers, W. B., editor.] *History of the Arkansas Valley, Colorado.* Chicago, O. L. Baskin and Company, 1881.

Walgamott, Charles Shirley. *Six Decades Back*. Caldwell, Idaho, The Caxton Printers, 1936.

Walker, Tacetta B. *Stories of Early Days in Wyoming: Big Horn Basin*. Casper, Prairie Publishing Company, 1936.

Walsh, Richard J. *The Making of Buffalo Bill*. Indianapolis, The Bobbs-Merrill Company, 1928.

Walters, Lorenzo D. *Tombstone's Yesterday*. Tucson, Acme Printing Company, 1928.

Walton, W. M. *Life and Adventures of Ben Thompson, the Famous Texan*. Austin, the author, 1884.

Waters, Frank. *The Colorado*. New York, Rinehart and Company, 1946.

Webb, Walter Prescott. *The Great Plains*. Boston, Ginn and Company, 1931.

———. *The Texas Rangers*. Boston and New York, Houghton Mifflin Company, 1935.

Wentworth, Edward Norris, *America's Sheep Trails*. Ames, Iowa State College Press, 1948.

Wharton, Clarence R. *History of Fort Bend County*. San Antonio, The Naylor Company, 1939.

Willbarger, J. W. *Indian Depredations in Texas*. Austin, Hutchings Printing House, 1889.

Williams, Amelia W., and Eugene C. Barker (editors). *The Writings of Sam Houston*. Austin, University of Texas Press, 1938–43. 8 vols.

Williams, Mary Floyd. *History of the San Francisco Committee of Vigilance of 1851*. Berkeley, University of California Press, 1921.

Willison, George F. *Here They Dug the Gold*. New York, Brentano's, 1931. Revised edition, New York, Reynal and Hitchcock, 1946.

Wilstach, Frank J. *Wild Bill Hickok*. Garden City, New York, Doubleday, Page and Company, 1926.

Wooten, Dudley G. (editor). *A Comprehensive History of Texas, 1685 to 1897*. Dallas, Texas History Company, 1898. 2 vols.

Wright, George F. (editor). *History of Sacramento County*. Oakland, Thompson and West, 1880.

Wright, Robert M. *Dodge City, the Cowboy Capital*. [Wichita, Kansas, Wichita Eagle Press, 1913.]

Yoakum, Henderson. *History of Texas*. New York, Redfield, 1856. 2 vols. Facsimile reproduction, Austin, The Steck Company, 1935.

Ziegler, Jesse A. *Wave of the Gulf*. San Antonio, The Naylor Company, 1938.

Index

Index

Index

Index

Index

Index

Index